Exalted Quest
You Have But One Quest to Live, Exalt It

Kindred Light

BALBOA
PRESS
A DIVISION OF HAY HOUSE

Copyright © 2019 Kindred Light.

All rights reserved. No part of this book may be used or reproduced by any means, graphic, electronic, or mechanical, including photocopying, recording, taping or by any information storage retrieval system without the written permission of the author except in the case of brief quotations embodied in critical articles and reviews.

Scripture taken from the King James Version of the Bible.

Balboa Press books may be ordered through booksellers or by contacting:

Balboa Press
A Division of Hay House
1663 Liberty Drive
Bloomington, IN 47403
www.balboapress.com
1 (877) 407-4847

This book is a work of non-fiction. Unless otherwise noted, the author and the publisher make no explicit guarantees as to the accuracy of the information contained in this book and in some cases, names of people and places have been altered to protect their privacy.

Because of the dynamic nature of the Internet, any web addresses or links contained in this book may have changed since publication and may no longer be valid. The views expressed in this work are solely those of the author and do not necessarily reflect the views of the publisher, and the publisher hereby disclaims any responsibility for them.

The author of this book does not dispense medical advice or prescribe the use of any technique as a form of treatment for physical, emotional, or medical problems without the advice of a physician, either directly or indirectly. The intent of the author is only to offer information of a general nature to help you in your quest for emotional and spiritual well-being. In the event you use any of the information in this book for yourself, which is your constitutional right, the author and the publisher assume no responsibility for your actions.

Any people depicted in stock imagery provided by Getty Images are models, and such images are being used for illustrative purposes only.
Certain stock imagery © Getty Images.

Print information available on the last page.

ISBN: 978-1-9822-2180-5 (sc)
ISBN: 978-1-9822-2178-2 (hc)
ISBN: 978-1-9822-2179-9 (e)

Library of Congress Control Number: 2019901565

Balboa Press rev. date: 02/19/2019

To my beloved children who have inspired me to dig deeply into the
fiery core of my own being, to reach beyond the farthest stars
of the cosmos, to expand my heart immeasurably,
and to discover the joy of living

Contents

Acknowledgments ix
Introduction xi

1. The Quest 1
2. Until We Meet Again, Fair Soul 10
3. The Wedding of Sir Ego and Dame Ego 23
4. Double Divine 41
5. Attempted Escape 50
6. The Ecstasy and the Agony 60
7. The Black Hole 64
8. Doing Time 72
9. The Unwinnable War 92
10. The Special One 114
11. The Moment of Choice 124
12. Why Do I Care? 138
13. Acknowledging Unacknowledged Resistance 149
14. Double Trouble 162
15. The One Truly Serious Philosophical Problem 178
16. Love, Heroically 190
17. Breaking Up the Band 202
18. A Higher Octave 212
19. The Script of Creation 225
20. Exalted Quest 239

About the Author 245

Acknowledgments

I have great gratitude for my fellow knights who have encouraged and supported my grail quest. You know who you are. Each of you has contributed in a unique way to my expansion, understanding, and compassion. Both our fellowship and sparring have blessed me in many ways. I honor you for your noble quest. May you be blessed, protected, and guided in every step you take.

Introduction

For many years and through many crises, I despaired at the disparity between my life experience and the spiritual teachings I explored. While I was inspired and encouraged by the words of saints and sages, I did not understand how to activate divine power to transform myself, cope with difficulties, heal my wounds, cultivate mutually beneficial relationships, and experience divine love. I couldn't make it real. I couldn't activate the wisdom and power in my own life.

Increasing desperation brought me to my knees before the divine, finally demanding that I be comforted, instructed, and healed. Teachers and teachings appeared to reveal the next steps in my journey. Increasingly, I sought to change myself, my attitudes, and my beliefs to allow the divine to enter and change me.

Slowly at first and then more quickly, I watched as stubborn aspects of my life changed as I transformed. Moreover, each step revealed deeper insights and truths, a higher perspective, more compassion, and release from anxiety and fear. This quest became the purpose of my life as it healed my life. The teachings came alive for me.

My challenges are of the garden variety that touch every life, family, and organization. As I see others struggle as I have, I feel compelled to share what I have learned in the hope that it will help others. I have seen firsthand that it only takes one person changing for an entire family to transform. I hope this book touches that one person who is willing to change for the benefit of many around him or her. Each of us who does our part contributes to the healing of humankind. It is the highest purpose for our lives. As our consciousness ascends to the higher realms, the view gets better and better.

Although we are eternally blessed, holy, and beloved, we are blind to this until we learn to walk in the light. Our blessed heritage awaits us at the end of our quest. Seize it.

1

The Quest

Napa Valley, a mecca of luxurious, chic lifestyles, was the glistening backdrop as I walked down the garden aisle in my handmade silk wedding gown and my nearly glass slippers from Harrod's in London. Prince Charming and I exchanged vows in the vineyard of an elegant winery overlooking the valley and then celebrated our wedding with the finest cuvee the winery could offer.

But I was in for quite a surprise about the exact nature of my happily-ever-after. While I would go on to have all the world desires, each prize would become another link in the shackles I would later wear in jail. Still, somewhere deep within my being was the knowledge that my quest for the grails of love, joy, security, and purpose could be exalted for a higher ideal, and this notion captivated me and drew me upward. Each link would then become a key to my liberation in a way that I had yet to understand on the day of my fairy-tale wedding. The conscious unlocking of each of those links would ultimately lead me to true love, peace, and my happily-ever-after.

In each of us lies the heart of a knight on the quest for the grail. With all our passion and might, we seek the grand adventure that will fulfill our wildest dreams and hearts' desires. We seek what will make us feel whole, satisfied, free, joyful, exhilarated, and, most of all, loved. What makes it difficult in practice are the million and one forms and turns a life path takes—each deceiving us, concealing the direct path, and leading us down glittering streets to dark dead ends.

Unforeseen circumstances arise, disasters loom, and bridges fall. We seek the camaraderie, friendship, support, and loyalty of our fellow knights traveling alongside us in the hope of completing the quest for our mutual benefit. Yet sometimes their rivalry, betrayal, and abandonment confound us and obstruct our paths as they head off on their own quests for their own grails. Over time, these distractions overwhelm us and cause us to lose sight of our true heading. We become enthralled by battles with circumstances and each other, losing faith in and forsaking our own quests.

There also lies within each of us a wise one who exalts the quest, has the wisdom to overcome the obstacles, and assures our victory when we heed his sage advice. Learning to tune into this loving guide, this inner knowing, transformed the direst circumstances of my life into beautiful diamonds of joy and pearls of wisdom. Silently, he waits for each of us to beckon him to heal our wounds and reveal the highest path for our lives. As part of us, he is available to all, at all times, without regard to race or creed, no matter how far we fall or how desperate our circumstances become.

The wise one's role is to guide, teach, heal, and save us. He gives us hope, inspiration, courage, and insight. He sees both our divine, perfect nature and our paths through our human lives. He does not wish to control or punish us. He knows nothing of guilt and shame. He does not ask for blind allegiance. He helps us to build faith and trust in him through experiences. He never gives up or forsakes us, and he never is more than a thought away.

The wise one sees our lives from a higher perspective and aligns our true natures, desires, and spiritual growth with the flow of creation. He is in tune with the universal consciousness and the fabric of creation that is woven from something like the Higgs boson particle. This subatomic building block contains the information and energy that governs the material world and orchestrates a fantastic odyssey of cosmic proportions for each of us. When we learn to attune ourselves to these higher realities and exert our will in alignment with these powerful forces, we realize the highest purposes for our life.

The wise one is in tune with the laws of creation, governing the quantum soup of energy and intelligence, that manifest the material world for our benefit, betterment, and highest good. The natural laws of biology, cosmology, chemistry, astrology, physics, psychology, sociology, evolution, and other forces of the universe conspire to lay the unique path for each of us to reach the exalted states of expanded consciousness and unconditional love. The interactions, interdependencies, and interrelationships of this cosmic machinery are beyond the understanding of the knights, our lower selves, without the aid of the wise one.

The wise one taps into the universal consciousness of humankind—the world of thought and pure consciousness—that links us with creation. Throughout the ages, many masters, teachers, saints, sages, and enlightened ones have embodied this understanding, represented this field of divine love and essential knowledge, and offered teachings of eternal truths. We may think of the wise one as the higher part of our own consciousness, sometimes known as the silent witness, who is able to attune with the universal consciousness and the teachers and avatars that are available to guide us.

In our loud, demanding, cyber, advertising, material world, the wise one can be difficult to find. He speaks in inspiration and intuition rather than words. He is the state of flow in which we are being, not thinking. He is in the present and never the past or future. He never regrets or worries. He speaks only with love and never with fear. He knows what to do and say in every circumstance for optimal effectiveness because he is aligned with the Creator, the forces of creation, and the universal consciousness connecting us to our fellow knights.

When he is activated, our words will have just the right energy, tone, facial expression, and body language to respectfully and kindly get our message across. If we start to seek the wise one and allow him to lead, we will quickly see that we become more effective in the world and our relationships. Over time, we see blocks and obstacles melt away and our relationships improve.

Perhaps this sounds too good to be true. If it were true, everyone would be doing it, and we would all be living in heaven on earth. *What's the catch? Where is the wise one hiding? Why can't I see or feel him? How do I activate this in my life?*

Here's the dilemma: the wise one is the silent witness who waits patiently for us to recognize and call upon him. He will never force himself on us. More problematic is the nature of the knight, the other part of our being, vying for control of our lives. Both the knight and the wise one exist within our consciousness, and we make a moment-to-moment choice regarding which one we listen to. Until we become familiar with the wise one, we allow the knight to function on autopilot.

The knight, Sir Ego, is the eternal spirit attached to this body, this suit of armor. He was born into a quest that he doesn't understand. Sir Ego wants to be a righteous warrior; however, he can be plagued with vices, weaknesses, and faults. Over time, he finds himself in bitter battles with his fellow knights and external circumstances that seem to stand in the way of his quest fulfilment. The wise one can be called upon to expose and remove the root causes of these imperfections, traverse these obstacles, and reveal the diamond self that shines perfectly within.

The primary goal of Sir Ego is to attend to the needs of the body for food, water, shelter, and so on. When Sir Ego is detached from the wise one, he thinks that his quest is of his own making. He establishes his own goals and path, without the benefit of the holistic perspective of the wise one. He knows neither what will work nor what will make him truly happy, so he searches in vain, chasing shiny objects and falling into ditches. He fails to maintain good relationships and collaborations with his fellow knights. He searches in ignorance, which leads to frustration and despair.

The quest is analogous to an online multiplayer video game in which the wise one directs his knight to interact with the game and other knights. As the wise one learns and masters various aspects of the game, he advances to higher levels in pursuit of the ultimate victory.

As you will see from my story, my journey went into desolate places from which it seemed there was no escape. Yet I did escape, and each step on the journey revealed new insights, higher understanding, greater peace, more loving relationships, and true joy. In truth, Sir Ego desperately longs for the counsel of the wise one, but there is an impediment to this that he must learn to overcome.

The knight must learn to wield the mighty double-edged sword of energy so it is used in his favor rather than against him. At the lowest point in my journey, my inner state was filled with fear, anger, anxiety, and insecurity. These are low vibrations of energy. There are also high vibrations of energy, such as love, happiness, excitement, and affection to which we all aspire. These states of inner energy should be our guides to show us what to go toward (e.g., a loved one or an ice cream cone) and what to run away from (e.g., a fire or a lion).

We are wired to be attracted to things that arise the emotions of love and all its derivatives and to have a fight-or-flight response to things that arise the emotions of fear and all its derivatives. The fight-or-flight response is that blast of energy we get when we sense danger that throws our entire system into an emergency response mode, directing and activating energy to escape from or to fight with the oncoming danger. This system of instinctual behaviors was beautifully designed and has worked for a very long time to ensure the survival of our species by calling us toward potential mates and away from potential predators.

However, somewhere along the line, the system got overloaded. The fight-or-flight instinct developed a hair trigger. A minor criticism, disappointment, or setback arouses a DEFCON one response: all systems on full alert, attack imminent, prepare counterattack, and raise shields. Our minds are hijacked when the alert sounds and start spinning in circles, considering all possible scenarios, responses, and resolutions.

Habitual negative behaviors jump to the forefront to ferociously defend our pride, turf, feelings, and ideals. Sir Ego dons his armor for strength and protection, seizes his lance and shield, and engages the adversary. He feels an urgency and an imperative to act. There's no time to consult the wise one. The moments when we need the sage thinking of the wise one are the times we are least likely to stop and consult him.

This happens because Sir Ego gets overwhelmed with turbulent inner energies, triggering a blast of thoughts and emotions. Sir Ego has stored packets of inner energy for emergencies in case he needs to lift a car off a child, execute a perfect triple axel, or escape from an assailant. These are unseen energy vortices, like tiny tornados. When something triggers the energy vortex, it starts to open, and the energy begins to be released.

These energy vortices have vibrations that can emit the whole spectrum of feelings and emotions. So we will call them vibe-vortices, or VVs. Although they cannot be seen on an x-ray or CT scan, they are energetic realities and contain memories, images, conversations, experiences, and emotions. When something triggers a VV, it opens like a flower blossom. The energy is released, and we feel the emotions contained within or relive the experiences. This is why we can become hypersensitive to certain situations that remind us of our past or why we can't break habitual responses to certain triggers or replay scenarios over and over in our minds. The energy of the VV is compelling and attracts all of our attention. And we all carry a chest full of VVs that can be used to fuel our quest or incinerate our lives. I have done both and recommend the former.

We have habitual responses to this abrupt increase in energy. Sir Ego brandishes the lance or shield. When these emotions are strong, they can hijack our minds and take us right back to the emotional state of the original event. We simply haven't let go of resentments, grief, and fear of past events. We bring these emotions into current situations, where they don't belong and aren't effective.

The sudden release of these energies overwhelms us and demands our attention and action. This is the moment when I always blew it. I said the wrong things. I couldn't stop the addictive behavior. I tried to control people, circumstances, and things that were outside my domain. I was ineffective. I was not consulting the wise one, and the energy was too overwhelming to even consider him.

The quest is like a process of sorting through old boxes of VVs that have been unopened in the attic for years. These things have outlived their usefulness, yet somehow we haven't let them go. What we need to do is empty the chest of VVs, the artifacts stored in our hearts, minds, and energy bodies. The artifacts are all the memories, good and bad, we hold on to: all the incidents of love and happiness as well as pain and fear and everything in between. The quest is one of releasing all these items from their storage chests until nothing, save our essential nature, our divine nature, is left. That's when we become clear channels for the divine to flow naturally through our beings to other beings. Divinity is where we came from, and it's where we return. We decide how long we will tarry.

My storage chest was filled with some very good memories, but there were many, many bad ones, some so terrifying I didn't dare look at them, lest I be turned to stone. But it's when the chests in our souls are emptied that we awake, alive and fully present to each moment. We are free to enjoy the magnificence of our planet, the love of every being, and the bliss of our divine heritage.

But we are very attached to the things we've stored in our chests, if only at a subconscious level. We believe they are us, they will free us, they will save us, and we can't live without them. We think we need to fix some of them and undo others. For some of them, we want vengeance and justice. We need a debt to be satisfied. We allow the things in our chests to define and bind us. Some terrify us in the darkest hours of the night. We bond with one another around our fears and indulge our victim stories.

We can't forget the time we peed in our pants in front of our third-grade class. We can't forget the abuse or crime we witnessed, experienced, or committed. We defend the contents of our chests, building a fortress with them. We rationalize, justify, excuse, blame, and even deny what we've stored. Because we can't tolerate the bittersweet experience of looking at what we've packed away, we try to arrange the world outside so it will not disturb the contents of our soul's chests and throw us off. Subconsciously, we do everything we can to keep these items in place, shoving them back in whenever they inconveniently pop out.

Over time, I learned to master this blast of energy, and it improved everything in my life dramatically, as well as the lives of those around me. When Sir Ego was his loudest, shrieking about how to get the situation under control, I learned to turn to the wise one instead. The insights I observed and the techniques I used can help anyone traverse this same rocky road successfully.

Every time, turning to the wise one resulted in a higher outcome, a more effective way of being, and a transformation in my consciousness. Persistent problems melted away. Fear gave way to love. Weaknesses disappeared. Hate-frozen relationships thawed. Positive habitual behaviors overcame negative ones. Battle scars healed. Peace and calm arose from the chaos.

I had it all backward. I thought I needed to get the outer world to behave before my inner world would settle down. For years, I continued this misguided pursuit, chasing outward, worldly success, despite the increasing inner turmoil it cost me. I would obtain the objects of my desire, only to watch them slip away or turn bitter and cause me pain. It was when I began to slay the inner dragons that the outer world began to look better and better. It had actually been magnificent all along, but I had accumulated fears and resentments that obstructed my view. I had a tendency to hold on to things that no longer served me.

I want to show you how I learned to take things out of my chests, release the energy they carried, and witness miracles in my life. Wounds that never before healed seemed to fade away and disappear. Virtues like acceptance, kindness, compassion, and humility, which I had long and unsuccessfully tried to cultivate, wondrously appeared.

And this wasn't just for me. As I changed, my circumstances and relationships became less chaotic, frustrating, and obstinate. It seemed these energy blockages had been holding negative puzzle pieces in my life. As the energy released, these negative qualities and situations were washed away. Truly, I found that we don't have to become good. We are good, and we just have to allow the veil that hides our intrinsic goodness to fall away.

There are many ways to release the stored energy patterns in our chests: meditation, massage, yoga, and energy-healing modalities such as Reiki and reflexology, to name a few. I have used and use all of these on a regular basis, so I know they are effective. But I also have a heavy-artillery secret weapon. I have learned how to take advantage of the moment when a VV is activated to use the energy in a productive way that became the rocket fuel for spiritual growth.

I learned to recognize the moment that Sir Ego was out of alignment with the flow of creation and to seek the wise one to bring me back into alignment with the flow of creation. When the VV exploded and Sir Ego readied for battle, I learned to press pause. In this split second, I learned to call upon the wise one for guidance instead. I learned to allow the VV energy to flow through me. I learned to wait patiently until the wise one responded in his loving and effective ways. And I learned to seek the moral of the story, the lesson behind the VV.

My quest is revealed to me one VV at a time. As each item popped out of the chest, the VV began to open, which represented the next step in my unfolding, the next lesson I was ready and able to learn and integrate. Looking back, I see that I was searching everywhere outside for wisdom and salvation, yet the next step was always right there, right in front of me. I did not need to find the *right* relationship, career, pilgrimage, retreat, teacher, book, or religion that would save me.

Each step of my individual, unique, custom-made path to salvation is being presented to me moment by moment. And if I miss a turn, it will be presented to me again and again until I get it. The magnetism of the

VV continues to draw the perfect lesson circumstances toward me until I release it.

I did not need to figure it out or fix it. I just need to be mindful of the state of my energy and the choice of response. Each one of us has the perfect treasure map and lesson plan within us. Every person's map is custom made exactly for him or her to attain the highest purposes for his or her life. That is the path: each moment, in the matter right in front of you, chose to liberate the VV. Choose love and not fear. This exalts each step on the quest.

For me, for many years, I accumulated more VVs. All kinds of traumatizing and terrifying things happened—the untimely death of my mom, years of infertility, an abusive marriage, alcoholism, imprisonment, bankruptcy, losing custody of my children, and my daughter's attempts at suicide—all traumatic and potentially devastating things. My fear and its array of forms grew—grief, depression, anxiety, anger, despair, and many others. Fear consumed my inner world and doomed me to the unconscious repetition of negative, self-defeating habit patterns until I met the wise one.

While I was in the darkest legs of my journey, I only saw the back side of the tapestry, filled with knots of pain and fear and no discernable patterns. Now I see the front of the tapestry and the magnificent vista that has been woven. I see that my path was perfect and beautiful, and each step on this quest brought me to a new level of understanding, love, and compassion for myself and others.

2

Until We Meet Again, Fair Soul

My mom was an Erma Bombeck mom. With a houseful of four boys and one daughter, she was the stage director of a chaotic play. Props and actors randomly flew across the set. She was real and flawed, and she laughed about that. In fact, she laughed at all the little dramas of life that would cause others to bumble, stumble, and fall. Apparently she was quite in tune with the wise one and unconsciously understood the cosmic joke that her humanity was a playful parody of her perfection. She radiated this divinity. In her presence, I felt loved, cherished, precious, and perfect. We adored each other.

Growing up, I was nurtured in the celestial sunlight of this love, but I was not instructed about its source and the connection to the wise one within. I embraced the role of a knight, honing my skills for the quest, battling my brothers for the lead, and querying the world for information about the nature of the grail I sought and the atlas mapping my quest.

The rowdy roughhousing of my brothers annoyed me greatly. Someone was always screaming in pain; another person was always screaming in conquest. Restless bodies and previously inanimate objects would fly up and down the stairs of our three-story house, across the untidy living room, and often precariously close to my face. But I could always find refuge in the kitchen with my mom, helping her with the dishes, dwelling in her calm eye at the center of the storm.

One day, a fire started in the living room, and nonchalantly she seized the dishpan full of water and extinguished the fire. Even that didn't qualify as a 9-1-1 in my mom's view of the world. She was the rock, the foundation, the stable center, the philosophical problem solver, and the practical wise woman. She was kind to everyone, saw the best in each person, and had no enemies.

There was something in the way my mother saw me that felt delicious, as though I were a scrumptious treat she savored. While she didn't expect or demand that I be successful in worldly ways, she was always pleasantly surprised by it. So I could never disappoint her, only impress her. She was genuine, and she was genuinely interested in me. I felt special.

I remember when I was in seventh grade and got in trouble for shoplifting, and she had to ground me. I missed my Friday night outing with friends, ice skating and gossiping under Philadelphia's starry winter skies. My mother and I sat in the basement, where she held me as I cried tears of guilt and shame while my brothers played ping-pong. I felt safe in her arms as I absorbed the lesson, delivered with few words and much love: what I had done was wrong, but I was still lovable and loved. She enforced this parenting boundary without judgment on me. I had made a mistake and had a lesson to learn, but I was not unredeemable.

Mom humbly allowed me to be the know-it-all of baking, cleaning, and laundry. She looked on as I blossomed in competence and self-confidence. I was grateful to be of service, the hallmark of my true love and devotion to her. Pleasing her was compensation enough. It was a special privilege to make dessert and prepare the house for her monthly bridge club. We were a team, laying out special china and paper napkins that matched the tally sheets for her honored guests. Mom's close circle of friends shared joys, sorrows, household hints, and life lessons.

You could tell my mother anything, and she would never judge you. Even my teenage friends and my sisters-in-law were closer to her than to their own mothers. My mother listened to every word of a person's saga. Although she said very little, each pearl of wisdom she did utter was spot on. I still live by her counsel today. During her last days, I would find friends and visitors in the kitchen with her, pouring out their usual complaints about a bad back, bad husband, or bad luck at bridge. She, fully aware she was dying, comforted them.

Mom incessantly crooned in a tone-deaf melody, "You are my sunshine, my only sunshine." Mom's sentimental ditty fostered a deep sense of well-being in me that lasted long after the echoes of this tune were silenced.

And she could laugh at herself. Some of the things she found funniest were her own quirks, like her culinary disasters or the piles of laundry she'd "misplace" in the basement (causing me to wear my brother's underwear to school on several occasions). She made it okay to be imperfect and taught the virtue of humility by example.

When we'd watch our family slideshow of photos throughout the years, the funniest ones were of her in some embarrassing moment, like a bad-hair day. The family favorite was taken at the beach, when my mom tried to put an inner tube over her head and it got stuck at her extra-large bosom. It wouldn't go down or up again. She laughed at her photos right along with us.

Mom didn't engage in a barter system of love. She didn't keep score of what she had done for us against what we had done for her. We didn't have to be a certain way or do a specific something to receive her love and acceptance. She gave of herself and her love absolutely, unconditionally, and constantly. Her repertoire did not include guilt, manipulation, coercion, power trips, or controlling, demanding, and punitive strategies.

I didn't know it at the time, but my mother's love was an expression of the Creator's unconditional love shining through her. When she looked at me, it was as if she wore mirrored sunglasses in which I saw a beautiful reflection of myself—worthy, whole, and lovable. And no problem was insurmountable. Everything would be all right. With Mom, it felt good to be alive. I was comfortable in my skin and in my place in the world. Because of her, I wanted to be better, speak better, and do better.

My father, on the other hand, was a first-generation German American, a World War II veteran, and a blue-collar father of five kids. He was strict, stoic, disciplined, and tough; Sir Ego was dominant and strong in him. His wise one expressed as a passion for nature and animals, but he spent most of his time working as an auto-parts salesman to support his family. He was hardworking, setting aside his personal desires to earn a living and support his family, but it seemed he grew to resent us.

What I knew of him that mattered most to me was that I couldn't seem to do anything to earn his love, which I desperately sought. He loved his animals and his garden, but he didn't seem to like people much at all, especially kid people. Specifically the kid people in our house.

I wanted to be a part of his world. I followed him around in his garden, where he expressed all the nurturing proclivities he had. Our one-acre lot was half lawn and half garden, and it was meticulously maintained. Dad knew a lot about horticulture, cultivating all kinds of flowers and shrubs, bountiful in every season under his green thumb. He rarely harvested the precious blossoms for display inside the house. This gift was reserved for visits to his mother. He shared colorful dahlias the size of dinner plates with her.

I also followed my dad down to his fish room, a coal cellar filled with eight fish tanks brimming with marine life. He looked after baby seahorses, hundreds of Siamese fighting fish, exotic lionfish with poisonous quills, and goofy clown fish (long before Nemo). I sensed he only found me annoying, but I did learn enough about each his hobbies to carry them into my adult life.

Each evening, while my mother tended to parenting duties, my father escaped to his fish room, where he would also consume a six-pack of beer. I never saw him drunk, so I never thought he had that kind of a problem, but his temper was explosive and terrifying. Occasionally he would be so enraged that he would chase us with a wooden spoon. I didn't have to run up the steps faster than my dad; I only had to run up the steps faster than one of my brothers. Whoever trailed at the bottom was the one who got whacked. It didn't matter who committed what crime or whether there even was a crime. Annoying my dad constituted grounds for the wooden spoon.

My father's answer to every request was "No!" If I pressed him for an explanation, I got "Because I said so!" I vowed never to say this to my own children.

My eldest brother was subject to the Vietnam draft in 1971. Guys were drafted according to their birthdate. The birthdates were randomly selected and given a draft sequence, and the smaller numbers were drafted first. On the day of the draft selection, we all sat in quiet anticipation of the number that would determine my brother's fate—all of us, that is, except my dad, who was tending his more beloved garden.

My brother's birthdate came up as an 87, in the first third of a possible 365. He was at risk. I went out to the garden to tell my dad. He was watering the marigolds, and I was interrupting his important business.

I said, "It's eighty-seven," assuming he would know what I meant.

He replied, "I don't care. We are not going to the swimming pool," and he added for good measure, "because I said so." He seemed completely unaware of the gravity and significance of the occasion.

I was stunned. Sulking away, I muttered, "Eighty-seven is John's draft number."

When I was sixteen, our family went on vacation to Florida. This was infinitely better than the other vacations my dad had chosen for us, spelunking in Laurel Caverns or mounting and photographing cannon monuments in Gettysburg. Alas, my dad found a way to ruin Florida when he started talking about a day to visit the Everglades.

Swamps? I wanted to soak up every minute of sunshine, beach, and ocean that I could, so I announced that I would not be joining this day trip.

First, he said, "Fine."

So I put on my bathing suit to head for the beach, but he stopped me at the door. He would not be mocked and demanded that I go to the Everglades. I went, and I made him pay with a bad attitude for eight hours straight.

I was terrified whenever he'd say to me, "I have a bone to pick with you." I don't recall ever learning from him that I'd done anything of sufficient consequence to fit this ominous pronouncement. It was always justified by a mental rap sheet my dad kept for each of us. At any given moment, he could recite the crimes my brothers and I had committed since birth. Throughout my adult life, I was haunted by a sense of guilt for some kind of capital offense I must have committed. At any moment, the judge and executioner might arrive for my sentencing.

I sought vindication from my father's judgment by becoming a perfect student in school. I hoped my academic accomplishments would suspend my father's harsh sentencing of me. I wasn't distinguished in sports or music, popular, or flirty. But I could get straight As.

My father's response was, "What? No A-pluses?"

I was just never enough to earn his approval and love. Looking back, I think maybe my father was joking about the A-pluses. Still, it was beyond him to give me the loving approval I desperately wanted to hear from him.

Unlike my mom, my father was all about guilt, manipulation, coercion, power trips, and controlling, demanding, and punitive strategies. He had no other strategies, and he didn't offer love even when we complied with the strategies he had. The best my brothers and I could hope for was to avoid that wooden spoon.

When I looked into my father's mirrored sunglasses, I saw myself as flawed, not good enough, unlovable, unworthy, and guilty of a crime I could never pinpoint. I did not understand at the time that my father's reflective sunglasses were filtered by his own wounds and fears, all the things he carried around in his chest. He was trying to get rid of items in his chest by throwing them at me, projecting them onto me. I absorbed these negative projections into my own self-image and started carrying them around in my chest. I felt small and wounded around my dad, and I reflected this back to him in a vicious cycle of projections.

I could not understand how the relationship between my loving mother and my unloving father worked, but it did. I almost never saw my parents fight or even seem out of sorts with each other. Without question, my mother was the peacemaker in our family, the glue that held us together. She neutralized and accommodated my dad's weaknesses. I wonder if my mother worked things out with my father in private.

Maybe she acquiesced and then processed her dissent with her bridge club. After all, that was how marriage worked in her generation. My mom's accommodations were an incredibly loving sacrifice for our family, which made our home a warm and nurturing environment. Her accommodations were also a lesson I silently and unconsciously learned about how marriage works.

Now I see my mother and father as the two parts of me that always seem to be in conflict. My mom represents the wise one, who believes in divine love, appreciates beauty and sanctity, and is eternally wise, secure, accepting, and content. My dad represents Sir Ego, who keeps a list of all my sins and grievances, my faults, and failures. Sir Ego is naysaying and self-flagellating while selfishly placing my interests above the well-being of others and thereby attracting unpleasant relationship consequences. For many years, these two forces battled within me for dominance.

Our family holidays had a Norman Rockwell quality to them. I cherish these memories. Although our home was not fancy or elegant, the fire of my mother's heart roared and warmed our home's cozy ambience. Mom created memorable holidays on a shoestring budget. The holidays were festive pandemonium. After the feast but before the table was cleared, we could count on my youngest brother, Greg, to be swinging from the dining-room chandelier, playing in a mess of spilled gravy, or hiding in the cupboard while my older brothers battled in sword fights and wrestling.

One Christmas, a blizzard kept us from driving to my grandparents' house just one mile away. My mom wouldn't miss a family holiday for anything, so she had us trudge the snow-covered streets, hand in hand, singing Christmas carols and bearing sacks of gifts.

I left Philadelphia to go to college in Virginia. But when I graduated, I was ready to return to my hometown to be near my mother. I took a job at a top accounting firm in downtown Philadelphia. I visited Mom every weekend and telephoned her every day.

Then I found a nice guy, Sam, a controller for a local chain of discount stores. He was willing to go for the American dream with me: marriage, a fine house, china, crystal goblets, and kids. I was twenty-four when I married Sam. We enjoyed more material success than most people attain in their lifetimes. I remember consciously thinking that without a rank on the dean's list to impress others with, I would show my worth by buying the best of everything: a house in the most prestigious neighborhood, an array of Waterford crystal, a Burberry trench coat, and a Mercedes Benz sedan.

But the truth was that I never loved Sam in the way you want to truly love your spouse. Sam from Cornell was safe. He was a steady, solid, reliable accountant who was also funny and handsome. He would have offered me the moon if he could. I never saw an ugly reflection of myself in his sunglasses. If I had given him the chance, I think he would have loved me forever. During our first year together, we seemed to have everything until my mother was diagnosed with malignant melanoma, the bad kind of skin cancer.

The doctor thought he had removed all the cancer in a minor surgery. But a few days before Easter, we returned to my house after shopping on a sunny spring day. My mom and I sat at the kitchen table, chatty and happy. Suddenly out of nowhere, she began to violently convulse and vomit. She lost consciousness in a grand mal seizure. As she regained consciousness, she was calm, and I was able to remain calm with her and take her to the emergency room.

Bewildered and terrified, I had embarked on a journey to hell. It turned out the cancer had spread to Mom's brain and lungs. I didn't want to believe what my mother already knew: this was a death sentence. I don't know how she did it, but my mom accepted this news peacefully and gracefully.

For the next few months, my life was a recurring slog through denial, anger, bargaining, and depression. Acceptance was only to be seen in my mother's eyes, a reflection that I could not comprehend. I quit my job to take care of her during the week while my dad was at work. I wanted every last precious moment with her.

My mother and I didn't speak of our feelings about her death, except on one occasion. We were lying on her bed on a rainy summer day. It was gloomy inside and outside. With tears in my eyes, I told her how much I loved her and said she would be in my heart forever. In her pale blue eyes, all I saw was love, along with no fear and no anger.

Like an angel of peace, Mom nodded demurely and wisely and acknowledged, "Yes. I have that omnipresent bond with Aunt Emma."

I did not know that the brain tumors would pull her into a deep fog and that there were not many more opportunities to talk about our feelings.

I dragged her to a few specialists, who tried some treatments with zero probability of success. The side effects caused Mom's quality of life to deteriorate. She endured these treatments because she saw that I needed her to try them. She didn't complain, but I don't think she would have endured them otherwise.

She would say, "I have taught my children how to live, and now I must teach them how to die."

I finally surrendered, ending the toxic treatments and my pursuit of a miracle that was not to be. Because the tumors in Mom's brain created swelling, she faded away mentally before she faded away physically. In her last few months, our "conversations" were conducted in silent communion. What little Mom did say was for my dad rather than for my brothers or me. I was deeply hurt, but in retrospect, I believe she was relying on him, which was appropriate. Perhaps it was unbearable for her to think of what the loss was doing to me, which was painfully apparent in my eyes.

Each weekday, I arrived early in the morning to relieve my dad so he could go to work. I cared for Mom, did the housework, prepared dinner for Dad, and then went home to prepare dinner for Sam. I closed out the day with wine and finally fell asleep, to wake up and do it all again the next day. I watched my mom slip further into oblivion with each passing day. The world I once knew was being blown apart in a slow-motion explosion of epic proportions.

I did not think that a twenty-six-year-old should have to watch her fifty-six-year-old mother die. Unlike me, my grandmother (my mom's mother) courageously and nobly watched her daughter die. I did the best I could, which meant suppressing most of my emotions and thoughts so I could persevere. Each day there was a new challenge, which was more personal, more intimate, and more unwelcome. I spent hours suctioning the mucus out of her throat so I could spoon-feed her a few bites of mushed something. Then I cleaned up the vomited mushed something moments later. The child became the parent. I helped Mom with all her personal hygiene, eventually mastering the skill of changing adult diapers. No manual can really teach you how to attend to your dying mother.

There were moments when I didn't think I could continue. One day when I was helping Mom walk from her bed to her chair, she fell a few feet short of the chair. She was almost six feet tall and much heavier than I was. I could not get her back up. So I just stayed on the floor with her and cried. When my friend came over, she helped me get Mom into her chair at last.

Near the end, Mom's bridge club friends came to see her. By this time, she had a very difficult time eating, and on this occasion, she began choking. Time stood still. All I could do was watch, conflicted. Questions raced through my mind: *Should I let nature take its course? Is this how she'll go? Is this the day? Is there any point in calling 9-1-1? Will her friends understand if I don't call 9-1-1? Am I ready to let her go?* Before I had the answers to any of these questions, Mom coughed and recovered. That was not the day.

When Mom did pass, I had the honor of being with her. For several days before, she was confined to bed, and the hospice nurse told us that pneumonia, the death rattle, would take her soon. The curtains were drawn throughout the day, and the only thing to do was wait and wait in the dark and gloom.

On the morning of December 10, Mom repeatedly stopped and started breathing again in a coughing fit. I knew this would be the day of her passing. I could feel it. I could feel her fading. I could feel her surrender. And I could feel her peace.

I called my dad at work and insisted he come home, all against his wishes. We had a brief talk in the kitchen when he arrived. My dad had seen his parent die and believed that Mom could go on like this for days. I wondered if, like me, he wasn't ready to let her go. We both went into the bedroom where Mom lay, serene, frail, and hauntingly pale. I imagine she sensed we were there. She was not conscious, so there were no beautiful, memorable good-byes. Within a few minutes, she simply let go. Her final exhalation. The end. Her pain and suffering were over. Mine had barely begun. There were no longer caregiving tasks to fill my days. There was just emptiness, a vast black hole, an absence of love, the end of happiness, and the beginning of grief.

We dressed my mother in the dress she had bought and worn for my wedding. I wrote a beautiful eulogy, but my dad wouldn't let me present it at the funeral. Maybe he couldn't bear to hear a heartfelt eulogy. I was too broken to insist. A minister who hardly knew my mom spoke at her funeral instead.

Christmas Day arrived two weeks after my mom's funeral. Two Christmases before, I had been married in a holiday celebration. My bridesmaids wore red velvet and carried red roses. My mother stood at my side. One Christmas before, my tree had been decorated with dozens of reindeer and unicorn ornaments in the midst of a house full of holiday decorations. Mom had helped me bake Christmas cookies while she described her biopsy to me. This Christmas, I stood in the kitchen, peeling potatoes as tears rolled down my cheeks. My family and I were automatons, going through the motions of holiday preparations. The empty chair at the head of the Christmas table extinguished the holiday spark in each of us.

I felt so much pain in the days that followed that sometimes I could only howl like an animal. The pain was deep, powerful, and engulfing. If my neighbors hadn't known what happened, they would have thought someone in my house was being tortured. I visited the cemetery often, a beautiful site with a gazebo nearby, but I couldn't see anything beautiful at the time. All I wanted was to claw my way back to her, to lie down in that coffin and return to the womb to rest in peace with her. No one would ever love me the way she did. And I would never love anyone again the way I loved her.

I didn't have much of a relationship with the Creator at this time in my life, so I found no consolation there. During my mandatory attendance at catechism class years before, I had affirmed the Sinner's Prayer as a precaution. In case it was true, I didn't want to risk eternal damnation. My analytical mind dissected the teachings of the church and the Bible, which aroused in me a deep respect and admiration for a loving Creator and a man named Jesus.

But a heartfelt love affair had not yet begun. I believed in ESP, yogis in the Himalayas who could sit in breathless ecstasy for days, and Jesus's miracles. I understood them all to mean "there is more to the cosmos than meets the eye." But the creeds and commandments I'd memorized years before offered me no insight or solace.

There had to be more to life, more to comfort me, more meaning to this loss, more to the story of my mom and me, and more to salvation than rote prayers. My love for my mom felt eternal, though her body had not been. This tremendous loss started me on my conscious journey to understand the mysteries of the cosmos. Despite the sterile education I had received about the Creator, I had an inner knowing that there was more to the story.

I wanted to understand why we existed and the purpose of this life that already seemed pointless and painful. I needed answers that would explain the injustice and suffering of the world. Surely there was something more profound to be unraveled. When I analyzed the material world, I saw that no matter what a person created, it would eventually disintegrate, and the only benefit was whatever was enjoyed during the ride. I concluded that the material world was a sham.

I'd had this realization on occasion even before my mother passed away. Once I announced to her, "The only purpose of the universe must be to help others because that is the only thing that lasts and reverberates."

Nonetheless I had embarked on the material treadmill anyway until my mother died and the treadmill stopped and I was abruptly catapulted into the abyss. Now my agony demanded relief. I became a conscious seeker, and my first teacher appeared.

Someone gave me an Edgar Cayce book that was channeled by one of his close associates after the famous psychic's death. It described a just and loving reincarnation process at work in a reality greater than the one we access with our five senses. There was a purpose to our existence, our various lives, on a journey of lessons leading us to the perfection of the Creator, of goodness, beauty, justice, and love.

This information allowed me to believe that my mother was still with me. She did often come to me in my dreams, and I marveled, *You look well. What would the embalmer think if he saw you now?* I wondered how long she would stay ... and then she was gone again.

Still, this was not consolation enough for my broken heart, though it fortified my belief that there was more to life, a greater purpose, and a way to hold life's tragedies and know that life was still worth living. I accepted that there was a greater reality outside of my present awareness and under the guidance of a loving Creator.

I didn't yet know how many ways a person could mess up his or her life, but the idea of a curriculum with lessons and an illuminating graduation made sense to me. The Edgar Cayce book explained the injustice and suffering of our world, which are failed lessons or, more accurately, lessons in progress. In the same way that I learned arithmetic first, then algebra, and finally calculus, I could count on life lessons of increasing difficulty, purifying my soul and leading me to the divine perfection of the Creator. But I still didn't know how to access this perfection to guide my life.

Psychics seemed to have a foothold in this world that was invisible to me, so I read a great deal of their writings and occasionally visited some. For the most part, though, I seemed to be left to my own devices to create a life worth living. Sir Ego did not understand how to access the wise one yet.

While the seed of spiritual awakening had been planted, it would be dormant for many years. I felt my mother's presence in my dreams, and I believed it was really her. But I buried the pain, grief, doubt, fear, and confusion in that chest of VVs and resumed a worldly life, chasing worldly things to distract myself. If there were some greater understanding to be had, it was on the other side of the grief. That was a journey I was not yet willing to take. I was not ready to let go of the idea that she shouldn't have died, that I could only catch fleeting glimpses of a greater cosmic view that would benefit both her and my soul in some unknown and unfathomable way.

This energy blockage became a dormant volcano in my psyche and required a great deal of energy to keep it from erupting. I didn't really blame anyone; I just resisted reality. I denied the loss of this divine and unconditional love and the gaping hole left in my heart. Sadly, this caused me to push away memories of my mother or to see them in a dark haze of sickness, not the vibrancy of her life.

3

The Wedding of Sir Ego and Dame Ego

Shortly after my mother's death, I returned to work in a profitable and stable (and boring) job as a manager of financial analysts at the same bank I had worked prior to my mother's death. I needed something more from my life, and I needed to fill the void in my heart. I needed to do more. I needed to be more. I was hungry. I was desperate. I was empty.

For two years, I sought to replace my mother with a child of my own, to regain the unconditional love that I believed I had lost. For two weeks of every month, I lived in hopeful expectation that I might be pregnant. But month after month passed of periods not missed, and each time I would reenact the loss of my mom. I watched all my sisters-in-law and friends get pregnant, and I was denied this precious gift, nay, this most vital human function. Each month's perceived loss was like a stream of grief feeding the flooding river of my rejection and abandonment.

I ached and ached and ached. *Why was this happening? What was the purpose of this suffering? How could I go on? Why should I go on? What kind of Creator allowed this? And why did he allow it to happen to me?* On many levels, I felt disowned and forsaken by the Creator of the universe who loved and provided for everyone else. It would ultimately be more than ten years before I conceived.

With a twinge of hurt and bitterness, I loved all the children being born when I was barren. I was a favorite aunt and babysitter, but those roles were no replacement. I could smell the sumptuous feast, but I could not partake. I was adding more and more hurts to my chest of anguish. My husband was incredibly kind and supportive. He gave me everything and anything he could. But I just slipped away. There wasn't enough there to fill the grand canyon in my heart.

Losing my mom and failing to get pregnant was more than I could bear. I didn't blame it on Sam, but I also could no longer envision a happily-ever-after with him. All I could see, for as far as I could see, were more weeks, months, and years of pain, loss, and grief. I was hollow, void of normal pleasures and pursuits. There had to be much more to life. I needed a big fix, a massive overhaul, a living reincarnation.

I concocted an escape plan. I quit my boring job, moved into an apartment in the trendy part of town, mingled with interesting new men, and hibernated in the womb of graduate school with the hope of being reborn in a new job in Silicon Valley, a bright new start in sunny California. I was really a sun and sand person. I took some consolation in my studies, believing they would be the future source of my professional redemption. Yet I wandered aimlessly between various men and my ex-husband, unable to find comfort during those two years.

Upon graduation, I was pleased to receive a lucrative job offer from Sun Microsystems, based on the San Francisco Peninsula. I believed fate was taking a turn in my favor, and I embarked enthusiastically on this new adventure. I moved into a fabulous town house with a fellow alumnus and started my new job. This was better. Now I would be living in a great place with a high-level job, and I would find a husband and start a family.

The first order of business was to get back on the childbearing train. I needed to find a husband or at least a baby daddy. One way or another, it needed to happen and soon. I wanted to recapture the rapture of my relationship with my mother and do whatever I needed to do to pursue this.

After my first year in California with absolutely no viable dates, I went to a professional matchmaker to expedite the process. I hired a husband and wife team, who put me through a series of interviews, questionnaires, and personality tests to make suitable introductions.

My first date talked about his triglyceride level—I don't know or care what that is—for a large portion of the evening. Pass.

Don was my second introduction, just before Thanksgiving. As we worked near each other, we had a lunch date at a great little café. It wasn't love at first sight, but he met all the criteria, so we set a second meeting. This time we met at a coffee shop near my office. He arrived with a single red rose wrapped in a sheet of newspaper and his boyish smile. The sheet of newspaper contained the locations of various Christmas tree farms in the area since I had told him that I enjoyed the thrill of the wild Christmas tree hunt.

How romantic and thoughtful, I thought. *And an invitation for a next date obviously.*

Deep in the Santa Cruz Mountains, we hiked, debating the merits of spruce, fir, and pine. Holiday spirit and adventure mixed to create an emotional cornucopia of excitement, passion, curiosity, and intimacy. I was falling fast.

Don was a handsome, charming, wealthy divorced father. His two children—sixteen-year-old Lauren and eleven-year-old Bob—lived with him. Don was also a brilliant inventor and entrepreneur with a successful technology business that he had developed.

Perception and attribution were two things I had learned about in business school. I perceived these very few facts about him and, on that basis, attributed many desirable qualities to him. For example, he was obviously a great father since his children lived with him. Without specifics, he alluded to his ex-wife as being somewhat troubled, uninterested in the children, and guilty of inflicting deep emotional pain on the children and him.

While this didn't quite reconcile with the facts that she was a teacher (who was disinterested in her own children) and had recently completed her PhD (which seemed smart and stable), I accepted his version of the story. I empathized with his great pain and envisioned a way we could heal together and save each other. He was also willing to have more kids. Obviously he was the perfect package.

We did really fun things. For New Year's Eve, we went to the Exotic Erotic Ball. We were stunning and sexy in our matching black tuxedo jackets, hot-pink cummerbunds, bow ties, and top hats. Underneath, he was shirtless and wore black silk boxers. I wore a black silk teddy. Even at this decadent and outrageous San Francisco event, we were a photo favorite. Everyone stopped to take our picture. This was a world-class party. We dirty-danced and celebrated the first moments of 1990, a new decade.

The next morning, we joked and laughed about the wonders of wine. Don mentioned that he'd almost gotten a DUI once and described that near miss. Easily I acknowledged that I had not been so lucky and had received a DUI after my birthday celebration the year before.

The next few months, we spent every possible moment together, basking in the warm glow of infatuation, intimacy, and intoxication. Except for Christmas. I had planned a visit to my family in Philadelphia, so we spent many hours on the phone during those festive days.

I was touched when he confessed, "I really like you and feel so close to you. I haven't felt inclined to play any games with you, like I have with the other women I have dated."

I was also mildly alarmed. *What games?* But I ignored that.

My hunger and trust allowed me to open like a spring blossom, revealing my deepest thoughts and desires. Repeatedly in February and March, Don invited me to move in with him. I declined. It was just too soon, and we didn't know each other very well.

"You could be an ax murderer for all I know," I joked.

I wanted to live with him. I did not want to risk letting this one slip off the hook. However, there were the children to think about. It is one thing for two adults to move quickly in and out of relationships, but the children had already experienced enough loss. I did not want to move in only to move out and hurt them again. I had to be sure.

Don and I talked about how our relationship affected the children. He mentioned the family therapist they were working with to help them over the divorce turmoil, and he invited me to attend a few sessions. I was impressed that he was an enlightened and committed father. At least those were the qualities I attributed to him. I agreed to go.

After the first session or two, it seemed Don and I had a few things the therapist could help us with, so we met with her separately. We had some situations. She called them miscues and said they very common in early relationships. Now I see these miscues were a result of one or both of us experiencing an exploding VV and becoming emotionally hijacked and irrational.

A conversation would be going very well, and quite suddenly it would take a disastrous turn with mutually exploding VVs. It wasn't about any conflict in substance; it was more something I would say, a tone of voice, or a facial expression that would trigger memories of his ex-wife, prior life, or random strife wounds. The conversation would begin an irrevocable descent into what the therapist called a tar baby. We would get stuck in a push-pull mud-wrestling match. He would pull away, and I would need reassurance that everything was okay. I would be stuck apologizing and trying to rescue the conversation. My desperation and fear made matters worse. He would withdraw more, defending himself by attacking me.

The therapist assured us that these were normal relationship foibles and we could endure them if we committed to stop threatening to end the relationship when in the midst of these crises. VVs triggered Sir Ego's fight-or-flight instinct. Threats flowed freely during the explosions. But, I reasoned, every relationship has its ups and downs. I committed more and harder to accommodate these miscues, suppressing all the fear, anger, and hurt that arose.

Our relationship only had ups and downs, highs and lows. There were no in-betweens. And the ups were so worthwhile! When I shared my dreams of basking in the South Pacific rays on Tahiti, Don said we should go.

"Of course we should go," I replied.

Several weeks later, he inquired about the status of my passport application.

"What?" I asked.

"We really are going to Tahiti, and you do need a passport. How about leaving April 30?" he asked, as if to say, "Cream or sugar in your coffee?"

Oh my God, I completed my passport application the same day. Exhilaration, delight, elation, and joy filled that vast hollow spot in my heart. The rightness of the world was manifesting before my very eyes. I was taking my place in the palace of exquisiteness that I had longed for, and my quest was looking promising.

After we booked all the reservations, I was laid off from my job at a start-up software company. I didn't care. I was on my way to Tahiti. With student loans to pay and no financial reserves, I finally agreed to move in with Don after we had returned from our trip. He wanted to take care of me, and I needed to be taken care of. It must have been meant to be. I now know it was, but not in the way I thought at that time.

We stayed in a Club Med that had little bungalows built over the pristine, shimmering, turquoise water and sugary white sand of Bora Bora, the crowning jewel of Tahiti. In the open air of the hut, all night you could hear the gentle lapping of the water just below the bed and the lizards scurrying across the thatched ceiling. If paradise were lost, we had found it.

It was a very small, intimate, couple's kind of Club Med. It could not have been more romantic. I have traveled to many exotic island treasures, but this resort on Bora Bora stands out as the most delicious, sensuous paradise. We spent many moonlit dinners drinking wine and dreaming up a beautiful life together. Gazing into Don's eyes, as crystal clear a blue as the azure water below, I fell in love. My knight in shining armor had arrived on the flight to Papeete. If anything could fill the void in my heart, this was it. I drank it in.

A remote island has little light to compete with the stars. Bora Bora's night sky had abundant twinkling stars. I felt that my mother watched over me. Surely she was smiling over this relationship, ensuring I would find the love I had lost that December 10.

I was hungry for love, and Don was forthcoming, showering me with tokens. Infatuation and lust are an irresistible combination, and they fed the hunger in my heart. I did not know that love is not hungry, empty, and insatiable. Love is abundant, omnipresent, and overflowing. I had these two things confused.

A few months later, we went to the Black and White Ball. It was on the opposite end of the cultural spectrum from the Exotic Erotic Ball, formal and elegant. *Trés* elegant. This was the start of my little black dress collection. I was adorned in a sexy, one-shouldered, backless cocktail dress. This time, Don wore the whole tuxedo. We were eclectic, sophisticated, and indulgent. It was everything I thought life—or I—should be. I easily ignored, denied, minimized, rationalized, and justified the imperfect part of our relationship. No relationship was perfect. And this one was worth fighting for.

My new job was taking care of the house—chauffeuring Bob to school, baseball, basketball, and friends' houses and overseeing the preparation of a beautiful candlelit dinner each night. Even if Don and I went out to dinner, we would come home to find Bob having a candlelit dinner of chili cheese bread, his favorite. Don traveled a lot for his business, and it was very convenient to have live-in help.

Luckily, Don's children liked me, and our new family unit seemed like a blessing to me. Soon Don and I became engaged, which seemed as natural and beautiful as anything I could have wished for. At last, all the pain was melting into a sea of love and happiness. Don made me feel treasured as well as special, worthy, and lovable. He had a naïve, boyish way of revealing his pain and making me want to heal and care for him. And he cared about my deepest fears, hurts, dreams, and desires, probing them to understand what made me tick. At last it seemed like I could redeem myself through his love, despite never having been able to earn my father's.

At the time, I did not understand that our relationship was Sir Ego versus Sir Ego. I did not understand that relationships don't work very well without the counsel of the wise one. I also didn't understand that each knight has a different preference for the lance and shield. As in any good sparring match, a balance between the use of the lance and the shield yields appropriate boundaries that characterize healthy relationships. Toxic relationships are defined by one partner using the lance predominantly while the other uses the shield mostly. This is why they find each other, stay together, and will be attracted to the same type of relationship repeatedly.

The miscues continued and even escalated after I moved in with Don and his children. Sadly, the VVs gained energy and power with each miscue. Often it was so subtle that I couldn't figure out where the conversation had gone wrong. What I did know was that I had failed to make him happy, to love him unconditionally, and to relieve his pain. He was quite clearly displeased about that. I understood that I needed to get it right or I would be rejected and abandoned. I would not let that happen again. I would not fail to earn his love. I increased my efforts to make our home life fun, cozy, and loving.

Sometimes I had a bad intuition, which I ignored, that things he said weren't all true: weird things, inconsistent stories, or unfair accusations about my motives and behavior. I befriended a coworker of his who told me the story of his DUI. It was not truly a near miss, but a direct hit, and she had picked him up at the police station the next day.

Why would Don lie to me? I am a naïvely open and honest person, easily revealing all my deep, dark secrets. I couldn't quite understand that he would intentionally lie to me, so I denied that it was happening. I couldn't prove it anyway.

If I pointed out the inconsistency, he snapped. "You are just like Phyllis [his ex]."

No, I will never be like Phyllis. I will always love you more, and I will never hurt you, I vowed to myself. But no matter how hard I tried, I kept falling into the same trap.

I mentioned to a counselor that Don never apologized after we fought. *Just like a man*, I thought. But deep inside, I acknowledged that he took no responsibility for our conflicts. Although Sir Ego might send flowers the next day and be extra kind and loving, he never discussed his role in our miscues or his plan to address them. It all seemed to be on me. And I was willing to do whatever it took to make the relationship work.

Over time, the troublesome situations got louder. We went to my graduate school friends' out-of-town wedding, a few months before our own. Many other friends from graduate school were there. It was a fun weekend of festivities in Napa, including a day of wine tasting on the party bus, a rented van. On the bus, I spent most of the time talking to a male classmate about his marital problems. This made Don jealous, although I was unaware of it.

Later that night, when we returned to our hotel room, Don badgered and harassed me. I tried to go to bed, but he poked at me, trying to engage me in a fight. "Why did you bring me here if you don't want to be with me? What's going on with you anyway?"

We had both had a bit of wine. I couldn't make any sense out of what he was saying or what he wanted me to do. So I took a pillow and blanket to the couch in the other room. He followed, pulling the bedding away. He continued to harass me, alternately demanding that I come back to bed and I leave the room. I curled up in a ball and cried. He finally went to bed and left me to cry alone for the rest of the night. As always, the next morning, we both pretended nothing had happened.

We traveled a great deal during the two years before we married—always fun and always first class. We had a life of privilege and abundance.

It was intoxicating, even addicting. Sir Ego is easily trapped by material pleasures.

I didn't flinch when Don asked me to sign a prenuptial agreement that my attorney suggested was "mean-spirited." It was understandable to me: he had been hurt by his first wife, and I wanted him to feel safe. I wouldn't hurt him like that. It wasn't about the money for me. I had excellent earning potential and would never need his money if we split up.

More importantly, we were leaving for a three-week trip to Europe in a few days. I certainly did not want to cause a fight at that moment. By now, I was keenly aware how painful it was for me when we had miscues. I would do almost anything to avoid this nightmare, often conceding increasingly important battles.

The trip was planned around Don's business meetings, with lots of time for sightseeing, shopping, wine tasting, and magnificent, expense-account meals. The memory that stands out to me was the Schlosshotel, a five-star hotel in Germany that had been a castle. I could feel the royalty in the air when we walked into the lobby.

The front desk clerk spoke to me in German because she could see my German heritage. "Ich spreche kein Deutsch." Everywhere else in Europe, people recognized me as an American. But in Germany, I looked right at home.

Each guest room was uniquely and exquisitely appointed. We had a tiny balcony overlooking the stunning gardens. The restaurant was both elegant and intimate; the romance was off the charts. The delicious food was paired with luscious wines. After dinner, the sommelier described the dessert wine offerings of their legendary German late-harvest Rieslings. Don ordered one for us to share, but I interrupted him. According to my currency exchange calculations, he had ordered a thousand-dollar glass of wine. A thousand dollars for three ounces. On second thought, he selected a fifty-dollar choice.

Enjoying these experiences made me feel cherished, loved, and special. I would cuddle up with Don and imagine he could make me feel secure and happy forever. He could take away the pain of being me. He could fill the hole in my heart left by my mother's passing.

Again, I didn't flinch when he tricked me into signing a quick claim to take my name off the deed of our new house. It was wrong of him to not tell me why I was meeting him at the attorney's office or what he was asking me to sign—until the moment the attorney presented it to me. Don read me right and knew I would surrender against my better judgment. I was past the point of thinking we could have a reasonable conversation about a conflict in front of this attorney; I knew Don could and would provoke and befuddle me. Anyway, it wasn't about the money, I rationalized. He needed that to feel secure; I didn't.

I started to flinch slightly when he asked me to enter into a real estate transaction that was not entirely kosher, to provide a tax shelter for his rental property. Surely his lack of integrity in business dealings was not going to affect our relationship. *No one was perfect, right?*

These indiscretions bothered me more than I realized. First, I strive to have a high standard for personal integrity, and I was taking my first steps down from it, although I ignored it at the time. More importantly, our inability to manage the most minor conflicts had traumatized me to such an extent that I was now unwilling to attempt to address more significant disagreements. Sir Ego surrendered his lance immediately and took cover behind his shield.

I hated myself afterward for being weak and allowing myself to be tyrannized. I was hypervigilant to ensure I wouldn't ruin a perfect evening by touching a VV, his or mine. Yet sometimes he came home from work irritated and confrontational. I learned not to ask why, as this would cause me to become the target of his negativity. Such miscues were no longer swept under the carpet by the next morning. I would be shunned, ignored, and stonewalled the next day, sometimes for multiple days.

The cumulative effect of the miscues was taking its toll on me. One day I was hysterical and paranoid, unable to grasp or explain what was happening. I packed a bag and fled to a friend's house. On the way, I stopped at a bookstore and picked up a book on emotional abuse, which described things like gaslighting, baiting, circular conversations, and normalizing bad behavior. Although I vaguely identified with concepts in the book, I could not embrace them as my reality.

In fact, my reality had become quite hazy. I questioned what had really happened. *How were my perceptions so different from his?* This could not be happening to me. I could not see the facts through the haze of my desire for and attachment to this amazing life.

When he called me to ask me to come back, he said, "We will work it out. It's okay." And without any plan to improve the relationship, I took all the blame and went home.

Toxic relationships are a dance. One party has a pattern of behavior that is intended to shape and control the other party's emotional responses, with Sir Ego favoring the lance. The other party unconsciously agrees to this dance, believing he or she is responding submissively out of love, with Sir Ego favoring the shield.

It was often not what Don said, but the way he said it that bothered me, as if I were disgusting, repulsive, or even insane. Over time, he grew more unreasonable and irrational with me, as did his insistence that I was crazy and explosive. My confusion, desperation, and frustration caused me to act explosively, justifying his behavior and condemnation. My VVs just got too big and too numerous to contain.

I stuffed all this into the chest because we were planning our wedding, which was going to be held on the grounds of a scenic, lush winery overlooking the Napa Valley. All our relatives were coming in from Philadelphia and Indiana. It would be a unique and elegant affair. My gown was being handmade of imported silk, matched with perfect pearl-colored heels that I had bought at Harrod's in London. The wedding cake was ordered: three tiers of sumptuously flavored cheesecakes in raspberry, dark chocolate marble, and vanilla crème. The winery's finest champagne would be offered, among other wines and refreshments. We were taking dance lessons and had a waltz routine choreographed to Elvis's "I Can't Help Falling in Love with You" for our wedding dance. I couldn't cancel this.

Don and I had arranged to honeymoon in Greece: one week in Athens, one week chartering a sailboat to sail the islands, and one week on Santorini, the gem of the islands. The sailboat included a captain who would navigate the isles, beaching us each day on a tiny, secluded slice of utopia.

In Santorini, we stayed in Oia, a little cobblestone street on a hilltop sprinkled with white stucco buildings and cobalt-blue church domes. Our chalet, midway down the hillside, required climbing one hundred steps, with a donkey to carry the luggage. This was the fairy tale come true and the happily-ever-after. I could not—would not—admit that this was not a good idea to break off the engagement. The grail was within reach, Sir Ego's resolve was strong, and the wise one was not consulted.

It was a stunningly beautiful wedding. The honeymoon was delicious, exotic, and hedonistic. And when the honeymoon ended, the palace door shut tight after me, and I found myself trapped in a dungeon. For years, there were no more trips, balls, friends, or parties. There was not even a night at the movies. The whole affair had been a bait and switch.

At first, I complained about it, but the emotional repercussions were too severe.

***

"I was talking to my college roommate, Carrie, today, and she invited us to dinner this weekend. Would you like to go?" I inquired hesitantly. I surveyed Don to gauge his mood, hoping to see his lighthearted smile. I was disappointed to see a blank look, masking his calculating mind as it formulated a response.

"No, I don't want to go there. It's too far away," he declined, mildly returning my gaze of evaluation, estimating the strength of my resolve.

"Okay. We can invite them here," I countered with a slight smile, ever hopeful.

"Her husband is too young. I don't have anything in common with him," Don declined again, unyielding and staunch.

"I thought you liked him. Well, let's do something fun, maybe with someone else. How about your friend Joe and his wife? We haven't seen them for a long time. Or maybe a movie?" I continued believing we were negotiating in good faith.

"I don't want to invite them. Why do you always need to stir up shit?" he spat back, his crystal-blue eyes ablaze, throwing down the gauntlet.

"I'm sorry. I just want to do something this weekend. What would you like to do?"

"I don't want to be bullied into anything with your friends whom I don't even like. Evan [Don's psychiatrist] says I need to stop you from putting your needs above mine in a selfish and unhealthy way."

I felt nausea swell up as my heart dropped into my stomach. *Here we go again.* On a good night, I would have stopped there, slumped down, and disappeared. But I did not on this evening.

"It is perfectly normal to want to do something fun on the weekend," I asserted while silently screaming, *I am normal!* in response to the implied diagnosis of pathology by a psychiatrist I had never met and who probably never said such a thing.

"It's *always* about you and your friends. You don't even care what I want."

"What?" We had stopped having my friends—or any friends—over long ago. "I don't care whose friends we invite over. I just want to do something fun this weekend."

"That's really weird!" he accused with disgust, the coup de grâce. I always panicked when he wielded this sword, my unknown and indeterminate fatal flaw exposed.

My face contorted in rage. I shouted the truth, "You are the one being weird. You are the one being selfish. You are the one bullying me. I am trying to cooperate and negotiate with you, and you are acting like a jerk!" I was shaking, out of control, frustrated, and confused.

With a composed smirk, he announced his victory. "There is really something wrong with you." He ambled away to his office, reclined in his supple leather chair, and poured himself a nice drink.

Thoughts racing, I ran to our bedroom and replayed the conversation a million times. *When did it go wrong? What did I say? Was I being selfish? Was I a bully? How can I fix this? I am not okay. This is not okay. I need to apologize and repair this. We should never go to bed angry. I'm calm now. I'm sorry. I'll go talk to him.* I forgot that we'd replayed this scene a thousand times and there was no happy ending.

I went into his office. "I'm sorry. I didn't mean what I said. I didn't realize you didn't like Carrie's husband. Let's start over. What do you want to do this weekend?" It was a peace offering spoken with guilt and remorse.

"I don't want to do anything with you. You are crazy and selfish," he declared, guiltless and superior. All traces of anger were gone; he was calm and methodical. Uninterested, he returned to a *Sunset* magazine article on Italian herb gardens.

He was right. I was acting crazy. This was crazy. Maybe I was crazy.

A few more attempts at reconciliation were met with equally dismissive responses. I surrendered, skulking away to collapse in my pool of self-pity. *What the hell just happened?* I wondered again.

The next morning, I lay in bed awake, uneasy and unsure of his state of mind. Tentatively, I brushed my hand against his back and snuggled closer. Without a word, he pushed me away and got out of bed, dressed, and went to work. I called later, but he didn't answer the phone. I left a voice mail, offering to take him to lunch. He didn't respond. I thought, *I have so much to be grateful for. I should stop complaining and give more.*

***

Don seemed to know that certain phrases triggered my VVs. He dropped these phrases anywhere in the conversation where they would cause maximum effect. Examples of these phrases included any reference to his ex-wife (I couldn't be like her), his psychiatrist (the ultimate judge condemning my behavior), or the final judgment, "That's really weird." (I wasn't even human; I was beyond redemption.) In this way, he could provoke me in front of others, even counselors, and they could not detect it.

And we went to many counselors, at least four, repeating the same pattern. I would watch him calmly and confidently paint a picture with factual details and subtle innuendo combined with seemingly innocuous untruths. The resulting picture received by the therapist was far from my perception of the same situation and was always a very unfavorable portrayal of me. Blindsided, confused, and VVed, I would become slightly hysterical defending myself, thus affirming Don's accusations. My personal therapist later told me this was a common therapy scenario between a controlling husband and a controlled wife.

My dawning realization that Don did not attend these counseling sessions to work out issues on his side of the street, but to prove my guilt and have me "fixed" eventually ended these attempts. I saw too that he took the children to their counselor to have them "fixed" as well. No wonder that ended without progress.

Over time, it became easier and easier for Don to provoke me because my stuffed chest of hurts was overfull, almost exploding. I found it was easier to accept the guilty charge and silently commit to do better, be better, and be lovable, all to make this work.

Unwittingly, I had made a deal with the devil. In return for an extraordinary life of wonderful material things and the opportunity to have the children I craved, I had to be accountable for Don's happiness, not just my own. It seemed like a good deal at the time, but it was far harder to endure than I expected. I had watched as my mother managed my father and our family's well-being. I thought I could do it too. I could make this work. I wanted to make this work. I had to make this work.

For some time, I made excuses for Don's behavior. My excuses fell into one of two categories. One came from a focus on Don: how he had been so hurt by his first wife that he needed me to accommodate the wounds and dysfunctional behaviors those wounds caused. The second came from a focus on me: how I would be loved and have a happily-ever-after; how I would make this man love me, as my father never did; and how I had to make this work because my biological clock was ticking louder and louder. Everything was perfect because it couldn't *not* be perfect. I couldn't stand for this not to be perfect.

All the secrets I had shared with Don in our intimate moments became weapons he now wielded against me. He continued to study me, discovering my every fear, hurt, weakness, and fault. We were intimate enemies.

Each time he pushed a button, I vowed again to become better, stronger, and more lovable. I wanted the pain to stop, and if I took responsibility for every toxic exchange, then I could get the pain to stop. But my strategy also strengthened Don in his dysfunction because he was never faced with taking responsibility for our problems. I didn't challenge his desire to control me, which fed something unhealthy in him. In fact, I believed I was the reflection I found in his mirrored glasses.

Just as my parents' glasses had reflected their internal state back to me, Don's glasses reflected his internal state, not the truth about me. Sometimes when I looked at Don, he reflected back to me the same lovable person I had found in my mother's glasses. I saw my beauty, my perfection, and my passionate and amazing self. He knew I needed and wanted this, and he was sure to offer it often enough to keep me engaged.

But other times, Don's glasses showed the same me I'd found in my father's glasses. I saw my weaknesses and failures, my inability to make him happy, and the needy black hole that seemed to be me. In time, I would come to see that this is the nature of Sir Ego as it attempts to control the people and events in the world around it. It would be a long time before I realized that we are all guilty of this manipulative behavior at times.

Don's cunning and charm enabled him to manipulate the reflection I saw in his mirrored glasses. He gained control over me through my emotions. With flattery, he manipulated what I saw. With guilt, he manipulated what I saw again. With empty affection and gifts, he manipulated, and then with punishment and disgust, he manipulated. He always kept me off balance. I lost touch with my internal compass, my intuition. I became more concerned with the images he reflected back to me than I was with seeing the truth of our relationship. Don became my god.

Sometimes he was triggered too much to be able to hide behind the mask of cunning manipulation, and then his self-loathing and fear were exposed. At these times he terrified me. I only needed a few of these experiences to learn that there was a dragon inside Don that I did not want to unleash. I became vigilant against the dragon's release. I did not understand that I didn't deserve this, I hadn't caused this, and I couldn't control this. My misguided and failed attempts to fix my relationship resulted in my developing maladaptive behaviors and coping skills. Most notably, I passively submitted, drank, and denied. Every day I stuffed emotions into my chest, challenging its capacity of containment.

Part of my implied agreement to make Don happy included always reflecting a nice image to him, no matter what he did to me. Rather than confront him with his troublesome behavior, I continued to treat him as if he were loved and loving. Or I did so as best I could, given my deteriorating emotional state. In this way, I manipulated too. I manipulated what Don saw. I forgave and excused him and tried to love him. I believed I could love him enough to make all the pain—his and mine—stop.

The world I saw through my glasses was a canvas for love, truth, integrity, and good intentions. I assumed Don wanted this too, and I projected the world I wanted onto him. I confused whom he really was with whom I wanted him to be. Who I was and what I wanted did not even enter into our relationship. It was all about Don getting what he wanted from me. And I allowed my enslavement. I lost myself.

These emotions had not seemed present in my parents' marriage. My father had not ruled over my mother, and she had not taken the lower path of absolute surrender to him. Both had taken a higher path, where he allowed her to lead in nurturing and family activities, and she allowed him to lead in the practical and financial realms. They each played to their strengths and compensated for each other's weaknesses. It was brilliant and robust, and it reflected great love, trust, and admiration between them.

A few times I thought I could break free by just physically leaving Don, but I found that I was still emotionally and mentally bound to him. Four times I stormed out and went to a friend's house, swearing never to return.

Then Don would call me to say, "Everything will work out."

And I would come back because I wanted to believe that everything would work out. I could not end this dance, no matter how much it hurt me. Sir Ego ignored the wise one's intuition.

In my pain, I reached out for spiritual solutions and self-help books. I wanted all aspects of my life to be exactly how it was on the material level, without the relationship dysfunctions. Eventually I exhausted the self-help shelf of the bookstore. No human effort on my part could control the miscues that were ruining my life. In frustration and despair, I could not control my reactions to his behavior. He had me. If anyone needed a miracle, it was me.

I found Marianne Williamson's books, *Return to Love* and *A Woman's Worth*, and I believed. I believed there was a Creator of love who removed all fear. I began to study *A Course in Miracles*, as Marianne Williamson suggested. Mesmerized by the poetic, insightful, profound, and revolutionary words, I fell in love with the *Course*, abbreviated *ACIM*. It explained the fear, pain, and suffering of this world and the most exquisite solution, love. I learned one thing for sure: this was not the life the Creator had planned for me.

ACIM was dictated to a scribe by an inner voice that identified itself as Jesus Christ. Without denying the Bible, the voice exhorted readers to seek a deeper and more mystical understanding of their spiritual journey. He asserted that the universal grail of self-realization can be attained by many paths and is foretold by many teachers. Alas, there may be false teachers and false grails on our quest, but these also teach us. They teach us what love is not. The wise one within each of us will lead us on our unique, personal, and individualized quest to transcend Sir Ego and reach the exalted grail.

My understanding was limited and colored by the denial of my situation. I prayed fervently for the Creator to fix my life, my husband, and my marriage. I learned transcendental meditation, which boasted a myriad of positive effects, and hoped relationship healing was one of them. I struggled with one foot on each side of the fence: one foot in the love and will of the Creator and the other unwilling to depart from the will of Sir Ego. I wanted to keep my relationship, material things, and hedonic life of wine, escape, and pleasure. I was sure these would make me happy and save me from the emptiness. Surely the Creator could see this and fix them.

I used words of love and forgiveness to justify turning the other cheek in response to each of Don's innuendos, insults, and attacks. I studied and meditated and meditated and studied, expecting miracles that were not forthcoming. I did not understand that miracles required demolishing the dysfunctional aspects of my life and rebuilding from the ashes. First, I had to relinquish my fears and choose love. Codependence and enabling arise from fear, not love.

Over time, failing to produce any improvement, I relinquished this pursuit and decided that having a child was the imperative. A child would fill the hole in my heart and give my struggle meaning. This was the deal breaker: I would leave Don if he did not live up to his promise to have children with me. After four years of stalling, it was time. I was thirty-six.

4

Double Divine

I don't know why, but Don agreed to another trip to Tahiti. We added New Zealand and Australia to our itinerary. We were back in the zone.

I planned an incredible trip, filled with sensory delights. It is amazing what money can buy. From Tahiti, we went to the island Huahine and stayed at the Hana Iti resort, where Diana Ross celebrated her fiftieth birthday party. Our accommodation was a multilevel, open-air tree house, literally built around the trunk of a huge tree. The bathroom afforded privacy but was still open to the elements, and the showerhead protruded from the tree trunk while water from the shower streamed down rocks into the ground. No wonder the natives were restless. They weren't living in this rustic opulence!

The highlight of New Zealand was a dolphin-watching excursion. We sailed out to find a pod of wild dolphins to play in the wake of the boat. I have always had a special affinity for dolphins. Experts say dolphins are as intelligent as humans. I say they are far more intelligent: they don't have wars, poverty, hatred, or crime. If we had found a pod in shallower water, the excursion operators would have allowed us to get in the water and swim with them. I missed the opportunity that time, but I would swim with wild dolphins on future occasions.

The lowlight was Don getting mad at me about something and saying he was not going on to Australia, that he was booking a flight home. Did he think I was going to argue with him?

I said, "Fine, but I am going on to Australia. Do as you like."

It turned out this was an empty threat, and we continued on to Australia the next day.

I shared my father's interest in the world of the sea, and I arranged for scuba lessons on a small private island in the middle of the Great Barrier Reef. The only thing on the island was a five-star resort, a one-of-a-kind experience. We had to take a small seaplane to the resort and land on the water. Our accommodation was rustic and elegant at the same time, a plush bed covered in mosquito netting and lavish linens.

Scuba diving on the Great Barrier Reef is arguably the best diving in the world. I was instantly addicted. It's unlike snorkeling, during which you are an observer of the other world of the sea. When diving, you are a part of that world, a colorful, iridescent, peaceful ecosystem. It surrounds you as you depart from the flatness of our earthly world into a world where you move up and down, flying through wonders. It expands your thinking about what is possible when you see this world of exotic shapes, textures, and colors. There are diversity and harmony as well as simplicity and interdependence. I wish I could live there.

In addition to diving, we sailed a little boat around the island to a tiny, deserted beach, a postcard vision of lush tropical flora, fine white sand, and turquoise water. It shimmered in the sun like a million diamonds and stretched out into infinity. Palm fronds danced in the tropical breeze; the sunshine bathed us in warmth and vitality. Our picnic basket overflowed with crab, lobster, brie, croissants, and an Australian Riesling. We were King Titan and his mermaid queen, seated on fine white sand thrones, overlooking our aquatic kingdom and the heavens beyond. The surreal beauty and harmony of this picturesque scene contrasted invisibly with the power struggle of our demons concealed just beneath the surface of our awareness.

When we returned to the United States, I stepped right back onto the infertility train, which increased my desperation to have children. After some time, Don agreed to do in vitro. We succeeded on our first try. Twin girls! Imagine my ecstasy. I felt rich, abundant, and fulfilled.

My pregnancy was a wonderful giddy time, both for myself and my relationship with Don. We had fun again and planned for a happy family. I remember the two of us sitting outside under the moonlight, wondering what our children would look like and whom they would favor. We shared the ultrasound introduction to our new family members in awe and delight. My hope that the goodness in Don could triumph over the darkness was renewed. I felt worthy of his love and respect. Perhaps he had a protective instinct for me during my pregnancy. It probably helped that I quit drinking and Don cut down.

When the girls were born, my joy was overwhelming. So was the work! But I didn't care. I was willing to do whatever it took to be happy and loved. Now I was successful.

There is no love as sweet, profound, intoxicating, and illuminating as the love between a mother and her newborn … and her other newborn! Although we hired a part-time nurse to help us adjust, I did so well with the girls that the nurse left ahead of schedule. Chris and Nicole were easy babies, and my instincts were good. We established a rhythm and synchronization quickly. I became adept at feeding them both at the same time and at the many other tasks only an octopus could have accomplished better. I was overflowing with love, joy, and fulfillment.

Lauren and Bob loved Nicole and Chris. What a big, happy family we were! Everything was going to be fine. Sir Ego hid behind his shield of denial.

Maybe a part of me also quietly thought that now that I had my children, I would be fine with or without Don. I suspect Don knew this on some level. I was unwilling to play games now. It wasn't just that I was too tired, which I was. I quit trying to earn Don's love. The twins gave me love without Don's toxic price tag. I looked into their eyes and saw the perfectly loving reflection of me I had seen when I looked at my mother years ago, unconditional love at last.

Something else happened too. I became a lioness, ferociously protecting my young. I might have been willing to tolerate Don's abuse toward me, but I was not going to tolerate his emotional manipulation with our children.

My new intellectual passion was learning everything possible about good parenting and loving boundaries (something of a challenge for a codependent like me). I read and reread every book I could find until I had marinated my brain long enough to behave accordingly, even under the duress of two crying kids. My wise one was channeling my mother, and I felt confident and rewarded.

From my studies on twins, I concluded that I would resist the temptation to dress them alike all the time. They weren't bookends. However, I did usually get mix-and-match outfits for holiday photos because it really is adorable. By the time they were eighteen months, it was hard enough to get them to put any clothes on to get out the door. I couldn't imagine the added complexity of ensuring they were matching.

Around age two, Nicole adored her half-brother Bob and began dressing like him. She duplicated his habit of wearing gym shorts underneath and sweat pants over top. I had to wash clothes every night to ensure the uniform was available each day or there would be an eruption. She insisted on getting her hair cut short like his and would not wear any clothes she considered feminine. By age four, Chris also followed this tomboy trend. I could see that I wasn't going to be attending adorable ballet performances filled with tiny pink tutus, as I had imagined. Gracefully, I surrendered this selfish desire.

In truth, I loved that they had a passion about themselves and did not discourage this self-expression. I packed up the Laura Ashley velvet toddler dresses with lace collars wistfully and embraced this new reality. From then on, both dressed like boys, convincingly. Throughout elementary school, they would never use the bathroom because other girls would ask them to leave the girls' room. Their teachers would always agree with me, even though many other mothers advised me against it.

My parenting prowess made it all the more intolerable when Don would cut in with his version of parenting. Most of the time, he left me alone, even when I desperately needed another set of arms. When he did intervene, it was not what I wanted. For example, Don and I agreed to follow the Ferber method, letting the girls "cry it out" in order to teach them to self-soothe and fall asleep. Picking them up after a crying spell would teach them to cry for a longer period next time.

Don complied by day, but at night, he would act as if I were cruelly allowing my kids to be traumatized. I would sit right outside the door of their Pottery Barn Kids periwinkle nursery to assure Don that I was not going to let anything bad happen. But one night, he stormed past me anyway and picked up Chris to soothe her.

The next day, I approached him in his office. "I see that this method of crying it out isn't working for you. Do you have any other ideas? It would be good if we could get on the same page about this."

"I am not going to discuss this. You are just going to do whatever you want anyway."

I stood there in total shock as he accused me of the very thing he had done and was doing right then. I was starting to understand the concept of projection, although it was very challenging at first. Don showed me, with clarity, how he projected his wrongdoing onto me. Eventually I saw that many of the untrue things he said to me and about me were really about him. Perhaps the look of loathing he gave me was due to him projecting his demons onto me and attacking them. I didn't know it at the time, but I was getting an extraordinary lesson into the wily ways of Sir Ego.

A primary concept in *ACIM* is Sir Ego's use of guilt and the projection of guilt onto others as a means to escape its fundamental fears. It is a very slippery concept. I was getting a front-row seat in the VIP box to see this defense mechanism at work. It stopped me cold in my tracks. I spun out mentally, trying to understand how I was guilty and he was not.

Don sold his company just before the girls were born. He was looking for a new venture and spent most days in his home office. Crying babies were common but most unwelcome to him. I had carefully planned my parenting style. Don's ad hoc interventions were usually in direct conflict with my approach. Take biting, for example. If one girl bit the other—a big problem with the twins because neither was developmentally mature enough to stop the cycle—I would put the offender in the playpen in the other room for a time-out.

Then Don would go in, pick her up, and take her for a walk outside. The lesson? If you bite your sister, you get special Daddy time. The twin who'd been bit would stand at the door, feeling left out and crying, victimized a second time. My heart burned.

Don would also wait in the girls' room to cuddle them whenever he heard me send them to their room for a time-out. Instead of learning to change their behavior and self-soothe, they learned to be emotionally dependent on Daddy. This seemed to send a message to the girls that disturbed me: "Mommy is mean. Daddy loves you. You don't need to feel guilt or remorse for what you have done. Look to Daddy for your emotional stability. I manage whether or not you feel bad."

Our family room, where I was stationed most of the day, resembled a jumbled preschool, with wall-to-wall toys, toddler paraphernalia, and two of almost everything but not quite everything. So the issue of sharing became another controversy with Don. When the girls fought over something, my response came down to one of three choices: (1) get a different (hopefully duplicate) toy, (2) take turns, and, if that failed, (3) give the toy a time-out.

Don thought this was an absurd approach. He believed that whoever got the toy first should get it and that was just tough luck for the sibling. It reminded me hauntingly of his belief that his needs were more important than mine.

By the time the girls were three, the friction between Don and me was untenable. I had a full and happy life with the girls. We attended Mommy-and-me classes and made great friends. Our social life was filled with playdates, swim lessons, beach trips, and afternoons at the park. I had two friends who each had her own twin girls, the same age as Chris and Nicole. We referred to the six girls as the six-pack. Nothing could be cuter than the panoramic picture of the six of them sitting at the edge of our pool, wearing little bathing suits covered in butterflies, polka dots, and rainbow-colored fish. I thought I had quarantined the toxic part of my life and built a separate life of enchantment and adventure with the girls, but my friends saw what I wanted to deny, that my marriage was becoming very destructive for me.

Don wasn't part of the happiness I'd found. He could no longer have me on his terms, where I placed his needs above all else. And he did not like the lioness I had become. In his view, I had reneged on our deal. I no longer cared about making him happy. I had found the love I wanted in my daughters' eyes. Without Don's consent, I had subconsciously cut a new deal.

I was willing to stay in the marriage as long as I could stay home with our children, an experience greater than all the traveling and material things. But Don's desire to control me persisted. He escalated the frequency and severity of his attempts. Somehow he expected being meaner to me would motivate me to become nicer to him. Again, I was seeing the inner workings of Sir Ego magnified in great detail, affirming the concepts of *ACIM*. Obviously being more loving to me would have been the right way to enliven the love in me, but Sir Ego sees that as weakness.

Unable to control me with fear, as he had in the past, Don's VVs increased. He couldn't get his inner or outer world under control. Without a connection to the wise one, a loving solution, or even an effective solution, Sir Ego became more controlling, angry, volatile, cruel, and overt. It became harder and harder for me to deny that something was dreadfully wrong in Camelot. My fear and VV explosions increased as I teetered closer to the edge of hysteria.

I was too intoxicated by my life with the girls to realistically assess my situation with Don. I was also too intoxicated by wine and denial, the only two effective solutions I had for the frenzy that lay just beneath the surface of my armor. Don and I were both heavy drinkers. Although he continued to drink for hours after I went to bed, Don said I was the one with a drinking problem. I was busy with my full-time job of caring for the kids. I drank a little too much after they went to bed, but Don was sitting in his office—and possibly drinking—all day. I could not reconcile his accusations with my reality. Still, he played on my guilt about drinking. Alcohol was not the only problem in my marriage, but it was a problem we both had. And it exacerbated our other problems.

Don set about collecting evidence of my "badness." He began secretly recording our arguments. After finding recordings a couple of times, I became alert to the pattern. When he argued, he would take a break and then return, very calmly baiting me. Don kept the recordings in a safe, as evidence for some judge at some future hearing. He also kept the letters I wrote him, in which I apologized for my part in our arguments.

One evening, I noticed that a video camera was recording us. I grabbed the camera and started to remove the tape. Don tackled me to the ground, wrestling for control of the recorder and refusing to free me—until I bit him! Naturally he photographed the bruise on his arm, using my camera to compound my guilt and his illusion of blamelessness.

The years of psychological games and the stress of caring for my twin babies wore me down. His abuse went from subtle and covert to threatening and overt. My panic and paranoia rose. Don played on all my fears like an orchestra conductor, knowing just how to tease the flute of vanity, tickle the ivories of insecurity, and reach a crescendo with the bass drum of guilt and shame. Bing, bam, boom!

I had a sense that he was scheming something, but I didn't have any evidence. Then one summer evening, I brought the girls home after dining with our friends. I walked into the kitchen to see half a beer on the kitchen table, an empty glass of wine on the counter, and an open bottle of sake. Don was the only person who'd been home. It was going to be a bad night.

It got worse. I heard him talking on the phone with my dad. I got the sick feeling that they were comparing their rap sheets of my crimes. Dad was the perfect partner for Don's tirade against me. My heart sank. I had been willing to overlook my own hurt to allow my girls to have a relationship with their grandfather. It turned out that my dad was a much better grandfather than he was a father. But now this fragile truce was being violated.

The next day I called my dad, and he immediately launched into a heated tirade against me. One of his main grievances was that I hadn't helped him take care of my mother when she was dying. *What? That was how he remembered it?* He was also angry that my mom had used an inheritance from her aunt for to pay for my college tuition instead of his dream of a hobby farm, which he later got anyway. He also reminded me that I had never paid back the thousand dollars they gave me for the down payment on my first car. I offered to send him the money. I hadn't asked him for another cent in twenty years. It was clear to me that if I were going to leave my husband, I could not count on my dad.

I had tried to make these two men love me, and it had come to this. It appeared I could do nothing to become good enough to love. I didn't understand that I was looking for love where it couldn't be found.

That same evening, there was another incident. Don said he would add my name to the title of the house when he refinanced it. While the prenup I had signed made sense to me before we had children, it didn't make sense anymore. I believed I should share in the financial security Don enjoyed. It meant a great deal to me when Don offered to add my name to the title. It was a last shred of hope, some basis for healing our relationship. But when I found the refinance papers on the kitchen table and asked Don where I should sign, he said I couldn't be added to the title because of my poor credit. The only credit I'd had in the last seven years was his, and it was impeccable.

The next day, I called the mortgage broker to find out what kind of error could be on my credit report.

"I didn't run a credit report on you. I don't know anything about you. Don said he lives alone in the house," she told me.

Not only had Don denied my request to be added to the title, he was denying my existence. Terror and dread blazed through me. What was most disconcerting was the oblique nature of the threat. Nothing made sense. I couldn't see the whole puzzle, though the few pieces were visible, dark, and menacing. I became very paranoid. I feared Don could be taping my phone calls and calling my friends. Who knew what?

5

Attempted Escape

Over the next few days, I confided in my closest friends, who agreed to help me get out of my marriage. Their concern for me had been growing for some time, and they were ripe to help me take action. I trusted their judgment because I could not trust my own. Almost every VV in my chest was firing at maximum velocity, and my reasoning faculties had long since flown the coop.

That weekend, Don and I were supposed to go to the beach for a few days with the kids. He decided not to go, given the recent turmoil in our relationship. I invited my friend Donna and her twins to join us in the town house on the beach we had reserved. The girls and I often took vacations with our friends, without Don. What a delightful sight for a troubled soul: four three-year-old girls huddled around a campfire on the beach, roasting marshmallows for s'mores, all covered in gooey chocolate and toothy grins, giggling and chattering. Donna and I discussed how her husband, a partner in a law firm, could provide a reference for a divorce attorney.

The sooner the better, I thought.

Don sent me flowers and a note, saying that everything would be okay.

When we returned home, I was edgy, and my mind was restless. Even with my growing resolve to get out of the marriage, I was still struggling to acknowledge it as a failure. I really wanted everything to be okay. I loved the idea of being married. I loved my girls and my stepkids. I loved our family. I loved being a stay-at-home mom. In fact, my self-esteem, at an all-time low, made the concept of getting a job and being a single parent seem overwhelming. It was forbidding, intolerable, unimaginable, unattainable, and dreadful.

Somehow all of Don's malicious intentions toward me boiled down to one infuriating point for me, his phone call to my dad. I needed to confront Don about this.

"I could kill you for talking to my dad like that and destroying our fragile détente," I said.

Don walked away. I followed him into the garage, where he reached for a utility knife. "I am such a bad person. I should just slit my wrists and get it over with."

I walked away from him and his theatrics. He would do anything but take responsibility.

When I went into our bedroom that night, Don was holding a bottle of sleeping pills. "I should take the whole bottle."

But he put them away and got into bed. Next, he opened the nightstand drawer and pulled out a gun. Before I could interpret the unfolding events, he said, "I wish I could die and join my dad."

Don had a gun in the nightstand drawer! What the hell was going on? Was he really suicidal?

This man, whom I had loved, was obviously in great emotional pain, whether he was truly suicidal or staging a desperate theatrical performance to my detriment. Yet I felt little compassion. I was on insanity overload. His behavior was just too volatile, too irrational, and too bizarre. Everything was unraveling so fast. Everything in my chest was jumbled. *Was I crazy? What was true? Who was I? What was mine? What were my problems, my obligations, and my responsibilities? What were my rights?* I had lost my bearings, and I could not see which way was up. In scuba diving, when you lose your bearings, you look at your air bubbles, which are always going up. I had no air bubbles to show me the way.

That night I took the gun, hid it, and went to bed in the guest room. But I didn't sleep. The next day I called Don's therapist and told him what had happened. He invited me to come see him on his lunch break, which was just after his appointment with Don. Upon arriving, I was struck by his unconcerned demeanor. Even if he were discounting Don's suicide threats, I expected him to see that they were the sign of a seriously disturbed mind.

"Did you threaten to kill him?" he asked with slight disdain.

"What? I was angry that he had caused trouble between my dad and me. I said something sarcastic like that, not a real threat."

Don had told him that I had seriously threatened to kill him. As the conversation proceeded, it became clear to me that he believed I was an unstable alcoholic and the cause of all the problems in the family. The conversation crushed my hope that help would be found there. I realized the insane nature of the conversation I had unwittingly embarked on. I was face-to-face with an alter ego of Don's who believed everything he said and showed me a mirror image of the demon he had portrayed me as. Suddenly, with nauseating clarity, I saw the reflection of his own demons. *How could I ever fight this delusion?*

That was my great mistake. I thought I had to fight it. This situation would have been an appropriate one in which to use denial, denying the delusion that he had conjured. For many years, I would instead fight with this delusion that I had made real in my own inner world. I accepted his projection of his demons onto me and came to believe and enact his perspective of me.

He was a genius at planting seeds of ideas in the minds of therapists. Their sessions would nurture the seeds until they blossomed into Don's version of reality. Denying an accusation to a therapist is confirmation of your guilt. I didn't even try.

Although we did not agree on the cause of my marital discord, Don's therapist and I did agree that it had escalated to a breaking point and that we should separate. He asked me to remove the pills and weapons from the house. I took the pistol, a rifle, and a pellet gun to a friend's house and inventoried more than a hundred narcotics from the safe, which I took to a safe deposit box.

Based on our independent conversations with his therapist, Don and I began to discuss separating over dinner that evening. Things were different now. My naïveté was gone. I was aware of his veiled threats about custody and money and couldn't ignore my uneasy feelings during our conversation.

I had always been aware of his habitual lying but had never seen the purpose. He would lie about the most innocuous things. He could take a fact and spin it 180 degrees from reality. I knew he wanted to keep me off balance. Now I saw that he was weaving a web and creating an alternate reality, his. In it, he looked good all the time, and I looked bad all the time. Once he devised and articulated this reality, he believed it, which made him very convincing when he painted the picture for someone else.

While he spoke to me that night, I devised the notion of a "truth index," which I used to evaluate the truthfulness of his statements. Most of his statements scored around 50 percent. I could see there was some truth in them, some factual basis, but I could also see that he was spinning facts to look like something else.

That night I learned the most important lesson of our relationship: 50 percent of what he said was not true, and I couldn't know which 50 percent that was. So I had to discount everything and trust nothing. The wise one penetrated Sir Ego's denial with the first sane thought I'd had about our relationship in years.

Our conversations about living arrangements and custody diverged. I realized this was going to be very complicated. My experience had shown me that Don would do anything to get his way. There was also the problem of money. He had all of it.

When I visited a divorce attorney, we discussed mediation. Despite the threat of recent events, we concluded that Don and I could mediate the situation and come to a mutually agreeable solution. The attorney joined me in my denial. She did not even mention filing for divorce and requesting custody, a grave mistake because I lost the first-move advantage. Instead she suggested that Don and I take a vacation from each other, which would not prejudice custody proceedings while we mediated.

Conversations with Don, however, stalled. We could not agree on how to proceed. He was not motivated to separate or mediate. I was extremely motivated. Each moment I spent in that house with him was another moment for him to gather his evidence against me. I was desperate, paranoid, and driven to get out of that house as quickly as possible. My friends offered the only compass I trusted. They helped me plan an escape.

But my escape required money I did not have. Don had me on a very short leash financially. A few months earlier, he had let me go an entire week without funding our joint bank account or renewing my expired credit card. He wouldn't even discuss the matter. He was trying to teach me some kind of lesson, but we never had a rational discussion about it to resolve the situation. So I got a credit card in my maiden name. I solved the short-term problem but was still plagued by the bigger issue.

"What would happen if you were in a car accident and I had no access to any money to care for the girls?" I demanded.

But Don refused to add me to any of his accounts. Instead he placed a check for $10,000 in my name in a file in his office for such an emergency. In my mind, this was an emergency, so I went to get the check. To my surprise, it was for $100,000, not $10,000. Moments later, I was on the phone with my lawyer. She told me to deposit the check immediately. I went to the bank and opened a new bank account with the check that same afternoon. It would take three days for the check to clear before the funds were available.

I launched into a flurry of planning for a move. I signed a lease for November 1 (one week away) for a nearby town house. I started accumulating spare furniture, which I stored in a friend's garage. I hired movers. Relief flooded me. The girls and I would soon be free of my tormentor. My whole plan was contingent on the funds from that check, so I counted the minutes until I could call the bank to verify that the check had cleared.

Meanwhile, I suffered silently at home, staying away from any conflict with Don. I assumed he would foil my plan if he found out about it, in order to regain control. I couldn't take that risk. I didn't want to stay in that house one more day than I had to.

On the afternoon of the third day, I was with Donna and the kids at the park when I called the bank. I was told that Don had stopped payment on the check the preceding day. He'd known about it and hadn't said a word to me about it the night before. The game of cat and mouse continued, and I was the mouse again.

My hysteria made me reckless. Donna was taking her family to San Diego the next day. I decided the girls and I should join her and stay in San Diego on vacation for the five days until moving day. I promptly made plane and hotel reservations, and then I ordered a bunk bed to be delivered to my town house on November 1. I shifted into a kind of emergency overdrive and ran as fast as I could to get away from Don. I couldn't see going home to him. I called him from the airport to tell him that we were going on vacation and would be home in five days.

He said, "Don't do this."

But I did. San Diego is a great place for three-year-olds. We went to Legoland, the San Diego Zoo, and Marine World. We drove up to enjoy Disneyland on Halloween and then flew back home to settle into our new town house. I had the girls call Don and leave voice mails telling him what they were doing each day so he would know they were fine.

My fears were fueled by phone calls with my stepkids, who informed me that Don was talking to an attorney about filing some kind of action. Lauren and Bob suggested that I talk to their mother, which I did. Her experiences resembled my eerie experiences with Don, including the bedside gun. Many things he had led me to believe about her were lies. *Had Don demonized her? And was he doing the same to me?*

When I went to pay the hotel bill with the credit card in my own name, it was denied. The bank told me that their fraud department had called my home to see if the unusual charges in San Diego were fraudulent, and Don had told them that the card was stolen. With the help of my valid driver's license, I convinced the bank that the card was not stolen and that the charges were legitimate. They reinstated my card.

I was on the run and afraid of shadows. But I shouldn't have been looking behind me because the devil was one step ahead of me at every turn. As we walked down the runway after our plane landed in San Francisco, Don was waiting with Lauren, Bob, and the police. Again my mind could not compute what was happening. Lauren and Bob took the girls. Don walked alongside me and told me that he now had sole custody of the girls.

"What kind of lies did you have to tell to get that?" I demanded.

He smirked and offered no explanation. I was so far behind in this game that Don didn't even need to engage with me anymore. He called the shots.

I told the police about the town house and my fears of returning home with him. The police insisted that Don not force me to go home with him. Finally he agreed to let the girls stay with me at the town house for one night. We left the airport.

Don had obtained ex parte custody order on the basis of an allegation that I was a flight risk. He claimed that my whereabouts had been unknown during this trip to San Diego and previously on the beach trip. He got sole custody without giving me a chance to respond. A hearing was set in another two weeks, at which time I would be able to respond.

Despite the fact that Don knew his allegations weren't true and that I had rented a town house nearby, he continued to claim I was a flight risk and wouldn't allow the children to be with me unattended. For two weeks, I hardly saw the girls. He had never been alone with them for one hour, much less overnight. And I had never been away from them for more than a couple hours. Each night they called, crying for me. But to Don, his charade was more important than their welfare. I went to the girls' preschool to see them and to reassure them that everything was going to be okay.

Although it didn't seem possible, my anguish, despair, and terror got worse. I was faced with the brutal reality of what Don was capable of, how unreasonable he was, and to what lengths he would go to continue to control me. I could only hope that the court would see what was really going on and set this right again in two weeks.

Don was attacking my motherhood, my most cherished role and identity. He defiled it with unjust allegations, and I spontaneously combusted in self-righteous rage. Fortunately my friend's attorney husband helped me to craft a crystal clear response for the court.

Don's allegation that I had $100,000 and was a potential flight risk was false. I had the evidence of his stop payment, dated before his sworn statement. This was a documented lie. Don's allegation that he did not know where we were when we were on our beach vacation was false. I had the receipt for the flowers he'd sent me to prove this. Another documented lie. Don's allegations that he did not know our whereabouts and thought the kids were in danger during our trip to San Diego were also false. He had saved the voice mails from the girls, so I recorded and presented them. Another documented lie.

Further I had evidence of Don's suicide threats: a narcotics inventory and sworn statements about the weapons I had removed from our house weeks earlier. Finally I had evidence of my fully furnished town house, which reflected my commitment to live nearby and co-parent. How could I lose?

The day of the court hearing, Don and I were first assigned to meet with a custody mediator, who would make a recommendation to the court.

I spoke of the weekly activities the girls and I enjoyed with friends, the Mommy-and-me classes, swim lessons, music circle, and the playdates. Don had nothing to say. The mediator recommended I get primary custody, with Don getting Wednesday night dinners and every other weekend.

Despite all this, the court ordered fifty-fifty custody, alternating weeks, pending the results of a complete custody evaluation that would take three or more months to complete. As scared as I was of Don, I was much more afraid to leave the girls alone with him 50 percent of the time. There was absolutely no way I was going to let that happen to them. I moved back home while we waited for completion of the custody evaluation. I would not accept my freedom from Don unless it included the girls.

Christmas was coming. Don and I agreed to call a truce so the kids could enjoy a good holiday. I shoved the entire emotional trauma into my chest. I made everything as normal as possible for the girls. But anyone who has ever gone through a divorce knows that the kids feel the tension.

My brother and his family were coming. It would be a welcome distraction. Part of my agreement to return to Don's house involved keeping the town house and some cash in case I changed my mind and wanted to move back there. Since the town house was vacant, I offered it to my brother and his family for their stay. The girls and I spent most of our time with them during their visit.

One evening when we were at the town house, Don called every half hour, more intoxicated each time, asking when we were coming back.

Finally he said, "Just stay there. It'll be better."

Of course, that was fine with me. But after we had all the kids in bed, Don showed up, banging on the front door and telling us he had the police with him. He was incoherent. Eventually my brother called the police, and they took Don away. The officer was kind and told Don to quit drinking or he would lose his kids.

After that night, Don quit drinking and started going to Alcoholics Anonymous. This did improve things. In some foolish way, I even started to hope again. It wasn't that I thought Don and I could have a good marriage, but I feared the unknown more. My hope was that our lives together could be tolerable. You know, it's the devil you know versus the devil you don't. My self-esteem had fallen so low that I lacked any confidence in my ability to get a good job to support my girls as a single mom.

Don's sobriety lasted only a few months, and my fortitude weakened. I had even failed at ending my marriage. For several months, Don and I bounced back and forth between therapy and the custody evaluator. During this time, Don bought a business two hours away from the house, and for months, he spent most of his time away. I could easily have gotten custody at this point, but I didn't. I decided it would be better to move near Don's new business, where the cost of living was lower. We could give it one last try, and if it didn't work, we would be in a better place to raise kids as single parents.

The emotional and mental fortitude I lacked caused me to fall backward. I was not ready to give up being a stay-at-home mom or the financial security I'd known. I was willing to sacrifice myself for my girls. In retrospect, getting out of my marriage and creating a healthy and stable life for my girls would have been better than what was about to happen. But I was too far gone then to do that.

It was fun to buy a new house and furniture, making a fresh start. The girls would be attending kindergarten in a new neighborhood, and it was a great neighborhood for families, unlike our previous one. We quickly made lots of friends, and the girls became involved in lots of activities. It really was a good move for the kids. I desperately hoped that everything would get better, and I was feeling better too. But I was only kidding myself.

Don was very busy with his new business and was rarely home, which was fine with me. He gave us a parting surprise. One night he mentioned that someone at work had a litter of golden retriever puppies. My only response was to "get a girl."

Two nights later, I was making dinner and looked outside to see the girls playing with the new puppy. Chris wanted to call her Mary. I suggested Sierra, and that stuck. Sierra was great puppy therapy for the girls. But she didn't come from a litter that belonged to someone at work. Don had bought her from a breeder a hundred miles away that he'd found on Craigslist. Truth index: 70 percent.

Don had another surprise for me. Several clues showed me that he was having an affair. I couldn't decide which offended me more: the perfumed handkerchief under his pillow, the Taurus-Leo love report I found in the printer (Don is a Taurus; I am a Sagittarius), or the time the girls and I returned home from a weekend trip and I found all the framed photos of me turned facedown.

But my heart was already so broken that Don's infidelity didn't add much hurt. If he left me for someone else, surely he would free me more easily and advantageously. Guilt, if he felt any, could be good for my cause. What did hurt was the idea of another woman playing a stepmom to my kids and usurping our financial security.

We hadn't been in our new house for four months before Don bought another house and moved in with his new partner, a woman twenty-five years younger than he was. But that was Don's MO, get custody of the new girlfriend before she figures out what he is really like.

Busy with his girlfriend, Don accommodated my wish to have the girls most of the time. He also suggested that he would be benevolent in both custody and the financial settlement. We went into mediation with two different mediators. Both times we negotiated an amicable agreement that Don took to his attorney, who nullified all the cooperative terms and crafted a one-sided settlement instead. I refused this bait and switch. It was a common game Don played. He would act like the good guy in mediation and then have his attorney do the dirty work.

On the day of the girls' fourth birthday party, I received word that my dad had passed away. Relief was really all I felt. I wouldn't have to face his not-love anymore. I inherited enough money to buy me time to indulge my broken heart, fight with Don, and not find a job.

My biggest problems remained inside me. I was emotionally devastated and depleted, and I could not imagine being able to get a job. In fact, I resisted the reality that I needed to get a job and that my new role was as a single, working mom. I was not dealing with the issues that needed to be dealt with. I was trying to wish them away or undo them instead—as if ignoring them would make them go away. Sir Ego was lost in the tornado of his VVs.

6

The Ecstasy and the Agony

I was so devastated that I couldn't imagine being employable, so I invested in a website development franchise. Being my own boss sounded good, and it was a welcome relief from the cruel master I had. Had I been on my game, I might have been able to make this sweet self-employment opportunity work. However, I was in tears as I prepared business proposals to submit to prospective clients, so I don't think I exuded the kind of energy that inspired their confidence. I submitted a lot of proposals but got very few signed contracts. I vacillated between false bravado and despair.

Daydreaming of my former life of exotic escapes, I Googled Club Med and scuba diving. Turks and Caicos—hmm, that had always been on my list of potential vacations. I needed a treat, and that seemed like just the right prescription. I had Don and his girlfriend, Barb, babysit while I had fun. The clear turquoise waters of the Caribbean would be a welcome change. Without much thought, I booked the trip. Surely my dad would approve of this way of using my inheritance. Maybe? Probably not. But I did not have to submit to him anymore either.

At my Caribbean destination, I could feel the balmy sunrays melt away the sticky, dense layer of depression. I came alive when my toes sank in the wet sand, and I fell into the warm, caressing, and cleansing waves. I was a million miles away from my troubles, inner and outer. For just a moment, I could feel the rightness of the universe as I floated on the salty surf.

Arriving at dinner, I was directed to the singles' dining room, where I was seated next to my soon-to-be beloved. I assumed my relationship signals would be as dismal as my business flop, so I didn't expect what happened next. Nick, the charming firefighter next to me, wore a $2,000 Ebel watch that matched mine and was also in the throes of marital dissolution. Magnetism beyond my understanding pulled us together in a whirlwind of intoxicating currents. Before we knew it, we had danced the night away and were not quite skinny-dipping in the moonlight.

We spent almost every moment of the week together, captivated by the romance and enchantment of our tryst. In perfect attunement, we enjoyed everything the Club Med had to offer. We mingled and giggled on a dive boat skimming over crystal waters and cruising past pristine shorelines to deliver us to the surreal delights one hundred feet below sea level. As we glided along on the resort's catamaran, a friendly wild dolphin, Joey, appeared, playfully skipping in our wake. We jet-skiied through the bay at top speed. We dirty-danced amid foam spray and flowing wine. Everyone thought we were newlyweds. Our infectious, intoxicating infatuation overflowed in fits of laughter and smiles, kisses, and caresses. All my pain melted away in the glow of his eyes, consuming the desolation and despair. I was hooked, big time.

However, Nick was straightforward and adamant that our liaison had no future. He was done raising his kids and was not interested in helping to raise mine. He said words that I did not hear: he was not reciprocating what he saw in my eyes. The week that seemed to last forever would—and did—end in a resolute good-bye. Kissed by the gods and rejected, I returned home to hell. At least now I had a fantasy, a joyful memory to relive, a hope I could be loved again. I resumed my dismal existence.

Two months later, Nick called and invited me to visit him in Santa Cruz for the weekend. Overwhelmed with joy, I rushed into the arms of my beloved. This began an eighteen-month love affair that would bring me to the heights of ecstasy and the depths of despair.

We each had significant amounts of free time. His job as a firefighter afforded frequent four-day weekends, and my self-employed, shared custody arrangement afforded me equal playtime. We played epically.

We called it extreme dating. We went on several exotic scuba-diving vacations to Cozumel, Key Largo, Belize, and Honduras. Each was more breathtaking than the last. We rode his motorcycle up the coast of Big Sur and lunched on the cliffs overlooking crashing waves. We went wine tasting all over Napa, Sonoma, and many other Northern California wine regions. Everything was first class: the finest hotels, bed and breakfasts, spa weekends, formal events, and fine dining. I acquired a new collection of little black dresses. We indulged every appetite and exploded in sensual feasts of intoxication, infatuation, and romance. Every moment we were together was a new shade of bliss.

Love flowed through me and from me like a fountain. I was giddy and delighted. I made friends at the gas pump and the grocery store. I flirted with the wine sommelier and the dive master. It was even sweeter than my love for my mother. Everything inside me was open. My heart exploded with butterflies, rainbows, moonbeams, and lightning bugs when I was with him. I envisioned that I could heal from the devastation piling up in my psyche. I hoped again that love could be my reality instead of the ever-present toxic vapors arising from my chest of VVs.

Consistent with my former pattern of denial, I refused to look at what was really happening beneath the veneer of rapture. First, Nick continued to affirm that, despite his love for me, there was no future for our relationship because of my children. I pushed away this truth and continued to hope that he would eventually concede. I knew how great a sacrifice it was to become a stepparent. I didn't want my children to have a reluctant stepparent. However, I pushed that idea out of my awareness also.

Second, I began to realize that Nick leaned toward a life of superficiality. He put subtle pressure on me to wear dangly earrings, high heels, miniskirts, and string bikinis. These things made me feel both wildly desirable and a bit uncomfortable. He was clearly making me into a sex object, but did I mind? For a divorcée at age forty-five, it was seductive to know that I still had it.

My life became a bipolar nightmare. When I wasn't with him, I was wrestling with deep despair that could only be relieved by a rendezvous with him. At some level, I knew I was not dealing with the fundamental issues of my life. I needed a stable job and a persistent commitment to my emotional, psychological, and spiritual well-being. I was adrift and awaiting the savior that Nick was not to be.

As the life I longed for and the life I was leading grew further and further apart, I used wine to alleviate my awareness of the incongruence. Wine and denial had worked before and would work now.

When Nick finally found a new girlfriend whose kids were grown, I exploded into dejection and desolation. Although I had tapped into an ecstasy that originated beyond Nick, I attributed it to him. With his departure, joy was extinguished from the universe again. All that passion and supercharged energy got shoved into my overflowing chest.

Wine became my only friend.

7

The Black Hole

The cacophony, inside and outside of me, was just too loud for me to handle—too harsh, too demanding, too challenging, and too intense. In my inner world, I had stored up too many toxic emotions, too much fear, too much disappointment, too much anger, and too much confusion. There was no peace or security to be found, only pain. It was a pain so intense, penetrating, vile, and excruciating that I could not bear to look at it. I was too sensitive. I had let in too much negativity from others. I had embraced their condemnation of me. I had established no boundaries. My chest was overflowing.

My outer world kept coming at me hard and fast: my mother's death, my abusive marriage, the workload of caring for my twin darlings, and the insanity of the war I was engaged in. I had learned a few things. First, I could not control unfolding events. People die. Second, I could not create the situation I desired, a happy marriage and family. I could not control the toxic nature of my marriage. Third, I was just plain bad, a failure, unlovable, unworthy. The world was out of my control and did not care for me. It would not love, protect, or support me.

It was not any one situation that caused my downfall. Rather, it was the notion that my one little person was in an incredibly scary, unpredictable, uncontrollable, unyielding world. There was no source of security for me—not within or outside me. Marriage, which many find to be a source of security, was for me the greatest source of insecurity. I was at the mercy of the unseen forces that jerked me every which way. I had made Don, then Nick, my gods, and each had rejected me. Each had expelled me from his universe of unconditional love and financial security and condemned me to the eternal hell of self-abuse that Don had carefully cultivated.

Primal fear screamed out at me at all hours of the day and night. My chest was overflowing with fear of being rejected by the Creator of the universe. Yet somehow, I had to function and take care of my family.

This was where the wine came in. The soft glow of alcohol diminished the harshness of my world. It suppressed my inner turmoil. It quieted my mental machinations. It kept the awareness of the insecurity and gravity of my situation just out of sight. It allowed me to keep going. I really felt like I would explode if I did not have my nightly intoxicated "vacations" from this fear.

Alcohol was a retreat from the daily battlefield. Drunk, I would lick my wounds, suffocate my hysterical emotions, and create a false bravado for the next day, one day at a time. It had never occurred to me that this short-term strategy would be my undoing. It seemed the only option. I was in survival mode.

Actually Sir Ego is no match for the planetary forces we face: the global economy, world temperature, drug cartels, HIV, Enron executives, and natural disasters. But most people have a sufficient amount of control over their individual lives that they don't confront that reality. It is much further below the surface until a tragedy strikes. For me, that reality was closer to the surface, and I had to find a way to cope with the pervasive anxiety that it produced.

I was a wine connoisseur—which was *clearly* different from an alcoholic—enjoying wine tasting all over California and Europe. I drank pricey wines in elegant restaurants in exotic ports. Sophisticated social drinking seemed totally acceptable … and fun.

I was a fun drunk. My normally introverted nature exploded. I became a dazzling orator, dryly humorous comedian, and insightful philosopher. That was how it all started. In college, I found out that ingesting alcohol changed a party from an intolerable boring affirmation of my undesirableness to a potpourri of endorphins. When I drank, I became dazzling and sparkly, not the brainy nerd with no dates. Every college student knows that a hangover is a testimony to the awesomeness of the party the night before.

I didn't even know that I was at the top of a very slippery slope, dancing on one foot, until I had slid down the long, twisted ravine and landed in the stagnant alligator-infested swamp at the bottom. Now I could probably spot a budding alcoholic at the beginning of his or her drinking career. Back then, I remember I just seemed to like it a little more than everyone else. I drank more, I drank faster, and I didn't have much fun if an event didn't include alcohol.

For twenty years I drank every evening—more than a couple glasses of wine—except during my pregnancy. While this style of drinking didn't affect my ability to conduct daily activities, it stunted my emotional growth and maturity. Instead of dealing with normal, painful emotions, I used wine to suppress them by shoving them into my chest. I also suppressed my inhibitions, which was not always a good thing. I did and said some things that should have gone undone and unsaid, had my frontal lobe been functioning at the time.

Alcohol magnified the dysfunction between Don and me. Despite how frequently it happened, it always took me by surprise when a lovely evening of dinner, wine, and intimate conversation turned suddenly ugly, based on one conversational misstep. There would be an overreactive emotional response and insufficient emotional control to recover. It could happen to either of us. The evening would be ruined, and someone had to be blamed. That was always me.

I didn't notice the downward spiral. Suppressed emotions got triggered. I couldn't handle them. I would drink to suppress them again. Then I had more suppressed emotions to get triggered. Soon everything all day triggered some VV that I had hidden away in there. The only coping mechanism that worked instantly was a glass of wine. It was immediate gratification.

The less I handled the emotions, the less capacity I had to handle them. I carved a habit pattern about how to handle them. Much later, in rehab, I would complete a survey that listed about fifty emotions and asked which ones I had used alcohol to deal with or enhance: joy, sorrow, anger, frustration, depression, fun, success, failure, exhaustion, loneliness, bondedness, and elation. I checked every single one.

By the time Don moved out, I was a time bomb of toxic emotional buildup. There was no release valve, just more painful emotions every day. Was I past the point of no return? If I had gotten a job then and quit drinking, could I have made it work? I doubt it. Each time I suppressed the emotions of a crisis, I was stoking a fire that was getting bigger and bigger inside. It would not have suddenly disappeared if I got my act together, as everyone admonished me to do from the sidelines. This train had to run its course until it ran out of fuel.

Don and then Nick had provided a governor on my drinking. Without adult supervision, I was in free fall. Anytime the fear and anxiety became overwhelming, I could have a glass of wine. When I was having the first glass, the ugly, tortured, hideous creatures would start to retreat into my chest of horrors. With each succeeding glass, they retreated further, and my feeling of well-being increased. There was zero chance I was going to let them come right back and no chance I was going to stop after two or three drinks. I kept drinking until I was sure they were gone for the night so I could not even see their menacing shadows in the dark recesses of my awareness.

The next day, they would be back all around me—suffocating, taunting, and accusing me. It was only a question of how long I could endure this until I popped the cork to start chasing them away again.

The clincher was when I would wake up in the middle of the night, paralyzed with terror and pain. I was not going to make it. I could not provide for my children. I could never be free of the tormentor that lived in my head. After one little glass of wine, I would be able to go back to sleep. One little glass of wine couldn't be my undoing. But it was because it was never just one. This scenario became more and more common until I was physically addicted. When the children were at Don's, I could designate drinking days. I would just drink and nap and then nap and drink throughout the day and night. I would not even pretend to do anything constructive.

I had become what I most feared. I had become the grotesque, hideous, repulsive, disgusting creature. I did humiliating things. I dishonored myself and my children. It wouldn't have been possible for me to have owned this shame any deeper in my being. I had integrated this whole nightmare into my self-image.

Within a year, I racked up two DUIs, one in Hawaii on the night of Don's wedding. I planned to scuba dive and drink my pain away, but instead I spent the night in jail. Why did he always win?

I managed to satisfy all the requirements and court obligations for these charges without Don finding out about them. I did have some trouble completing the six-month alcohol education program because I had to be sober to attend class each Wednesday at six o'clock. Some Wednesdays I couldn't make it because I was having a different kind of alcohol education at home.

Addiction hijacks the rational mind. Even in my sober moments, my thinking was irrational and unreasonable. My defense mechanisms of blame, rationalization, justification, and making excuses were world class. *The end justifies the means* became my mantra. My primary goal was getting the next drink and keeping the path clear to drink again the next day because those ugly, tortured, hideous tormentors still lurked about, and there was only one way to get them to retreat.

I am ashamed to say that it was a distant second goal to take care of my children. Deprioritizing them wasn't a conscious decision. It was survival. Without a drink to keep my internal volcano under control, I couldn't care for them. If the volcano erupted, holy hell would break loose.

I had a really bad habit. I would drink too much and call Don up. I would tell him what a bad person he was and how he had ruined my life. I was so stupid. I even left voice mails to this effect, which he saved and later used against me. The evidence would come in handy.

A friend advised me, "When you open the bottle of wine, unplug the phone."

My free fall was becoming obvious to my friends and Don. My neighbor invited me over for coffee one morning after we dropped the kids at school. How nice. She was the neighbor who also invited me to church. She was a beautiful, kind woman.

It was a lovely sunny morning as I walked across the lawn connecting our houses. I was feeling great. The day before, I'd had a good day. I had cleaned the house and organized my office. I was always *preparing* to look for a job, just one step short of the goal. It took some liquid courage to make me sit in my office and work on résumés or applications, and then quickly it became about the wine and not about the applications.

When my neighbor opened the door, I noticed that several, maybe all, of my other friends were there. It wasn't my birthday. What kind of surprise party could this be? Then I saw two of my brothers from Philadelphia. Uh-oh. To my shock and horror, this was an intervention.

Guess what happens in an intervention? All your closest friends and relatives get together and take turns talking about your drunken antics in front of each other. A woman from AA was there to talk about how if I quit drinking without going to rehab, I would have seizures.

My friends were the parents of my children's friends. These are the people I shared all the joys and challenges of parenting, ski trips, camping trips, softball games, volunteering at school, playdates, and violin concerts. I loved and trusted them. I felt so betrayed.

My secrets were clearly out of the bag. My adrenaline rush told me two things: these people were crazy and *run*. Which I did. I got out of that house and back to mine as fast as I could. My brothers followed me. I told them, without any genuine intent whatsoever, that I could and would quit drinking for thirty days. They had just flown in for the morning and had to leave in an hour to fly back home. I could tell them anything I wished.

They left, and I poured myself a glass of wine to neutralize the adrenaline rush. My feelings of betrayal turned to rage when I found out that Don had orchestrated this lovely intervention. I rationalized it as one of his plots to control me. If I had had any intention of giving this intervention serious thought, learning of Don's involvement dispelled it. In truth, this was an honorable thing he did for me. I had become what I feared and what he had accused me of.

This downward spiral was fueled by the insane idea that life all around sucks and the only good moments were when I was enjoying a glass of wine, like on the commercials. Total denial prohibited me from seeing that what I considered my best friend was really my worst enemy. I had made a deal with this devil. I allowed it to destroy my material world, my outward circumstances, and my physical body. I allowed it to poison and corrupt my mind. In return, I received a few hours of relief from the existential agony of what I perceived as rejection by the Creator.

No one else could see my tormentors. No one else could understand how I could be willing to make this deal and allow my physical world to crumble. A person can quit drinking, but he or she still must deal with these tormentors to create a life worth living. If I could not get rid of my tormentors, drinking myself to death did not seem like such a bad idea. Sadly, many have chosen this path. The VVs ran my life.

Every single day, I told myself, "I won't drink so much today."

Well, every day except for my designated drinking days. Those were guilt-free. But once I had that first sip of wine, it took control. Any shred of willpower vanished instantaneously. That was the grand illusion of my alcoholism: I just needed to cut down, not quit. I could drink in moderation like everyone else. Alcohol was my best friend, the only one that made me feel okay in the jungle of life. I could not give up my best friend, my only source of freedom from the pain, my only coping mechanism, and my only defense against the army of tormentors.

And I refused to believe that drinking was causing all the trouble in my life. I became a gold-medal athlete in the defenses of Sir Ego—excusing, blaming, rationalizing, and justifying. All these defense mechanisms built a fortress that shielded my awareness from the one truth that could free me: I had a drinking problem, and the only way out was complete abstinence.

So I would never say "I am an alcoholic," which would have nullified all my other defenses. In my heart, I knew this to be true, but as long as I didn't acknowledge the problem, I didn't have to deal with it.

The absurdity and imprisonment of my life were only invisible to me. Everyone else could clearly see the problem. Their judgment caused them to retreat from the scarlet *A* on my chest.

I blamed Don for everything. My demons and tormentors were his creations; he had trained me to abuse myself. He no longer even needed to be there to push the buttons. I thought I could never be free of this ill-begotten torturer. I hopelessly accepted the death sentence in hell that I believed would be my life from that point on.

I no longer had a first hour or two of soft glow. The moment the first sip hit my lips, the beast awakened, and it was a hungry, thirsty, demanding beast. A huge vacuum was sucking the life force from my being, and I felt powerless to stop it. Now instead of neutralizing my emotional turmoil, it added to it. Each day, I thought I would explode. I wondered, *Will it be a heart attack or stroke? Will it be a nervous breakdown? Or will it be suicide?*

I had a suicide plan, easy and painless. I thought I would just drink a lot, something different for a change. Then I would get into the car, with the garage door closed. I would turn on the ignition, open the windows, and escape into forever sleep. I considered this plan for months. Each time I came to the same conclusion. I would not allow my girls to lose their mother in an untimely way, as I had lost mine. I would not do this to them. No matter what the cost to me, I could not let them down.

Yet I was letting them down with every sip I took, and this added to my overflowing chest of failures and flaws. In some horrible way, I had recreated the situation with my mother. I was fading away and disappearing. I became more aloof and secretive because I was hiding my drinking.

Tragically, my daughters became my caretakers. They cleaned up the dinner dishes because I sat outside and drank. They got themselves ready for school because I was too hungover to get up. They slept in my bed to keep tabs on me, making sure that I eventually surrendered the glass of wine and came to bed. I once had shown them a beautiful reflection, but it was fading and faltering.

In the end, I have much remorse for the great pain I caused my daughters and would do anything in my power to help them heal from this. But at the time, I couldn't help them. I could not even help myself. So I was on my knees. I prayed to the Creator to save me.

And he did. He answered my prayer in a way that I did not see coming.

8

Doing Time

I woke up on the floor of a holding cell, where I had passed out hours earlier. This was my third DUI in two years. I would not be able to hide this one from Don, and I would not be able to shield the girls from its effects.

It was clear to me that I had had my last drink. I would never be able to drink again if I wanted to be in my children's lives, which I desperately did. In fact, I felt salvation depended on this, both mine and theirs. I did not believe that all my problems were a result of my drinking. At the same time, I hoped it was true because I could see no other way for all my problems to be solved. I had so many problems.

Something positive happened to me in that holding cell. Instead of feeling defeated, I was angry. I was supercharged. Although I was going down in flames, I was determined to rise from the ashes like a phoenix—bigger, better, and more powerful. The lioness awoke to annihilate the beast, and I knew I would not stop. I would do whatever it took. I would endure any humiliation and suffer any agony to make my life work and to become the mother my children deserved. Like the Cowardly Lion in Oz, I found my courage in that holding cell.

Somehow the divine spark reached me and inflamed my spirit. I discovered another image of myself, a divine image that I could embrace, not the image Don had emblazoned on my consciousness. I cried out to the wise one and was answered.

A Course in Miracles had taught me that my soul was divine and perfect, untouched by the dramas unfolding on this earthly plane. I was not this weary, imprisoned, alcohol-dependent body. I clung to this truth in moments of darkness and despair. I knew the Creator wanted my life to have love and meaning. I needed to find a way to align with that reality and surrender the pretense that I could make my life work without the Creator. I embraced the fact that there were two very different realities in my consciousness: the material realm of Sir Ego and his catastrophic circumstances and the heavenly realm of the wise one.

I spent three months in jail—not my usual five-star accommodation, not a castle, overwater bungalow, or tree house. No more little black dresses for me. Orange was my new black.

Courage is the strength to keep doing what is necessary in spite of fear. I needed a lot of courage because jail is a scary place. This is where our justice system puts people who cannot manage their own lives and are menaces to society. Check and check, I met the criteria. Looking back, it was the best thing that could have happened to me because it was the only thing that stopped me from drinking. I could not or would not do it voluntarily. I am grateful for this intervention. It saved my life.

It was sobering, in more ways than one, to sit in jail and look upon the catastrophic state of my life. Even the vast ocean of fear that had gotten me to this point was nothing compared to the fear I felt now. The intricate and fragile Rube Goldberg machinery that had worked every day to get me through a few more hours of wine and denial had stopped abruptly and was damaged beyond repair. And my previous problems were nothing compared to the problems this DUI would cause. During my three months in jail, I would lose almost everything.

First, I lost custody of my children. Don acted swiftly and obtained sole custody of our girls by my second day in jail. I attended several court hearings during my incarceration. In prison garb, handcuffs, and shackles, I was led to the courtroom to plead my case, seeking the right to speak to my children on the phone twice a week. Don's attorney fought that unsuccessfully. He would do well writing for the tabloids because his descriptions of my criminal behavior were filled with inflammatory wording.

Don and his attorney were successful in prohibiting my daughters from visiting me in jail and at the rehabilitation center. It would be five months before I had regular visits with the girls. The court appointed an attorney for the children and ordered him to arrange a visit before the next court date, to begin the evaluation of my relationship with them. This was the first of many court-ordered visits the children's attorney would fail to provide. He also failed to return my phone calls requesting these visits. For the next eighteen months, he would limit my access to the girls, ignore my phone calls, and charge me thousands of dollars for these services.

I lost my car. Although I was arrested a few blocks from my house and requested that my car be towed to my house, it was towed to a storage facility instead. I was unable to bail out of jail for six weeks, so it was sold at auction to pay the storage fees. I had taken out a loan against the car to pay my divorce attorney fees when I started running out of cash and credit. Now I owed the bank the balance of that loan, but no longer had the car.

I lost my house. My house was on the market and sold before I was released from the rehabilitation center. I lost all leverage in the financial settlement of my divorce. As I continued to fight for visits and return of custody of my children, I eventually settled for a small fraction of what I had expected. I incurred $50,000 in debt to pay all the expenses related to my DUI and the custody battle with Don. Eventually I had to file a bankruptcy. I lost not only my credit score but my self-esteem, my reputation, and my freedom.

I lost the support of my family and friends. Despite my frantic phone calls, no one would bail me out. No one would get my car. No one would visit me. No one would advocate for me. Where were all my intervention friends now?

I lost my jewelry. Although it was trivial in comparison to the other losses, it represented something to me emotionally. The stones represented my preciousness, entitlement, and worth. I recalled admiring the dazzling, perfectly colorless 1.2 carats on my ring finger. I secretly believed that showed all the world my value and the affluence of the gentleman I had been able to attract. In the end, I was forced to see that stones were just things without meaning. Their value lay in what they could be exchanged for.

When I ran out of cash and maxed out my credit cards, I sold jewelry. Ten thousand dollars' worth of diamonds sold for less than a thousand dollars. I needed the money to put food on the table. The remainder of my jewelry I gave as collateral to a fellow inmate, a drug addict, who cosigned my bail. It was never returned.

I cowered as the foundation of my life imploded, showering each brick on my broken psyche. I had built this rickety life, deluded about the security and love that I believed cemented it together, and it was crashing down on me. It seemed I had failed myself and my children in every possible way, despite having had the most loving intentions and many worldly aptitudes and resources.

The first few days in jail, I was hysterical, partially due to alcohol withdrawal symptoms, but largely due to my absolute inability to get any friends or family members to help me. Being thrown in jail and held there was a very unpleasant surprise. Bailing out would have allowed me to get my affairs in order before serving my sentence. As I did not have a job, I needed someone to cosign my bail, making this person mutually liable for $2,000 of bail expense and $20,000 if I didn't appear in court. No one would take on this contingent liability.

My new quarters were slightly larger than my walk-in closet at home. The cell had concrete walls painted drab, with bunk beds (metal shelves with two-inch-thick foam pads atop them), a toilet, a sink, and two concrete slab desks with stools. Instead of French doors overlooking my parklike backyard, a one-foot-square, barred, frosted window let in enough light to show if it were day or night, but no more.

Stripped of my clothes, jewelry, cell phone, and pride, I was given a jailhouse uniform and a welcome bag containing a bar of soap, a plastic spoon, a plastic comb, and a cup. Our day started at five o'clock in the morning, when the reinforced steel door clicked open to signal the breakfast call. Prisoners had to bring their plastic spoons and cups. If you lost your plastic spoon, depending on the mood of the guard, you might or might not be given a new one. Rule one: don't lose the plastic spoon.

I was grateful that my bunkmate, Beth, was kind, compassionate, and informative. She helped me to navigate the jailhouse routine, ensuring I did not inadvertently break a rule or anger a guard. Such behavior resulted in unpleasant consequences, ranging from solitary confinement to withdrawal of the few privileges we had—going to the jail library or out to the cement courtyard for an hour or purchasing personal care, stationery, and food items through the commissary.

Beth was also a twentysomething, slightly overweight, attractive mother of two small children and a devout Christian. Her crime was having consensual sex with a seventeen-year-old boy. She had been sentenced to a year in jail and would be a registered sex offender upon release, unable to live near or volunteer at her children's school.

The first thing I learned in jail was that no one's story started with "the actual crime." Beth had been molested by a family member, beginning when she was four years old. She confided that she could not seem to develop appropriate sexual boundaries despite how hard she tried, having been promiscuous most of her life.

Out of necessity, she was delving deep into her faith and seeking healing. She was a devoted mother and wanted to protect her children from the abuses she had suffered, but it was just more complicated than that. More than protecting them from being molested, she needed to heal herself to protect them from the consequences of her brokenness. Like me.

There was some help available for each of us, but not much. Nothing compared to what these people needed to repair their lives and heal their spirits. Once a week, a minister came in to conduct a service. Also once a week, an anonymous alcoholic held an AA meeting. Twice a week, we could go to the jail library, which was filled with self-help books.

This was welcome news to me, a self-help junkie. I read every book and did every workbook exercise that pertained to alcoholism, abuse, and forgiveness. Honestly, it gave me a lot of information but did not reduce the burn in my heart. It did not take any items out of the chest. It did not liberate the VVs. And daily, items were being added to the chest: suppressed fears, perceived injustices, and desperate outreach for help that went unanswered by family and friends.

Worst of all, I feared that my daughters' lives were being irrevocably damaged with each passing minute and I could nothing to protect them. I couldn't wait to get to rehab for support in these areas, but I was required to serve half my sentence in jail before I was eligible for rehab.

Beth told me about an inmate held in solitary confinement. This woman had been a nanny and was accused of shaking the baby she had cared for, causing the child to die of shaken baby syndrome. Her name was Maria, and she was Hispanic. This woman had been in jail for many months. She spoke almost no English, so other Spanish-speaking inmates translated her side of the story, which was that the baby had had some sort of seizure in its high chair. As Maria was picking up the baby to revive it, the parents walked in.

What I could see in jail was that Maria was devoutly religious and had the demeanor of a saint. Despite her challenging circumstances, including being separated from her own children, she never showed anger. Her warm, nurturing countenance didn't seem capable of holding impatience, frustration, desperation, or anger. I can understand that the parents wanted someone to blame for their baby's death, but this had become a tragedy for more than one child. After about a year of imprisonment, Maria was found not guilty and released.

I had a few other women whom I spent the endless hours with. My favorite Scrabble partner was a brilliant sociopath, one of the few available partners who could make words with more than three letters, a crucial requirement for an engaging game. Jean, a perky, petite, beautiful blond, had been charged with over 150 counts of insurance fraud. She had sold policies and used the money to buy methamphetamine. Obviously she was clever, but my amateur diagnosis of sociopathy was based on her shockingly callous and ruthless treatment of other inmates. She used the only weapon available, her words, which she wielded like a sword. They kept almost everyone else at a distance. Like so many others, she had been molested as a child and had acquired some very ingenious but nefarious coping methods, including a meth addiction.

Another professional criminal was Leslie. Her charges included identity theft and possession of controlled substances, actually a lot of both. She had a million-dollar bail and was putting up her house, an ill-gotten gain, as collateral. Meanwhile, she was victimized, like so many other inmates. Her so-called friends, fellow drug users, knew her house was unoccupied, and they broke in and stole all they could. I learned that this was commonplace in drug circles.

I was somewhat fascinated by Connie, a vivacious, authoritative, thirtysomething woman. Originally in the holding tank, she told me she had been arrested for having a scale and a minor amount of medicinal marijuana. She proclaimed her innocence for the guards to overhear.

Eventually her story unfolded. Her husband had been arrested several weeks before she was. He no longer lived in their house because he was living with his newly pregnant girlfriend. As a couple, they had been very high up in the local distribution chain for marijuana, a very lucrative business based on the description of the assets that had been seized and auctioned. Upon her husband's arrest, she knew she would be next and cleaned out her home of any incriminating evidence.

Despite their lack of ability to convict Connie of any substantive charges, the authorities were holding her as leverage in her husband's case. Connie and her husband, having expertise in all things felonious, had devised several ways of communicating with each other to keep their stories straight. Sometimes they would three-way call a mutual friend. Other times they would pass notes under the reinforced door connecting the men's and women's cellblocks. If anyone got caught passing notes or was even suspected of passing notes, the entire cellblock would be locked down for the day. That meant everyone was locked in her cells without access to the common room.

I always kept a large stash of books on hand to survive the long days of suffocating captivity. Each day Connie recited a series of Hail Marys as part of her Catholic upbringing. This was in sharp contrast to her repeated offers to "take out" Don. Of all the offers I had, hers was the most credible. But my answer was always the same, "Not on my karma."

Eventually I also realized she had no intention of changing her ways when she was released. This was all a giant game to her, a game of "What can they prove?" Long ago, she had lost sight of what was true, right, or moral. It seemed much like Don's behavior and eventually my own as I searched for a loophole to get out of my charges.

There were not one, but two, women in the cellblock whose mothers had had them arrested. Both had completed sentences for a third DUI and were still drinking. Even though they weren't driving, it was a violation of their probation to consume any alcohol. In desperation, their mothers had called their probation officers to have them arrested again. They faced a year in prison. Angry as they were at their mothers, it was clear that this was their mothers' desperate attempt to save their daughters from an imminent alcoholic death. If I drank again after I left the jail, that would be me, without any mother to call probation.

Many of my fellow inmates were young meth addicts. They had been abused as children and had become addicts by the time they were teenagers.

The maturation process seems to freeze at the time one becomes an addict. They were lost in a teenage world of hair braiding, eyebrow threading, using Kool-Aid as makeup, and fighting over the TV channel. They'd never had a chance to complete their education, develop employable skills, or mature emotionally, as I had. I had a world of resources that they did not have.

I was assigned to work in the infirmary. It would have been a welcome break from the tedium, but the head of the infirmary was a tyrant. Rumor had it that she had been nicer before her husband ran off with a former inmate.

There was a prisoner in the infirmary, an ancient man who was frail and terminally ill. I could not imagine what crime he had committed, as now he could barely commit an act of any kind, even self-care. Usually his door was closed when I was cleaning, and I only caught a glimpse of him through the partially closed shade over glass square in the door.

On one occasion, I had to clean his room while he had been taken out for some reason. I could feel the heavy presence of the reaper patiently waiting in this dismal, forsaken cell as I mopped and emptied the trash. The next day, I learned that the inmate had surrendered to the reaper. I was required to clean again, this time disposing of his standard-issue soap, spoon, toothbrush, and cup, his last possessions.

My thoughts returned to the moments of my mother's death and the days afterward, removing the no-longer-needed implements of human existence. I was crushed, reliving the overwhelming loss, acutely aware of her presence watching me in this darkest time of my life. Without any way of processing the intense emotions, I returned to the common room, crying. A very compassionate officer took me into a private office to release some of the weighty emotions overcoming me in a flood of tears.

No one is defined by the worst actions of his or her life. I was distressed and saddened to see the judicial process at work. It wasn't possible for justice to be enacted when those sitting in judgment could not see the whole of a person's life: his or her wounds, intentions, remorse, and repentance.

This time-out forced me to evaluate my life in the harsh light of sobriety and legal consequences. My study of *A Course in Miracles* assured me that I was divine and perfect, even in this seemingly impossible predicament. The wise one could navigate all circumstances, including these, for the good of all. There was a lesson and healing here for me. This knowledge reduced my defenses and allowed me to penetrate very deeply into the beliefs, thoughts, perceptions, and compulsions that had gotten me to this place.

The most pervasive and insidious notion was that Don was to blame and that his abuse had caused me to become a dangerous alcoholic who was destructive to my children and a menace on the road. However, *ACIM* is very clear that all defenses except forgiveness are double-edged swords that attack us as well as the other. What did this mean? I looked very closely and found several interesting and dysfunctional things about my inclination to blame Don.

First, he did not put me in jail. I did. As much as I hated to admit it, I had other choices in my response to his abuse. He did not make me drink when I was afraid. He did not *make me do it*. What he did to me and how I responded were two different things. Yikes. My emotions did not want to accept this, so I continued to lash out about him to anyone who would listen. But my mind knew it was true.

Second, focusing my attention on Don was just not helpful. It was painfully clear that I was being required to atone for my sins, while he was not … yet. A part of me screamed the third-grader's mantra, *It's not fair*. Yet another part of me finally saw that, regardless of his participation in how I had arrived at this broken state, his engagement, cooperation, or approval were not required for me to repair my life and heal my relationship with the girls. I needed to choose between fixing the problem or fixing the blame because, according to Pastor Jones at my church, "You can't do both."

This was a critical decision, one to fix my life, regardless of what anyone else did with theirs. *ACIM* identifies all transgressions as mistakes in need of learning and correction, not judgment and punishment. This was welcome news. I needed to hear that my mistakes were fixable.

But defining sins as mistakes had to include Don's sins as well as mine. I couldn't hold a view where my mistakes could be corrected and yet his were unforgivable. This is the choice of fear or love: love forgives all; fear judges all. I wanted the Creator's love and forgiveness, and I needed to give it.

Most importantly, I was locked in a war with Don for the privilege of parenting our children, a skirmish I was determined not to lose. He was going to be part of my life for many more years, and right then, he held all the cards. Granted, I had sustained an involuntary retreat from the battlefield. I had given him enough ammunition to annihilate me. But I would need to find a way to continue to victory, to be there to help my children heal from these traumas.

I sought the healing power of forgiveness with intensity. Once I had committed to moving from fear to love, opening the chaos and destruction of my life to the wise one's healing, the question was how. How could I activate the healing force, the divine intervention, the power of the Creator in my life? The how is forgiveness. This is the chariot that must be harnessed if one is to ride out of the depths of hell and into the glory of heaven. I knew one thing: forgiveness was the way to go. It was my lifeline back to sanity. Honestly, it was my only hope. I had to find a way to empty the chest of VVs.

Forgiveness was the dynamic act of volition that would bring me back into alignment with the divine flow of the universe. Frankly, I needed to receive forgiveness as much as I needed to offer it. By now, my compassion was allowing me to see the universal nature of our quest for happiness and the dysfunctional, desperate measures we were willing to take to survive, based on the well-intentioned but misguided direction of Sir Ego. I needed to learn how to hear and accept guidance from the wise one. Sir Ego had slammed into the wall and had no more weapons to wield.

I spent a great deal of time reading the Bible and every book in the jail library on forgiveness and the twelve steps, which include forgiveness steps. All these sources agreed that forgiveness is good and right, but none told me *how* to forgive—how to release the burning, self-righteous accusations that shrieked from the depths of my being. Having the idea in my head was not the same as having it in my heart.

The VVs exploded, constantly hijacking my emotions. But there was a tiny spark in my head that said there was a way out of this, and forgiveness was that way, however inaccessible it seemed at that time. The spark of the divine in my heart kept this hope alive in my darkest moments of despair. I knew the Creator had to be stronger than Don and my circumstances, despite a bit of evidence to the contrary.

Each time I had to go to court was like taking the last walk to my execution. Filled with trepidation and fear, I would will myself to take each step, while every molecule in my body screamed, "No!" I endured the barking orders of the guards and the psychic assault of the shackling. With ferocious determination, I endured whatever I had to so that one day I could be reunited with my daughters.

Don and the attorneys continued to thwart every effort or motion I made to pursue my relationship with the children, using each court appearance as an opportunity to revisit my crimes and assert unfounded accusations against me, a character assassination of sorts. For example, Don paid $5,000 to have the house painted and staged with rented furniture, brought in to create a model-home feel, when we put it up for sale. Don's court documents said he spent the money to repair the damage I had done, a very credible accusation, as alcoholics notoriously bash walls and trash carpets.

In another example, his court documents asserted that I had tested positive for methamphetamine use. In truth, the routine test was negative. Each assertion created a larger mountain in the eyes of the court that I would have to overcome in order to regain custodial rights when I was released.

Each one—the truths, the untruths, and the distorted truths—stung like a poisoned arrow deep into my vulnerable and exposed heart. I met every blow with the divine shield I envisioned around myself. I found courage in the depths of my being, which served me well during the long battle ahead. I faced my tormentors and became fearless, walking straight toward any obstacle that confronted me. Sir Ego was called upon to survive. Thick armor was required for protection from the vicious slings and arrows. The lioness separated from her cubs had found her power.

I tried in every way possible to maintain a positive relationship with our daughters, a seemingly impossible task. There wasn't much interesting to say about my life in my letters to the girls, so I started a storytelling interchange. This worked well with Nicole who loved to read and write. I started a story about several people stranded on an island, à la *Gilligan's Island*. After writing several paragraphs about their adventure, I would end the letter on a cliffhanger. My daughter would write the next few paragraphs and end with a new cliffhanger. We exchanged these letters several times a week, and they were the highlight of my life. They kept me connected with her, and I was impressed with her imagination and writing abilities. We ended up with quite a long and involved story that was entertaining to all my fellow inmates.

I used the few items at hand to create things to send to the girls. I made word puzzles for them to solve. I drew pictures, colored with Kool-Aid powder, of our visits to the lake. I became very creative in turning the stories of my fellow inmates into fables with good morals that the girls could understand.

As my circumstances did not fit in my worldview, I simply had to find a different way to understand the world and my place in it. This receptive thinking led me to look at the world in a different light. I questioned the nature of responsibility, blame, righteousness, and justice. I had many examples all around me of the failures of human attempts to wield these mighty swords.

The court systems have a very limited view of justice, looking only at the specific crime and not the events leading up to it. The courts are naturally limited to what can be proven. I was being punished for my transgressions while Don was not being held accountable for any. On the other hand, I had driven drunk more than three times. I learned Sir Ego likes to play a game of *What can you prove?* and *What can I get away with?*

Sir Ego is very present in the underpinnings of our judicial system. Jail is about administering punishment in a haze of guilt and shame. These are not conductive to healing or repairing a broken life. Experiencing these VVs opened my heart to a new level of compassion.

I watched my internal reactions to my state of disgrace and held tightly to a shred of dignity. I insisted that my circumstances did not define me, that I was holy, worthy, and lovable in the Creator's eyes. This was the seed, roused from hibernation, that would give birth to the new me.

I understood the material world to be a teaching environment, connected to a higher reality of unmanifested spirits. I wondered what I was to learn from this. I concluded that human justice was not just. Neither did it facilitate learning. This reinforced the idea of karma that was percolating in my consciousness. From the Creator's perspective, all things are known, and true learning and healing are miraculously possible. This omniscient perspective was required to see the truth of each person's state of consciousness and provide an effective healing and lesson plan for the next step on their quest.

While I did not know how to accomplish it, my mission became to embrace this reality. It cast my circumstances with Don in a new light. I could not condemn him unequivocally as I had in the past. There had to be some understanding, perhaps beyond my reach, about the justice in my life. I made it my mission to grasp this understanding. I befriended the wise one as my guide on the quest.

There was still much negative energy in my VVs that clouded my view of these deeper truths. I soon learned how much pain was involved in passing through this haze of ignorance and delusion. On the other hand, the pain of hitting bottom gives one the motivation to go to any length to alter the nature of one's reality. It is said that a person changes once the pain of staying the same exceeds the pain of change and not before.

I sat in jail for six weeks, unable to obtain bail, watching my children, my house, and my car vanish. Phone calls were very challenging to make from jail. We spent a limited time each day in the common rooms where the phones were. There were only a few phones relative to the large demand for them. Prisoners could only call landlines, not cell phones. You lost your turn if the person you chose to call didn't answer. People couldn't call you back. Even when I was successful in reaching my potential saviors, they would not help.

Finally a fellow inmate was released and agreed to cosign my bail. When Sue arrived at the jail, she was high on methamphetamine and wearing three morphine patches, triple the customary dosage. Several times, she passed out and fell off her stool onto the concrete floor. I was shocked that the guards were unconcerned and did not offer her any help or send her to the infirmary. Her life was in as much of a shambles as mine, but she had great compassion for my mountainous obstacles. After six weeks, she was released and cosigned my bail, and I was released.

The next day, Sue and her boyfriend arrived at my home, high on drugs, and demanded my jewelry. They said they would hold it as collateral in the event that I jumped bail. Afraid of a confrontation and believing they would return the jewelry upon settlement of the bail, I turned over all my remaining jewelry. I never saw it again, despite notifying Sue of my full payment of the bail. I suspect it was sold for drugs the same day I handed it over.

I also used this opportunity to have my last alcoholic beverage. Due to my emotionally overwrought condition and my six weeks of abstinence, I drank more and faster than my body could tolerate. I had only an hour or two of sweet relief before I was vomiting. Yet the dragon had been reawakened, and I alternately drank and vomited for twenty-four hours until my brothers arrived and officially inaugurated my permanent sobriety. This turned out to be a very memorable experience to help me maintain sobriety. It shattered the illusion that I could enjoy a nice glass of wine like other people. I learned how quickly and violently the beast could overcome me.

My brothers who had come for the intervention came again to help me. I was deeply ashamed for them to see what I had become. Their love and support were very gracious. I was grateful to have the opportunity to pack up my belongings and put them in storage before the sale of the house. They each gave me a few hundred dollars, which would be exactly the amount that I needed until I got out of rehab.

I made a surprise visit to my daughters at school, before Don knew I was released. I went to school during recess, found the girls on the playground, and hugged them. I told them how much I loved them. I assured them that I was getting help for my drinking problem and that we would be together as soon as I was well again.

As I expected, Don and the attorneys made sure that I did not see the girls again during the two weeks I was home prior to serving my remaining jail time. However, they did let my brothers spend some time with their nieces.

Although many correctional officers had a disrespectful, even humiliating, way of interacting with the inmates, a few did show genuine compassion. They were bright lights in a dark world, and I was very grateful for them. There was a rehab coordinator responsible for arranging my transfer out of jail. I often spoke to him about how Don was taking advantage of my imprisonment to take legal and financial actions against me. Despite the waitlist and paperwork, this rehab coordinator arranged for my transfer to a recovery home where my children could visit me. I walked out of jail, grateful to be leaving the punishment phase of my journey and anxiously anticipating the healing phase.

When I arrived at the recovery center, I was pleasantly surprised to see a country house next to a field of cows lowing softly. There was greenery in every size and shape as far as I could see in every direction, in sharp contrast to the cement courtyard of my jailhouse outings. The first task I was given was completing a short questionnaire that the director would use to determine the extent of my denial. I quickly and arrogantly completed the form and returned it to her.

She said, "You answered no where it asks if you have been institutionalized as a result of your drinking."

I looked at her, puzzled. She pointed out that I was in a rehabilitation facility and that I had just left a correctional facility. Yet I had still answered no. I often scored high on tests, and on this test too, I scored very high in denial. I had a lot of work to do.

Rehab turned out to be a safe haven, where I could lick my wounds and regroup. Between jail and rehab, I accumulated six months of involuntary sobriety, which became a solid basis for my recovery. The two rehab counselors who ran the facility, Laurie and Cathy, were like angels appearing in the darkness, and I still consider them among my closest and dearest friends. Both had done years in prison, struggled with heroin addiction, and triumphed, which prepared them to serve now as counselors. Finally I had allies. They stood side by side and fought every day for the women who came under their care, many of whom would not fight for themselves and, sadly, would never permanently get to the other side of their addiction.

The house was occupied by six women whose dysfunctions had created total chaos in their lives, plus a few children. There was much healing to be found in that house, in our group, and in the long walks I took every day, surrounded by nature. My usual destination was a little stream that bubbled and sparkled in the sunlight, reminding me of the gentle flow of life beneath the surface of our dramas.

It would have been a lovely place for my daughters Chris and Nicole to visit or even to spend the weekend, but Don would not permit this. The lioness paced in her den, watching, while the jackal imprisoned her cubs in his lair. The thing I feared the most was that he was harming the children in the same ways he had harmed me every day while I rotted on the sidelines.

The daily group meetings addressed various recovery topics, which helped me break through my denial and allowed me to slowly process and release the psychological toxins that had been accumulating for so long. Tears flowed. I came to understand my addiction and the path to recovery. The director of our program helped me to see that my addiction to Don was as toxic as my addiction to alcohol. She observed as I continued to call him and seek salvation from him, expecting him to help solve my problems, denying he was the author of many of them as he withheld visits with the girls and financial resources from me.

Soberly facing the pain and fear that I had locked away for so long was as excruciating as being separated from my children. But that is the journey to recovery. We must open the chest, look inside, and begin releasing what we find there. Not doing this work is what differentiates those who heal and recover from those who remain on the merry-go-round of obsession, compulsion, and dependence. A person needs effective skills to empty the chest.

Anyone can use the techniques I discovered. Once I let it all unravel—poured out the sorrows, screamed out the pain, and swore out the rage—a glimmer of hope sparkled ahead. It was the hope of a new life, without alcohol and without the buried pain and fear.

What unfolded each day among my housemates and I, in our lives and in our groups, was a study in human nature. We bonded in our desperation, allowing one another to process the pandemonium and turmoil of our lives, sharing our defeats and victories. We shared the joys of regaining custody of their children. In my case, we mourned defeat as we watched the courts favor Don so I would not see my daughters.

The value of group therapy—any therapy really—is directly proportional to one's willingness to go deep. Group therapy allowed me to become aware of my defense mechanisms when I saw them reflected in another person's story of woe. In those four months, the excuses, the rationalizations, the justifications, the denial, and (my personal favorite) the blame took on a shrill tone that I could detect when I heard them in others' mouths. So I looked within myself to see where these gremlins hid. What I found was only the tip of the iceberg, for I was still prey to their wily ways.

I was surprised by what didn't happen next. Although we spoke about the unspeakable demons within, nothing awful happened. No one spontaneously combusted, no dragon appeared through the mist, and none of our past perpetrators blazed in on the flames of hellfire. This was also true of the terror-filled moments I endured in court and in jail. Those suppressed fears, like the monster in the closet, disappeared when we turned on the light.

Could it be that the story I'd told myself about Don controlling and threatening me was really nothing? That what I had feared would destroy me was nothing? The VVs opened up. We screamed, we cried, we trembled, and we wept. But we did not spontaneously combust. What I had feared to look upon had no substance and no power to destroy me—except when it stayed inside me. Better out than in? This was startling news.

I learned the therapeutic benefit of releasing the energy of these VVs, which was better than suppressing them and shoving them back in the chest. But it was not as good as transcending them, which I would learn much later.

Two things lay within me at this time: the twisted tormentors of my psyche and the undying spark of divine perfection they had been hidden for so long. Rehab was where I began the journey of discovering that spark within myself, the wise one. It was where I learned that my memories, no matter how horrendous, could not hurt me in the present moment. The swirling energy of an exploding VV was uncomfortable to expose but was not an actual sword penetrating my armor.

Well, I had learned the nothingness of what lay behind me, though I did not foresee the battle that lay ahead of me. I had an Everest-size mountain of VVs within. An arduous journey would be required to liberate these tormentors. The wise one and Sir Ego were beginning to work together with courage and compassion to proceed on my quest.

My counselors and housemates watched in horror as Don flawlessly executed his custody lordship. He and the attorneys demanded that I be prohibited from seeing the girls without a licensed therapist present rather than the usual custody supervisor. We were unable to arrange this type of visit for six weeks. Therapeutic visits were normally reserved for cases of physical or sexual abuse, when the parent had traumatically injured the children. A counselor's assistance was required in such cases to ensure the emotional safety of the child.

Finally I was allowed to have supervised visits with Chris and Nicole. We cherished those moments! They were loving and kind to me and gave me the strength to continue when my reserves ran low.

A few weeks after our supervised visits started, their tenth birthday arrived in mid-January, and I arranged with the supervising agency to take them bowling, a favorite pastime of ours. Everything was arranged. The girls were thrilled and filled with anticipation. The brownie cake with peppermint frosting I had baked from scratch was ready to go. The portable DVD player and Harry Potter game discs were wrapped in purple birthday wrap and matching ribbon. The rusty rehab van with no heat awaited as my chariot to the ball.

An hour before my chariot was to depart, Don called. "I am not bringing the girls for the visit. I cannot contact their attorney to confirm his approval."

"What? This visit was approved days ago because the supervisor wouldn't have scheduled it without the approval," I retorted, trembling at the idea that he was canceling the visit.

"No. I can't confirm, and I don't want to get into trouble with their attorney." I could feel Don's smirk through the phone.

Crushed! Just like that. I could not imagine what convoluted thinking had led him to be willing to disappoint the children in this way. I did know that I would be blamed for it.

I had to call the girls to say that the outing couldn't be worked out. I assumed Don would listen in on the phone extension to make sure I did not defame his character, so I was very careful not to implicate him in any way that he could later use to accuse me of alienation of affection.

I couldn't help but wonder how it was possible for anyone to think that Don had the girls' best interests at heart. He was intent on keeping them from their mother, who was doing everything she could to make her way back to them. If I hadn't been in rehab, it would have been most difficult to hold on to the thin thread of sobriety I had managed to weave into my life.

Although I had been sentenced to more than four months in rehab, state funding ran out after three months. I was released early with about ten dollars to my name and no home to return to. I had developed a friendship with members of a local church, and they invited me to stay in their home until I could get settled. It was forty-five minutes away from my daughters.

I immediately began looking for a job, a car, and a house to rent. Without a driver's license, job, money, or credit, buying a car would be challenging, but I found someone on the internet who was desperate to sell. For a few hundred dollars and my commitment to make the remainder of the payments, I took possession of her car.

Shortly after my release, I had a court date and returned with excellent progress reports. I hoped I would be released from any further obligation. But I was not. I needed to complete six more weeks of jail time or rehab. My rehab counselor agreed to let me return as a housemother, which gave me credit and allowed me some freedom to look for a job and a home. I found a nearby storage facility and parked my car to keep that little secret from my rehab directors.

One day I called a headhunter with whom I had been working before my arrest. She had been very impressed with my résumé and had sent me on several interviews. But when I spoke with her now, I was shocked to hear her say that my sister had called and told her about my arrest. She said she just couldn't represent someone with my criminal record. When I explained that my DUI charges were misdemeanors, she relented, made some phone calls, and later called me back to say that she would be happy to continue to represent me.

But who had called her? What kind of criminal record was someone saying I had? I didn't have any sisters! The only people who could have retrieved her name and phone number from my answering machine would have been those who had access to my house: Don, his wife, and the realtor. (Your guess is as good as mine.)

I left the rehab facility during the day to take the bus (which was code for walking to my car and driving away) to job interviews and on house-hunting expeditions. I got a job quickly, one that started three weeks before my rehab release date. I also found a house to rent that would be available when my job started. Both were miracles.

Luckily this all happened quickly because my ownership of the car was short-lived. When I submitted a payment for the car, as planned, the credit company called me to say they couldn't accept my payment without authorization from the owner. But her cell phone was disconnected, so neither the credit company nor I were able to contact her. The credit company wanted to send someone to repossess the car, which would have jeopardized my position in rehab. So I immediately drove the car to the used car lot where the previous owner had purchased it and dropped it off. I only had that car for a week, but it served its purpose well!

It was surreal to start a job after the nightmare I had been living in jail and rehab. I had resisted a regular job for so long. But my life depended on it. I had to make this work. During the week, I was required to stay at the rehab facility, which meant a commute of four buses each way, every day. On the weekends, I was given a pass to stay at my house, where I settled in.

When I was officially released from rehab, I arranged the first supervised visits with my children at my new home. Don and his wife dropped the girls off for their first visit. What they found was a fully furnished, beautifully decorated, cozy home in a nice neighborhood, not far from them. And they brought our golden retriever, Sierra, whom I welcomed back. How I had missed her.

The wise one led me to everything I needed, just in time. I believe it was all predicated on my repentance. I saw that it didn't matter how I had gotten into my predicament; I was the one who had to take responsibility for creating my life and moving forward. I was the one who needed to heal the wounds and learn the lessons. Even if someone like Don had wanted to undo what he had done, which he didn't, it wouldn't have taught me my lessons or released my fears or healed my wounds. I embraced that I was divine, blessed, and protected by the wise one, even when my human circumstances were catastrophic. I learned that Sir Ego was unable to create human circumstances that could guarantee me happiness and security.

Even if I had them for a moment, the inevitable tides of change would wash them away. I came to believe that the Creator's justice was far greater than man's. I could relinquish my thirst for vengeance against Don, offering him the grace that I believed was mine. I daresay it was all miraculous.

9

The Unwinnable War

Based on the experiences of my housemates, who were quickly reunited with their children, I prepared for a forty-yard dash. But I was aware of the possibility that addiction could rob me of my children forever. Several of my housemates had lost their children to adoptive or foster parents. The possibility of this outcome steeled my determination. It was a good thing because I was unprepared for the marathon I had unwittingly embarked on, one laced with hurdles and obstacles.

A court hearing was scheduled for a couple weeks after my new start. Proudly, I could show the court my prestigious job, my well-furnished home near the kids' school, satisfaction of probation and legal obligations, completion of four months in a rehabilitation program, and a strong recovery support network. I entered the courtroom expecting to have 50 percent custody restored to me and suspension of visit supervision.

"Nicole's teacher called me because she is concerned about Nicole. She has been spending her recess time in the library," Don said to the judge.

I was speechless. I hadn't heard anything about this.

"Based on the teacher's concern, Don doesn't feel the children are ready to be with their mother unsupervised," Don's attorney added.

"We will continue this matter for another month so we can review the results of the supervised visits," decreed the judge without consulting me.

Flabbergasted, I stormed from the courtroom. I was filled with a dark outrage. Who were they to say what happened to my kids? What the hell had just happened? What did the library have to do with anything? It brought about another month of supervised visits. That's what it did.

At our next visit, I asked Nicole about the library.

"It's a hundred and five degrees on the playground, and it's air-conditioned in the library. It's just too hot for me," she replied.

I chuckled to myself, thinking Nicole always had been an avid reader and sensitive. When she was younger, she would explode if she were too hot, too cold, too tired, or too hungry. Her explanation made perfect sense. I saw that I had been ambushed in the courtroom, but my outrage had to wait until I was alone. We continued our visit under the watchful eye of the supervisor, who noted every interaction during our two-hour meetings.

"Well, that's a cool secret," I joked, my insides exploding with frustration, reliving VVs of Don's dominance over me.

The visits were challenging for me. A part of me was angry and humiliated about the circumstances. Yet I wanted to suspend that negative emotional activity during the visits so we could really enjoy the time we had together. Thankfully, the supervisor was a beautiful and kind woman who was pleasant and invisible during the visits. I planned special things to do, partly as a distraction for myself and partly to ensure the girls' enjoyment. They never uttered one word of dissatisfaction with me or our visits, and I was grateful for that. Beyond increasing the distance between us, any dissatisfaction on their part would have given Don more ammunition against me.

On the next visit, I planned for the four of us—the supervisor, the girls, and me—to walk to Target, which was a mile away, to buy a birthday gift for their favorite cousin. The supervisor approved this outing according to her supervised visits protocol. When Don and the children arrived, I asked him if he would pick the children up at Target at the appointed time instead of my house, and he agreed. I would walk home alone so the children would only have to walk one way. After the visit began, I explained the plan to the kids.

Apparently, Chris didn't like the thought of me walking home alone. She called her dad to ask if I could ride home with them, and he agreed. Believe me, I didn't want to ride with them, but I did. The supervisor recorded everything, so I upheld a high standard for my behavior and speech to ensure there wasn't anything incriminating in those notes. (Although it turned out no one ever read them, it cost all three hundred-plus hours and $13,000 worth of notes.)

In anticipation of the next court hearing, I sent another declaration to the judge extolling all my recovery activities and successful custody visits. Surely this would be enough basis to resume unsupervised custody.

But at the next hearing, Don's attorney said, "At the last visit, Mom instructed Chris to call her father and ask him to pick them up at Target. Mom knew this was against the supervision policy, so she put the child in a difficult position of calling her father and making this inappropriate request. This behavior is not acceptable, and we request that supervised visits continue. If the visits are not supervised, she may say and do other inappropriate things."

I could feel the thud of my heart hitting the floor. My stomach lurched. I was defeated again. My inner self shrieked hysterically while my face reflected stone-cold astonishment. Without any response from me, the judge concurred, and another hearing was scheduled in five weeks. I was given no chance to explain that, as the supervisor's notes would have shown, this was a lie.

Clearly I had watched too much television and believed that the courtroom was a sacred chamber of justice where lies were not tolerated. The reality was much fuzzier. There was no sworn oath, no compassionate jurors, and no slick defense attorney to ensure my rights were protected. There was just "he said, she said" or, in this case, only "he said."

Like most other members of my alcohol education class, I continued to drive while my license was suspended. There were simply too many places to be each day: work, errands, individual counseling, conjoint counseling, drug testing, DUI class, court appearances, probation appointments, recovery meetings, legal meetings, and so on and on. The penalty for a first offense driving on a suspended license was community service or a fine. That was a risk I was willing to take in order to ensure that I complied with all my other obligations.

One afternoon, I had a court appearance and a probation appointment, and I left work early to drive to these. When I got to the probation appointment, something was off, but I couldn't put my finger on it. The probation officer had me blow in the Breathalyzer three times, convinced that a zero couldn't be right. Even so, I was not suspicious enough to notice the officer follow me the six blocks to where I'd parked my car.

I was arrested for driving on a suspended license, a violation of my probation. Luckily I had a great relationship with my bail bondsman and bailed out in a few hours. Note to self: never burn your bail bondsman.

When I got home in the early hours of the morning, I found that Don had already picked up Sierra. He had also canceled my supervised Mother's Day visit with the girls, scheduled for that weekend. I hadn't called him, so there was only one other way he could have found out that I was arrested. The probation officer must have called him. Now I smelled the stench of the trap I had walked into or, more accurately, driven into.

A second offense was a big deal. I never drove again until my license was reinstated. In conversation, I would laughingly note that everywhere I needed to go required two buses, a taxi, a two-mile walk, and a mule. Actually that wasn't far from the truth.

I recognized that I needed to fortify my position based on my experiences with the legal system. The company I worked for had a relationship with the county probation office and the county sheriff, so I solicited their help. I approached my boss with trepidation and confessed my sins—that I was an alcoholic with nine months' sobriety and I had been arrested for a violation of probation, driving on a suspended license. I could sense his discomfort, but he offered support. Phone calls were made, and I was assured that I would receive a minor consequence, a fine or community service.

So I left work to go to my court hearing, expecting to return in a few hours. When my case was called, the DA stood and addressed the judge with additional allegations that after my arrest, I had continued to drive on a suspended license, that my husband had seen me doing so, and that I was driving on a suspended license with my children in the car. These allegations were lies. The last one was not even possible. The supervision of my visits with my children prohibited this.

I was stunned speechless, but it didn't matter because I was not offered the opportunity to respond. The judge remanded me to jail without further discussion. Presumed guilty. Next. My probation officer later told me that Don's new wife was in the lobby, orchestrating this catastrophe.

The nuclear bomb that exploded over Hiroshima was eighteen kilotons. The nuclear explosion in my being was at least twice that. As physics would dictate, I assumed Don had an equal and opposite reaction. This was the pinnacle of his domination over me. He imprisoned me physically and psychologically.

I used my one phone call to leave a voice mail at work, explaining how I had been duped and the predicament I was in. I had to divulge more about my circumstances to explain how the company's intervention had been trumped. I implored my boss to hold my position for me. It was a bad time to go to jail (is there a good time?) because I was in the middle of preparing a major presentation for him to present to the board of directors.

Although the DA asked that I be sentenced to sixty days, I was sentenced to thirty. The judge and DA were tough on me due to my alleged irreverence and incorrigible behavior. If I had lost my job over this, it would have been game over. The tiny, fragile seedling of a life I had been nurturing could not withstand a blow of this proportion. If I had lost my job, everything I had worked so hard for would topple like a row of dominos: my house, my car, my belongings, and my shot at regaining custody. It might as well have been a death sentence.

All I could do was languish in jail and pray for a miracle … which came in two days. I was released. I will never know exactly what miracle was performed, but the author was my boss. He earned my eternal loyalty by showing unearned faith in me. My probation officer was furious that I got out so fast. I had foiled her attempt to eradicate my threat to society. She continued to treat me with suspicion and distrust.

For two years, the attorney appointed for the children failed to provide a plan for the reunification of my children and me, to my great frustration. The children's attorney did assign a counselor to me. Optimistically I hoped she would help me to establish the strength of my recovery and suitability for reunification. I poured my heart out to her, explaining the toxic relationship and mutual substance abuse that had given rise to the unfortunate events preceding my custody struggle.

She sympathized, saying, "Don is running a covert character assassination." I was relieved that someone saw this. Finally, someone I could trust to help me. She also warned me, "You are going to have to endure the test of time and show who you really are. Your behavior must be impeccable, beyond reproach." I had come to this same realization myself.

Shortly after that, on a Saturday morning, I answered my door to find six probation officers, all adorned in Kevlar. They stormed in and searched the place. They administered another Breathalyzer test. Zero again. I was terrified, wondering if I could possibly have been set up. It would only take an empty wine bottle in my garbage to violate my probation.

The incident made me stunningly aware of how precarious my situation was. I was literally afraid to jaywalk on my nightly walks with Sierra, sure that could result in a prison term once Don got done with it. Over the next six months, fruitless searches by the probation department became routine. Eventually they stopped. I don't know if Don quit making allegations or if they just quit listening. In the meantime, I was the county's most wanted. If only the worst criminal in the county really was a three-time DUI with a minivan.

With vim and vigor, I took on this challenge. Knowing that I held the power to redeem my life steeled my determination. I could get an *A* in this. I would do everything asked of me for my own life and, more importantly, for my children. I had to get my life together, and I had to regain custody to protect them from the same relationship failures I'd had with their dad. More than anything, I feared they were being emotionally destroyed while I was helplessly sitting on the sidelines.

I complied meticulously with the terms of my probation and custody orders. I understood this was my last chance. Even a tiny slip could bring down a barrage of devastating consequences. One drink could put me back in jail. One angry outburst at Don or in court could jeopardize my chance for custody permanently. One failure to attend a counseling session, a recovery meeting, a DUI class, a probation appointment, a court hearing, or an alcohol screening test would be construed as disregard for the gravity of my situation, insincerity in my recovery, and possibly a relapse.

This knowledge motivated every moment of every day. I had to excel at work, recovery, and counseling. I had to excel at providing a stable home for my children. It all had to be perfect, beyond the reproach of the battalion of credentialed evaluators who held our fate in their hands.

Perhaps idealistically, I sought support and assistance from these professionals. Surely if I explained the nature of Don's emotional abuse and active addiction, they would help me to regain custody as quickly as possible. After all, that was what the entire matter was about, the welfare of the children in the face of active substance abuse. Now I was the well-documented sober one. I could prove it. I had alcohol screenings and eventually an interlock device on my car that kept records of me blowing a zero into the Breathalyzer, multiple times every single day.

The children's attorney also required that I have conjoint therapy with the kids and another counselor. At that point, it was costing me between $1,500 and $2,000 per month to meet the court's requirements, just to stay in the game. This continued for eighteen months.

With pure intention and professional conviction, the court-appointed family counselor wanted to reveal and heal the emotional wreckage she assumed was between my children and me. Each week, she would dig into the topic of my alcohol and drug abuse and how the children felt about it. Although I found it odd that she would lump me in with drug abusers, I didn't want to create any conflict with her. I needed to be 100 percent compliant.

If such wreckage existed, I hoped for healing as well. However, no matter how deeply she probed, there just didn't seem to be anything there. I could feel the shadow of mythical broken children of alcoholics. Somehow all the sins of all the alcoholic mothers were presumed to be lurking in my family. And she wasn't going to be satisfied until she uncovered and healed those imaginary wounds.

After months of no progress and the counselor's refusal to write any kind of letter for the court, Nicole simply refused to go there anymore. At the end of one of our last visits, the light bulb went on. The family counselor made a remark about my drug use, to my surprise.

"What?" I inquired, completely stunned.

"Oh, come on, you tested positive for methamphetamine," the counselor said in disgust.

"I have never even seen meth, much less used it," I countered.

She looked at me the way all counselors look at addicts denying their addiction. The familiar ring of Don's lies caused a million unprocessed fears to rise up. In my defensive state, I couldn't provide a response that did not have the putrid smell of a lame defense. Now I understood how far the covert character assassination reached. I walked out, cognizant of the prejudice she was operating under. In her mind, we couldn't heal until we confronted the ugly realities of my drug abuse and its impact on the kids. The surreal nature of the battle I was fighting became clear to me.

It dawned on me that I was the archetype of the alcoholic in this scenario. These attorneys, judges, and counselors saw themselves as righteous protectors of my children. They saw me as the epitome of every sin that every alcoholic ever committed. I was painted with a stigma that was far greater than me. How could I overcome that prejudice? Their jobs, their credentials, and their JDs, MFTs, and PhDs gave them power over my family. I hoped they would help.

Once again, I was learning about projection. Sir Ego imbued others with his own ideation, motives, intentions, beliefs, and behaviors. Their faulty assumptions had nothing to do with me. They simply weren't true. The faulty assumptions of my intentions, motivations, and behaviors did, however, say something about them. I triggered their VVs and some ghost of their past, other clients, or personal bias, and then they couldn't see me truly, clearly.

In the past, I had owned the false things Don projected onto me, but I was learning not to accept this anymore. I could see clearly that I was not what they thought I was and I could not afford to buy into their disgraced images of me.

Despite the assault on my motherhood and my inability to protect my children, I persevered in my quest for forgiveness. I tried to see this situation from all the perspectives of the players who blocked me. They had legitimate reasons to be skeptical. I had lied about my sobriety in the past. But I couldn't help but notice the paradox. Early recovery is very challenging even without such obstacles, and yet if I failed, no one would blame it on the obstacles that confounded every effort I made. Don and his attorney would congratulate themselves on predicting my failure and protecting the children from it.

The grotesque creatures from my chest had come alive. They were no longer confined to my psyche, imagination, and personal hell. They were orchestrating a hideous play that became my and my children's lives. The torturers' eyes were no longer lifeless but humanly alive and made me feel disgusting, humiliated, condemned, and ashamed. They were the faces of every attorney, judge, counselor, and social worker. Their minds were filled with a threat of indeterminate nature to the children. I felt thwarted, denied, blocked, punished, attacked, and denigrated.

I had to meet with these authorities in their armored fortresses, courtrooms, and offices, where the magical powers of degrees and titles made them right and me wrong. I had to speak with them civilly, cordially, and convincingly. I had to smash all my fears into the undersized chest and pray it didn't explode during the meeting. I had to look into their condemning eyes and deny the judgment, holding my divinity and my head up high. I had to discuss their irrational position as if it were rational. I had to listen to their false assumptions, conclusions, and "facts" that led to appalling decisions. And then I had to thank them and pay them. I repeated this over and over, week after week, and month after month.

It was unjust, unreal, and upside down. What was good for the children was declared bad; what was bad for the children was declared good. The active alcoholic became right; the sober alcoholic became wrong. Don's lies were regarded as truth; my truths were regarded as lies. The innocent one was imprisoned; the guilty one was free. But he, the insane, did not become sane. And I, the sane, did not become insane.

I came to see that the circumstances could be understood quite differently depending on the observer's point of view. What is truth? I needed to set my compass for a heading of the highest good and healing of myself and my family. I needed to seek the counsel of the wise one, even when I didn't like what it showed me about myself.

Tragically, like my own mother, I had abandoned my children. I relived this tragic loss every day from both perspectives: losing a mother and being separated from my children, agonies too profound for words. I can't know what it was like for my children because they still have not revealed this to me. But I am sure their suffering was no less than my own.

It was excruciating as my babies were metaphorically ripped from my womb. I couldn't protect or nurture them. I couldn't dry their tears or comfort their fears. I couldn't love them the way my mother had loved me. There were no more picnics at the lake, trips to the zoo, bedtime stories, art projects, intimate talks, and hugs and kisses. What we had were supervised visits, four hours per week, which I was very grateful for.

Spiritually and energetically, I was always with them, even when they weren't aware of my presence. There wasn't a day when I wasn't thinking of them, loving them, and praying for them. There was no limit to what I would endure to be reunited with them. I didn't care how long it took, how painful it got, and how hopeless it seemed. I would never quit, surrender, and really abandon my daughters. I was fearless, unstoppable, tenacious, and obstinate. I would not be defeated. Sometimes this is what it takes for a person who is stuck in the role of a victim to reclaim his or her power. The person must be willing to do whatever it takes to be victorious over his or her circumstances.

Everything I did was for them. I repaired every aspect of my life, constantly confronting all the demons in the chest of horrors without benefit of self-medicating. I studied *A Course in Miracles* like a monk and marinated my heart and mind in its message of love and perfection. The love of the wise one shattered the dark reflection I had internalized and instead emblazoned a divine reflection on my heart. I could and would do it. I would not stop until it was done.

As the custody battle wore on, I realized three things. First, I could never, ever, ever drink again. If I did, I would lose my kids, maybe forever. Second, the courts could only keep my children away from me for so long. In a few years, they would be old enough to choose, no matter what anyone did or said. Third, if I couldn't find a way to stay sober and purge my rage and fear, the girls would not *want* to come back to me.

My conclusion was that I alone determined the outcome of this drama. Finally I understood what I did have control over, my response to the situation. I could control whether I would find the wise one and the exalted path to reveal the divine power and love that would heal our family, or I would be destroyed by the weight of the burdens of fear, delusion, and untruth.

My resolve continued to be tested. Early recovery is a delicate time. Although I had developed some new coping skills, the deeply etched pattern of drinking the misery away still exerted strong influence. Each setback in my custody case, especially the ones that reeked with the stench of treachery and malice, would trigger the excruciating, overwhelming desire to self-medicate. The dragon would rear its menacing and dangerous head.

But my resolve was greater. The stubbornness that had prevented me from heeding advice to stop drinking was now my ally. Sir Ego now sought the grail of redemption with the same conviction the he had protected the grail of addiction. I would not be defeated, surrender, and fall into the abyss, no matter how hard I was pushed. My VVs became my friends. They were gateways into the fortress of pain I had built. Each time my efforts were thwarted, the VVs would unleash an avalanche of rage, fear, hurt, and pain. They were explosive, raw, enormous, consuming, and volcanic. It would be years before they were purged. If you think hell hath no fury like a woman scorned, you are wrong. Try taking her kids away from her.

I was deeply conflicted. Intellectually, I wanted to forgive and let go of the past to move forward. But my emotions were stuck in the pain. My wrath was overwhelming. My thoughts raced in circles. How could Don be so cold and calculating in his attempt to destroy me, someone he claimed to have loved? His cruelty was appalling and merciless. The torture of living with him was nothing compared to this attack on my motherhood. He shamed, humiliated, attacked, betrayed, and kicked me when I tried to get up. He systematically tried to destroy me or eliminate me from the girls' lives.

I wanted him to suffer and to know the pain I was feeling. I wanted payback. I dreamed of retaliation. I plotted it in my daydreams, painstakingly detailed revenge fantasies from which I emerged as the vindicated superhero and he as the desolate and defeated sufferer of eternal damnation. I wanted the truth to be known and justice to be done. And I wanted the cast of professionals that stalled my custody case to experience the hell they had created for my family, humbly correct their error, and vindicate me upon realization of the truth.

But I could also see the futility of these desires. Fulfillment of my revenge fantasies in no way would eliminate my pain or undo the wrongs. The wrongs were in the unchangeable past. My pain was inside me and was mine to liberate. No amount of exoneration, amends, or repentance on anyone's part would release the volcano stored in my psyche. I thought it would. But it would not. And I was never going to get it. I realized that I must forgive them, regardless of their willingness to admit guilt or make amends if I were to be free. I understood that I must learn to release, forgive, and purify. In this way, I alone determined my fate.

Despite evidence to the contrary, I knew the Creator's power was greater than Don's. It would have to prevail eventually, if I could hold on that long. Sir Ego's faith in the power of the Creator was growing.

ACIM declares the world is upside down because it is a world of fear. Love is the only antidote for fear; love is the light that dispels the darkness where fear lurks. There are only two choices, love or fear. I rebuked fear. I could see the damage that fear had done in my life. I persisted each and every day, despite my fear. I walked into my fear, confronting it.

My chest was wide open, and all the terrifying contents were exploding out at all times. There was no relief—nowhere to run and hide and no intoxication vacation where the hideous torturers were not present. As I had learned in rehab, I must allow the VVs to open, the fear to be felt, the tears to flow, and the heart to ache. It seemed that an endless flow of agony washed over me during these years. I had not yet learned to fully allow and nurture this energy release. A part of me resisted it, yet the imperative to heal was stronger. I wondered if it would ever end, if the peace beyond understanding would ever be mine. I was on my knees and praying that the Creator would hold me and show me love, despite my brokenness, as my own mother had done so many years ago. Sir Ego was ready to bow to the wise one who beseeched this divine love.

This image comforted me during many sleepless nights. Without this faith, I do not know how I would ever have continued to remain sober and functional. I knew that something deep within me—the wise one, my connection to the Creator—was responsible for guiding and protecting me. Something very real was sustaining me, and it was not in the realm of Sir Ego.

Sir Ego would never have been able to do that. Sir Ego was still stuck in the broken place. It offered thoughts and advice that were going in the wrong direction, downhill and backward into hell. I call these fix-it thoughts. Each hysterical thought it offered, like, "This is just too much. A glass of wine couldn't hurt," or "Just call Don or the counselors and tell them how ridiculous this is, how backward this is, and how much they are hurting the kids," had to be countered with strength, courage, and wisdom that came from beyond it. Each time Sir Ego offered these "helpful" hints, I examined them from a higher perspective and concluded that they were not sage advice. These were the behaviors that had backfired in the past.

Both of the girls played softball, and I loved to watch their games. Don got court orders to prohibit me from attending my daughters' games for one whole season. Why? Perhaps he wanted to keep up the supervision as long as possible because he was afraid that I would disparage him and his tactics to the girls. But I was not seduced by the short-term high of alienation of affection. It was bad for the girls, period.

When I could finally attend the games, I felt like I had returned from a war that the other parents were oblivious to. They were still talking about the color of granite countertops for their kitchen remodels. I couldn't relate anymore. It had been two years. Could they still be working on the same kitchen remodel? Perhaps they had moved on to the bathroom. On two occasions, Don was drinking alcohol slyly, and I had to watch the girls get in the car with him and drive home.

Each day my girls were held hostage, my fear for their emotional well-being increased. Ironically, my attempts to convey this concern to the army of professionals I was paying to help me hurt my cause. I looked like every vindictive alcoholic they had ever seen, trying to place the blame anywhere other than on my own shoulders.

One of the counselors said to me, "Don just wants to hear that you are sorry."

I had said that to every player in this drama a million times, and far more profoundly, I had backed it up with my actions. I had repented and was doing everything in my power to move in the right direction. Actions speak louder than words.

Christmas was bleak once again. All the girls' handmade ornaments adorned my blue spruce, bearing witness to the love and joy we once shared. Yet I sat there alone, filled with desolation and remorse. My daughters' photos adorned the walls, but their voices and spirits were missing. Their furnished bedrooms were unoccupied and unembellished, awaiting their future occupants' decorations and treasures. Wistful and forlorn, Sierra and I sat by a fire that could never blaze brightly enough to banish the gloom.

I took solace in Jesus's birth. I cried out to Him day and night, beseeching Him to comfort and console me in my darkest hours.

When I wasn't excruciatingly sad, I was outraged. I was filled with molten lava. Each setback became an opportunity for me to slay a tormentor as they blazed out the chest of horrors. They were also a test of my sobriety. Would I feel the pain as I held the hand of the wise one, or would I anesthetize it with my old friend, alcohol? This was a minute-by-minute, day-by-day battle for a very long time. I learned that the pain could neither kill me nor make me drink.

My willingness to feel the pain, to allow it to pass before my awareness, was only due to my shield of faith, my firm conviction that I was divine and the condemning screams of the tormentors were lies. I was not the grotesque, disfigured, horrific reflection that had been created in my psyche. I would not accept that anymore. So I learned to rebuke them.

I was defeated in many battles by my cunning, devious adversary, who seemed not to care about the collateral damage to our daughters. But I did not give him the one piece of ammunition that he needed for ultimate victory, a relapse, employment termination, or a public emotional explosion. Likewise, the girls did not give one shred of evidence against me. They never said a word or resisted whatever action was necessary to keep the reunification hope alive.

After a year, the judge grew impatient that the reunification was not happening. All the evidence pointed to my healthy and stable recovery. Finally the custody evaluation I had sought for so long was ordered, including psychological profiles, reference checking, home visits, and interviews with all family members. I sold my Waterford crystal to pay my half of the bill, $5,000. I believed that at last the truth would be revealed, Don would be defrocked, and the world would return to its rightful order.

Well, not quite. You see, I still believed in Santa Claus, the tooth fairy, and justice prevailing. In the end, the report accomplished the long-awaited result of recommending shared custody and overnight visits, but it favored Don. The evaluator found that Don and Barb were parents par excellence. His report asserted that I continued to lie about Don's abusive, narcissistic, alcoholic behavior. He drew this conclusion despite three facts listed in the very same report: (1) I did not lie to him personally, (2) my psychological tests said I was not a liar, and (3) my reference (i.e., my boss) said I did not lie to him. In fact, my boss affirmed that he trusted me to manage his company's entire treasury operation, overseeing millions of dollars personally. In conclusion, the evaluator wrote, "I don't know why she lies about Don." He presented these facts and his completely inconsistent conclusion to the judge, and no one questioned it.

During the course of the evaluation, the evaluator had led me to believe that I would be satisfied with the outcome. I took this to mean that Don and I would soon be sharing custody. In a pet shop afterward, I lost my heart to two tiny black-and-white kittens, littermates, twins for my twins, a homecoming gift.

On the next supervised visit, the girls' curiosity turned to delight when they saw the litter box and asked, "Did you get a cat?"

"No," I replied. "You got a kitten each."

The two tiny fur balls rolled around in a knot, climbed the curtains, licked our ice cream, and even groomed Sierra, licking the insides of her ears and other hard-to-reach places. The girls adored them. It was teary to see my daughters leave that night, but I assured them they would be with me and their kittens soon. I was mistaken.

When we took the report to the court to be affirmed, Don fought it, and it was not affirmed. It was part of the long-standing pattern. Don would literally agree to things with me in the lobby of the courtroom. When I repeated those agreements, as I had written them down, in court, his attorney would say that he would swear under penalty of perjury that they were untrue. The judge ordered that supervised visits continue for four more months. Unbelievable. Intolerable. Inexcusable. Unjust.

If anyone needed a miracle, it was me. My eyes lit up when an email about Colin Tipping's Miracles Workshop hit my radar. His book *Radical Forgiveness* had taught me techniques to come to a place of true forgiveness. I attended the three-day workshop with about twenty other people. The process of the workshop was to purge one's victim consciousness. Through a series of steps, we were guided to see the lesson in the perpetration and to forgive, releasing the stuckness of the situation and allowing for a miracle.

Colin's premise was that it only required the tiniest amount of willingness to forgive to create a crack in the dam. Although I knew in my head that forgiveness was the key to unlock my prison, unforgiveness still burned in my heart. That was about all I had, the tiniest amount, but it was enough.

I was the quintessential victim, hitting the undo button over and over, demanding to be right. I wanted vindication, punishment, and justice. I wanted to reveal Don as guilty, wrong, and condemned. I had to teach him a lesson so he would never do it again. I had to save the world from his perpetrations. I was vigilant for his repeat offenses, coloring his every word and deed with the shades of his guilt. I screamed empty screams that I did not deserve this, yet I had actively participated in it.

I was unwilling to deal with my current reality, living in a neverland that denied these violations, resisting the world as it was. We can never win the fight against reality; it will never conform to our wishes and demands. We must conform to it. Insisting on fruitless resistance is to hold horrors in our chest, refusing to liberate them until justice has been done.

Needless to add, this does not work. Justice, punishment, revenge, and vindication, these acts and thoughts do not liberate things from our chests. Over time, I would come to ponder the futility and absurdity of my demands. They could never help me remove my pain. My suffering would not be less if Don suffered. And the girls would suffer more again. The voice in my head was telling me a lie! I vowed to find the truth.

If Don were simply to confess and make amends, would this be enough? For some crimes, I would have accepted this and released that item from the chest, but not for these crimes. Don could not earn my mercy. Only grace would liberate those items from the chest. According to Sir Ego, punishment means getting what you deserve. Mercy is not getting the punishment you deserve. Grace is getting what you *don't* deserve, unconditional forgiveness. Mercy and grace are the ways of the wise one.

I reflected on a forgiveness circle that I attended. Colin had hosted it at a nearby church. This Native American ceremony allowed me to see that we are all wounded. All of us are victims and perpetrators at different times. We all make mistakes born of our hurt and fear.

For the ritual, the group gathers into a large circle, and various transgressions are called out. "If you have ever been physically violated, walk the circle."

Each person who feels so walks across the circle, thinking of the various occasions of this offense, hugging each person he or she meets, acknowledging his or her fellow victim, saying, "I am sorry that happened to you." As each of us contemplates our victimization, we both acknowledge that others have been victimized and receive their support in this mutual exchange.

Then the crime is flipped. "If you have ever physically violated anyone, walk the circle."

My mind went to frustrating toddler moments, when I picked them up and put them in the time-out spot. And the time when I bit Don as he wrestled me to the floor. Again, you hug each person you meet as you reflect on your offenses, offering, "I am sorry that happened to you."

We experience the pain of being a perpetrator and compassion for ourselves and others as both victim and perpetrator. As I walked the perpetrator's walk, tears streamed down my cheeks for the pain I had caused my children, and I was grateful for each hug and expression of empathy from my fellow perpetrators.

Something happened to me when I walked the circle as both the victim and the perpetrator—compassion, mercy, and grace. I understood both the victim and perpetrator are equally harmed by the interaction in a cosmic sense. "He that is without sin among you, let him first cast a stone at her" (John 8:7 KJV).

Oftentimes in my story, my victimhood contributed to my downfall. I consistently resisted reality: refusing to deal with my troubled marriage, my new life as a single working mom, and my alcoholism. In my denial, I created an alternative reality I believed in and I tried to enroll others in. It was a reality where my actions made sense although they did not fit the veritable circumstances. I exuded the angry, vengeful, toxic energy of victimhood, and everyone—counselors, attorneys, judges, and social workers—saw it. It was visceral. They could feel it. It validated Don's accusations about me. He played on their fears as he had played on mine, causing them to delay reunification.

Recognizing my divinity was a crucial element of my recovery, and I could not accept it without being willing to recognize Don's divinity. Forgiveness became an imperative. It was the other side of the coin of my redemption. I could not accept my divinity without accepting his. It was that simple. *ACIM* defines forgiveness as denial of the lower consciousness that we *all* are sinners in need of redemption and affirms the higher consciousness that we *all* are eternal, divine, perfect souls having a human experience that incudes mistakes, healing, and lessons. These options are mutually exclusive. We choose which of the realities we live in, that of Sir Ego or that of the wise one.

Of all the stories the workshop participants shared, mine was considered the most heinous and challenging because of the nature of the violation.

And it was still occurring. How do you forgive the rapist in the middle of the rape? How does Christ forgive the crucifixion as it is happening? Christ could do that, but could I?

This is possible only if you believe there is a different reality than this physical realm. I had to embrace a truth that this world is but a play, a drama designed to teach and amuse us, without effects on our eternal souls. I had seen the injustice of this world up close, yet I knew somewhere deep in my being that the universe was not without justice. It was in a realm that was invisible to the naked eye but not unseen by the wise one.

ACIM talks much about the change in perception required for the miracle to occur. This change in perception is always provided when we seek it. I turned my will away from seeking justice in this earthly plane and toward seeking truth in the divine plane. This was an act of faith, love, fearlessness, and desperation, for I knew not what lay beyond. *ACIM* is crystal clear that there is love and there is not-love, also known as fear. There is no combination platter. I had to choose. I could see that only fear lay on this material plane, and I was willing to take any option other than that. So I put my faith in love, the Creator, and a higher truth and reality.

In this higher truth, Don and I had engaged to teach other important lessons for our souls. He had done an extraordinarily good job, as I was being forced to look at the world in a way that I would not have otherwise. His strength and persistence motivated me onward when I might have fallen and failed. Although this did not instantly release all the Don VVs in my heart, it reoriented and propelled me in the direction where this could and would occur. There was simply no denying that I was on a much healthier and sacred path as a result of what had occurred, a path I had not found on my own. Little did I know that this fateful decision would eventually and astonishingly create a beautiful harmony in our family and functional co-parenting between Don and me. I would come to feel gratitude, affinity, and compassion for his role in our family, absent any negativity. This was a miracle, no less.

As I projected my victimhood on our children, it bound me to a responsibility to save them. The turning point for me was when I saw the Creator's eye view that my daughters were not damsels in distress that I needed to rescue. They were the unconditionally loving angels who were providing the incentive for my recovery, awaiting me at the inevitable goal line.

"Keep your eyes on the prize," my rehab director would admonish each time my self-pity started to engulf me.

The entire group cheered when this realization gushed out of my heart and through my mouth into the heavens.

I could see that our children had chosen us as parents, and they had lessons in this circumstance as well. Another seed was planted about my role in parenting as guardian rather than owner of our children. I came to see that we are all born into families that will set up many of our life lessons. There is no unfairness in being born into a family of greater or lesser financial status, cultural condition, or health. We chose just the right family for our lessons. My faith in karma as a benevolent force that creates challenging situations for our highest good was growing, little by little.

As a parent, I could have refused to release many VVs about the pain I caused my children and my guilt would have continued to be a heavy, dark cloud over our family. Colin explained that holding onto and defending my guilt and shame would have acted as a magnet attracting negativity from my children, perhaps in the form of attack and punishment thoughts and words. The river of forgiveness runs through us and purifies our own guilt and shame. And, those words of attack and punishment never did come, thankfully.

It also changed my view of my mother's early death and my relationship with my dad. I believe I chose to be born into that family, probably knowing what would happen. It certainly started my spiritual quest, which, although slow to blossom, was never totally absent. It also left VVs in me that attracted a bad marriage and drinking problem, which would eventually change the course of my life in profoundly positive ways. I was beginning to have some limited visibility into the higher realm, and the strength of it continued to grow in my awareness.

Forgiveness is the cure for victimhood. The powerful definition of forgiveness that Colin Tipping uses acknowledges that "cause" is not of this material world. The cause of everything is in a higher world, where lessons are planned, defined, created, and agreed to. The crime is a mistake, not a sin. Forgiveness is learning the lesson, releasing the offense from the chest, and correcting the mistake. If cause is not of this world, then no blame can be laid in this world.

This material world is a theatrical performance for the education and spiritual growth of the actors. In various lives, we all get a chance to play both the victor and vanquished, the prince and the pauper, and the hero and the villain so we may experience and understand all flavors of love and fear. Over many lifetimes, Sir Ego learn what attitudes, behaviors, and pursuits cause pain and suffering and turns to a higher path with guidance from the wise one. After the play is over, the murderer and his victim enjoy a good a laugh and a celebration of the art form. The murderer isn't taken to prison. He was merely playing the antagonist's role.

This breakthrough was the cornerstone of a foundation of love, compassion, and forgiveness upon which I would build over the next years, changing the course of my life and my family's.

Two days later, a visit with a mediator and Don gave me everything I asked for, including unsupervised overnight visits and shared custody. Even the mediator was shocked, given the high-conflict nature of our case. The only person not shocked was Colin Tipping. He had predicted it: when my energy changed, the whole situation would change. Without knowing it, Don felt his release from the grip of my judgment and condemnation, and he lost the compulsion to fight.

My newfound insights gave me power to change things in the material world. Wow. I changed myself, and Don changed. I surrendered the battle and won. All my resistance had been in vain. It had locked us in a battle of wills. This was a shocking and unbelievable discovery. In fact, I wasn't sure I believed it. However, it would prove to be quite true in time. Somehow the VVs bound us together, and when I released some energy, it had repercussions in Don's being.

It was clear that I had a choice. I could keep the explosive hatred and rage inside and simmering, possibly causing a relapse, or I could let it go. Despite the one-sided nature of the courtroom drama, the truth was either Don and I were both guilty, and I would be condemned to this angst as a criminal and a victim, or I could accept another perspective in which we were both innocent and I would be freed from this angst. I absolutely chose the latter; however, it would take a great deal of introspection to understand how to integrate this new perspective.

Simply stated, we choose to function on the level of the wise one that understands the greater reality. It makes healing, growthful, VV-releasing choices for the evolution of our souls and the highest good for those around us. Or we may choose to function on the level of Sir Ego, the lower self, which lives in fear of the world and other brothers, always brandishing the lance and the shield. Sir Ego is fighting the VV-holding battle to sustain a semblance of order in our inner and outer worlds, but in truth, it is his frenzied and unwitting attacks and defenses that darken his world and cause his suffering.

The brilliant dawn had finally come after the darkest night. I celebrated with my children that very evening, sans supervisor. Amazingly, the girls were weathering this storm quite well, from outward appearances. The later elementary school years are a child's golden time. Children of that age are self-sufficient in practical matters, yet not old enough to catastrophize about things. I considered myself lucky that our separation and reunification happened at this time. If the girls had been younger, the time away from me would have been more devastating. If they had been older, individuating teenagers, they might have rebuked me.

The bitter pill made our every moment together even sweeter. We just had major fun. We loved, laughed, snuggled, and reconnected. My daughters never reproached me for the horrible nightmare I had caused. Even that, I would have accepted with love and grace. I deserved it. But it never came. Their love was truly pure, unconditional, and far more than I deserved. My cup runneth over.

At bedtime, we would go into my room and cuddle up on my bed. Our rebonding included nightly back rubs and foot rubs with specially selected lotions and oils. I could not imagine a more powerful way to heal, no matter how tired my hands got. We laughed, giggled, chattered, and snuggled with Sierra and our kittens. The love flowed, and the joy spilled over. The girls slept in my room for the next year. Perhaps they were afraid I would disappear again and did not wish to allow that to happen. We all climbed back into the womb together, reunited at last.

Now my exotic vacations included them. They got certified for scuba diving, and we went off to Cozumel, Hawaii, and Grand Cayman. In Hawaii, we finally realized my dream of swimming with wild dolphins. The crew knew the daily route the dolphin pods took from their nocturnal deep-sea hunting to their midday sleep in the shallower water. The boat would cruise along until the crew spotted a pod of dolphins. Then we donned snorkel gear and jumped into the water to join them.

Fifty or more spinner dolphins filled the clear turquoise waters, to the right, the left, and below. True to their name, they jumped, spinning in the air and splashing joyously in the gentle waves of the bay. Their joy was contagious and visceral. I felt a natural buzz of endorphins, my heart expanding to encompass the magnificent experience. The dolphins were curious and friendly, and they came right up to my girls, touching them. Like me, the mamas swam blissfully through the water with their babies flanking them, theirs were football-sized darlings.

I had a new appreciation for even the most mundane tasks, which I considered privileges, of parenting. In less than a year, the girls demanded fifty-fifty custody, and Don put up little resistance.

The junior high years were delightful. The girls flourished in school and sports. Together they weathered the social turmoil that often swamps singleton children. The unbreakable twin bond, fortified in the dark times, seemed to immunize my daughters from the erratic relationship dramas of their peers. Through the years of my war with Don, it had to have been very hard on them. Even if I felt my bullets were righteous, who else could tell the good guy from the bad guy when bullets were flying in both directions? This thought alone often ceased my fire.

The forgiveness miracle continued to grow. As the battles ceased, I had time to heal, release the pent-up rage, and investigate the mistaken beliefs I needed to let go of. My sense of being persecuted ran very deep. As I faced each volcano of fear and anger about the custody battle, I would commit to release the destructive energy. Over time, that commitment brought new insights to the surface.

10

The Special One

One day, I awoke from a dream in which I could feel myself having both the perspective of Sir Ego, being in the dream, and the wise one, watching Sir Ego in the dream. First, Sir Ego is in a terrible place. It's a dark, threatening, cold, barren, and rocky cave. Terrified, Sir Ego lacks everything: food, warmth, companionship, security, and comfort.

Suddenly for no apparent reason, Sir Ego is now in an okay place. It is not nice, but it is much better. It is bare and gloomy but contains a table, a hard chair, and some scraps of food. Suddenly Sir Ego is returned to the terrible place and then begins to ping-pong back and forth between the two places with no apparent rhyme or reason.

As the witness, the wise one, I see that this was not under Sir Ego's control or discretion in any way. And just before I awoke, I saw the moment that Sir Ego makes two fatal mistakes. First, Sir Ego resigns himself to the okay place because it is so much better than the terrible place and he does not look for a better place. Second, he thinks I just need to figure out how to stay in this okay place and avoid the terrible place and begins to strategize how to hold onto the okay place. His strategies don't make any sense and aren't useful because he does not understand what determines which state he is in.

It took some thought to understand how well this dream represents Sir Ego's dilemma. Saints and sages tell us of the beautiful reality beyond the material world and the purpose of our life is to seek it, the exalted grail. Yet Sir Ego immediately forsakes that quest and begins his own quest to stay in the okay place and out of the terrible place. Then he exerts all his thoughts, words, actions, and will to stay in the place he desires and avoid the place he fears. These efforts are futile because he doesn't understand the cause behind which destination he finds himself.

I believe the cause that determines our circumstances is karma and our journey of life lessons. Sometimes our life lessons require us to go into dark and scary places to gain insight and understanding. Sometimes our life is lacking but tolerable, so we are lulled into a false sense of resignation that there isn't anything better or higher. The exalted quest is the higher path that takes us out of this ping-pong game altogether where we expand in wisdom, understanding, clarity, and love. This path leads to the higher realms of self-realization, true joy, and unconditional love, a return to our divine nature.

When karmic events occur that catapult us into the dark place, Sir Ego is quick to look for a solution in the material world rather than the spiritual world. *Why am I here? How do I get out? And if you are to blame for putting me here, you need to get me out of here. If you stole my money, my husband, or my health, you did this. You put me here in the place that I fear. And you must pay.* This is where I was stuck with Don.

When I first read *ACIM* during my toxic marriage, I saw forgiveness through the eyes of a codependent. "Forgiving" my husband for each violation was really excusing or rationalizing his behavior. "He's had a bad day, bad ex-wife, bad burrito, whatever. Or "His comments seem nasty, but they are really to help me grow and improve." This is not forgiveness. I was afraid of him, so I will excuse this and be nice. This was me trying to control Don's behavior so I could stay in the okay place and not be cast into the terrible place.

Eventually I did learn to have appropriate and loving boundaries with Don. But the forgiveness came first. It purified my intentions; hence my boundary came from a place of love, offered in kindness, without the foul stench of judgment condemning a boundary violation. I knew both the loving way I had redirected my toddlers away from the hot oven and the angry way I lashed out at Don when he touched my red-hot VVs. With love and patience, I could teach him, as I had taught my toddlers, that I would not let them touch the hot spot.

There was another misunderstanding about forgiveness that I needed to transcend. Forgiveness is not affirming that the perpetrator is guilty and offering him or her a stay of execution, keeping the offense noted deep in the recesses of my mind. Many books I read seemed to imply that forgiveness could be achieved by saying "You wronged me, but I forgive you," whether in private or public. Sir Ego would be affirming that the other knight caused me to land in the terrible place, but Sir Ego was willing to let this one slide.

In jail, I tried every book on forgiveness and wanted to forgive, but the overpowering energy and violated victim thoughts were persistent. I was not yet free of it. I was merely putting the incident back in my chest to VV another day. And I continued to pull it out and relive it, inspect it, and be vigilant for repeat offenses where I would unforgive this old charge. When I was still in this stage of forgiveness, I still judged every move Don made, made assumptions about his malicious motives, and reenacted the whole nightmare over and over in my mind.

That kind of karmic recordkeeping is the Creator's job, not ours. As I saw in my many visits to the courtroom, Sir Ego does not have the level of visibility to understand the karmic nature of the events. Forgiveness, in the highest sense as described in *ACIM*, is denying the fundamental error that you both have made that allows you to think something is wrong. In the divine plan of lessons, nothing is wrong. You did not put me in the dark place. My lessons, my karma, and my magnetism put me here. What is happening now is for my highest good, my expansion and my education.

When you forgive in this way, you identify with the wise one who has attracted the lesson in order to grow and purify, and you deny the illusory identification with the body for both of you. You take the wise one's perspective and deny the delusion of Sir Ego's perspective. As our wise one speaks in thoughts and energy to their wise one, it elevates both of us to a place we could not reach on our own. Before, we both believed we were bodies, and now we both have a glimpse of our divinity.

This is the exalted quest that the Course lays out. Every time that we honor our brothers by seeing the divinity beyond the knight's armor, we release a link of the prisoners' shackles that bind us to the terrible place and the okay place. We forge a new interlocking chain of compassion and freedom that takes us to the higher divine realm. We walk together, hand in hand, with our fellow knights into heaven or hell. Forgiveness chooses heaven. Sir Ego must be trained to take this path and seek this grail.

And nothing can be more beautiful. It tenderized my heart, breaking the crust that prevented love from penetrating. It allowed us to both share in the sorrow of our misguided belief in delusion and stomped on it with the truth and righteousness of our divinity. We see that every knight is stuck in the same misguided quest to find the bliss it seeks and salvation from fear, where it is not. I developed compassion for each subsequent layer of defense the ego built around this fear and saw that the crime was a correctable mistake, not an eternally damned sin. We choose to exalt the moment, release the VV, honor our fellow knight, and move on the next challenge in our grail quest.

I started to understand that karma may be difficult but is not cruel or punitive. Sir Ego often takes this victim perspective, but the wise one can show him or her that the terrible place holds a lesson and becomes a sanctified place when we learn the lesson. My greatest challenges yielded the greatest growth for me and improvement in my circumstances. We ascend the spiral staircase each step we take in learning the lesson, and we descend each time we fall into victimhood.

The war cries of the victim, "This shouldn't be happening," "You must undo what you did to me," and "you've stolen my happiness" arise from Sir Ego's need to feel special. How could you do this to *me*. Sir Ego is fighting the wrong battle. He wages war with the circumstance and his fellow knights rather than his inner VVs. Well, it *is* happening to me, and nobody can undo what's been done. I must find a way to make the best of the circumstances. I choose my response, not my reality. I'm not special. Bad stuff happens to me, like everyone else, and I alone must pass through the darkest hour. When you are going through hell, don't stop.

From Sir Ego's distorted perspective, he screeches that he doesn't deserve the terrible place, yet secretly believes he deserves the punishment. I both believed I didn't deserve the treatment Don gave me and I did deserve punishment for my transgressions. While Sir Ego vacillates between these unreal and unhelpful perspectives, the wise one sees the karmic perspective. From Sir Ego's distorted victim perspective, everyone else in the universe seemed to be doing just fine in his or her Stepford lives: perfect marriage, successful career, financial abundance, and trouble-free children. Somehow they received their hearts' desires, from which I was barred. I, alone and forlorn, needed to struggle for each moment of happiness. I found it in whatever devil's bargain I could make and drunkenly anesthetized the preponderance of moments of everything except happiness.

This was the thinking that I had to reverse. Either Don and I were both guilty of similar offenses as alcoholic parents, or we were both innocent in a grand lesson plan. Intellectually, this had to be true. Something interesting was causing me to have a lopsided perspective, to reject my punishment and demand it for Don. I learned that the reason it was so hard to see was that Sir Ego was attached to being special—specifically that I was especially good and he was especially bad. I wanted to direct the imaginary wrath of the Creator toward Don and deflect that wrath away from myself. As long as Don was guiltier than I was, I would be okay.

When I looked hard and deep enough into this idea of specialness, I saw it was a monumental inner construct that was going to take some work to dismantle. How could I be the one among billions who was special in the universe? Even if that were so, it could not save me from the forces of the universe! I was tiny Sir Ego, standing on a tiny planet in a tiny solar system in the infinity of the cosmos, shaking my fist and stating, "You must care for me and attend to my desires. Don't let anything bad happen to me. I am special."

Sir Ego seeks to be special, and this causes his competitive nature. *ACIM* tells us we are special by our inclusion in the universal consciousness, not by being excluded from the herd. Each person is absolutely unique. We each have a calling that is all our own and that only we can absolutely fulfill. We are each one whom the Creator waits patiently for, whom the Creator absolutely desires at his holy table of communion. We are each one whom the Creator absolutely loves, blesses, protects, and guides throughout the maze of many lives and lessons.

But not one of us is special nor the only one. The Creator has a unique path for each of us to purify our energy and awaken to the awareness of our true selves. The guide markers are our VVs leading us ever forward when we choose the wise one and looping back if Sir Ego fails to embrace the lesson. The wise one calls teachers to him when he is ready for more wisdom. We must travel our own path, following this sage inner guide. We cannot know the path of another as they cannot know ours.

When we stand in the truth, *ACIM* says we walk hand in hand with our fellow human beings into salvation. That is how the universal consciousness returns to its completeness, its essential unity, its perfection. We must move away from the necessity of specialness in order to accept our unique position in the cosmos, the divine plan, and the heart of the Creator.

When my specialness was not acknowledged by those around me, I felt persecuted, condemned, and crucified. But I was not alone on the cross of my own making. Remember, we are all interconnected in the eternal vibration of the universal quantum soup. Sir Ego, unenlightened by the wise one, wages a war against his fellow knights—of energy flow, psychological manipulation, and physical attack—for the prize of specialness at all times. Sir Ego proudly embraces his armor as a symbol of his separation from the other knights and the Creator. Sir Ego is on a quest of his own making toward worldly grails.

Sir Ego's guilt, shame, and fear of punishment must be eradicated from Sir Ego's awareness so he can continue attacking his fellow knights who appear to be blocking the entrance to the okay place. What could be a better place to project guilt and wrath than upon all the nonspecials, that is, everyone else within range? So we self-righteously declare our virtue and condemn our fellow knights. We are willing to march into hell, ramming them from behind, to ensure they go there one step ahead of us. That was where I was stuck during my custody battle, trying to crucify Don to save myself and, in reality, damning my own argument.

The wise one is ever joined with our brothers in the universal consciousness. Whatever we do to each other, we do to ourselves. Our thoughts do not leave their source, the energy of the universal consciousness. You get what you give. We are all interconnected, bound by each wisp or billow of energy our thoughts direct at another. Thus, each instant holds the potential to become an opportunity for fear or love, judgment or pardon, or punishment or liberation that we all will share. We walk together into heaven or together into hell. As we spend this moment in divine love, in eternity and in truth, we exalt it.

Trying to understand this idea, I pondered the image of a car accident. When another driver does something that really scares me, like dangerously cutting me off, I have a split-second impulse to hit him to "show" him. But

I resist this impulse. Why? Because my car will also be hurt, and I will have to pay for the repair of both cars. Therefore, I resist this urge to punish the other driver, to teach him a lesson. I had to break the connection between punishment and teaching. We teach with love, not with fear. Sir Ego is not receptive when he is afraid.

In the world of energy, our verbal or thought attacks work the same way. When we "hit" someone with attack thoughts or words and think *we* are unscathed, we are wrong. Our divine nature is hurt when we dishonor another person. Although it may be buried deeply below our awareness, we are hurt by our transgressions against others. I felt it during the forgiveness circle ritual. We create karma for which we will have to "pay" at some time in the future. We believe we can get rid of negative energy by putting it on another person in this way, but it is not true. Hitting a person with negative thought energy is exactly like hitting them with our car. Wow, I needed to be more careful with my thoughts.

Sir Ego wishes to hide these truths from our awareness so he may continue the quests of his own choosing. He would rather do battle with his fellow knights than acknowledge the unknown wise one. Sir Ego does not trust the wise one to make good decisions. He knows the wise one will ask him to surrender his vices and fears that the wise one may punish him for his past transgressions. So he creates layer upon layer of defenses, defending his battle plans, his false grails, and his dishonoring of his fellow knights, making us afraid to look into this quagmire.

ACIM says that darkness cannot hide, and this creates fear. But of more significance, there is nothing we should want to hide. All that is required is for these incorrect notions to be brought into the light to be dispelled, transcended, and purified. They do not need to be conquered. There is no war to wage. The Creator is not an adversary. The enemy is our ignorance, our fear, and our mistaken perception of ourselves and our identity. These mistakes require only correction. That is the goal of *ACIM* and all the scriptures and avatars, enlightened teachers. They come to reveal the truth, to eradicate mistaken beliefs about ourselves and our essential nature, to light the path that returns us to love. In this way, their goals are congruent. Their aspirations are the same. They come from the same all-pervading source, though the paths vary according to the natures of humanity.

My experience has taught me that there is nothing I wish to hide from the Creator. There is nothing that the Creator didn't create and there is nothing we can do to eternally destroy creation. We are neither especially good nor especially bad. We cannot bribe, flatter, or coerce the Creator. We cannot offend, attack, or betray the Creator. We can't hide anything from the Creator. There is no thought too toxic. There is no emotion too volatile. There is no idea too annihilating. Anything is better than keeping these things inside of me. I believe these are the VVs that keep many people from long-term sobriety. I know their explosions threatened mine.

The deeper we go, the more dreadful the thought we are willing to offer into the light, the more profound the transformation. This is why changes are so difficult to make at the level of Sir Ego. Like snapping the leaves off a weed, the roots remain and rise again. Offering lies to the fire of truth transforms them into lessons, love for all concerned, and permanent changes in our being, which removes fear at its root.

In addition to our desire to be special, Sir Ego engages in *special relationships*. The *special relationship* serves Sir Ego on his personal quest in the material realm. We have a certain expectation for our fellow knights because of their role in our lives: our parents, children, spouses, siblings, coworkers, neighbors, friends, and foes. Sir Ego believes it is fair to use our fellow knights to get our needs met on his personal grail quest and is willing to cooperate, to some extent, to meet their needs in return. And Sir Ego feels it is a give-and-take relationship, always a negotiation. A little bit of manipulation with guilt, flattery, or money is acceptable. Sir Ego may even keep a scorecard of how much he has given versus what he has received in each relationship. And he keeps score of contract breaches and injustices.

The Course implores us to offer each special relationship to the wise one for purification and to be used for the highest purposes for all parties, to seek a *holy relationship*. The wise one uses the *holy relationship* to advance our exalted quest, while Sir Ego uses the relationship to advance his lower quests. As a constituent of the universal consciousness, the wise one sees the highest purpose for both us and our brother. He weaves our quests together for the same sacred purpose, focusing the quest on the highest grail that strengthens both of us.

I prayed fervently, offering my relationship with Don to the divine for the highest purposes, seeking a *holy relationship*. It didn't have any immediate effects, and I wondered how *real* this idea was. Yet I was starting to see that he was my teacher and that I wouldn't be learning these lessons if the nightmare had not occurred. So this is an eternal perspective. Our relationship struggles don't make sense to Sir Ego, but the wise one uses them for our mutual benefit, and we will both learn our lessons and move to a higher step.

Once I understood the power of this insight, I incorporated this into my daily quest. I sought to make all my relationships sacred in this way. Every time I struggled with a relationship, I prayed for a *holy relationship* with this fellow knight. Why not? My experiences revealed that this was very powerful in transforming my relationships in positive and unforeseen ways, as this story will continue to reveal.

Most miraculously, one day I realized I had received self-forgiveness. As you give, so shall you receive. The Creator's forgiveness is given abundantly and unconditionally, but our capacity to receive it is determined by the extent to which we offer it. I realized I didn't carry that burden and stigma of guilt and shame anymore like many people in recovery do. I never intentionally focused on self-forgiveness. It just appeared as a reflection of the compassion I offered to Don.

It was a long and arduous process, and old habits die hard. Don sent me many emails that contained toxic attacks that had worked well in the past. I formulated many counterattacks in reply email. But instead of clicking send, I would click delete. I had developed appropriate and functional boundaries with him. Over time, he learned, like Pavlov's dogs, that I would ignore these attacks, and they would become more and more infrequent. I responded to the factual, practical parenting emails and deleted the rest.

Communications with Don improved every day: first by email, then by phone call, and finally by speaking to him in person at my daughters' softball games, without physical symptoms of dread, distress, trepidation, and apprehension.

My heart filled with love, and the Creator smiled with each act of kindness I directed toward Don. Soon I found that he would call me and have completely functionally and rational co-parenting conversations. We could even discuss controversial topics, which in the past would have been "evidence" for the other's poor parenting. Each of these positive experiences filled my heart in a way that was beyond the romantic love I felt for Don during our dating. I was learning to speak from my wise one to his wise one, and it was a profoundly divine experience. My heart was opening to a greater reality.

For the next few years, our family life became increasingly positive, and the girls were doing well in all aspects of their lives. It was almost unfathomable to believe the war was over and both sides had won. My gratitude and faith grew and deepened.

As I learned to discriminate between my defensive behaviors and this higher perspective, I saw similar inner struggles in my work life. Sir Ego brought his lance and shield to work, and I became aware that his defenses were problematic there too. My newfound compassion, understanding, and nonjudgement could serve me there as well. So I started to seek the wise one at work.

11

The Moment of Choice

For several years, my job was a source of great satisfaction and financial reward for me. Smooth sailing for a while gave me time to heal and integrate the lessons I had learned. I focused on my personal healing, recovery, and growth. I read voraciously and attended frequent weekend retreats and workshops, always with the theme of healing, healing, healing.

A promotion at work afforded me the opportunity to manage a large project that required cross-departmental cooperation. Up to that point, I had been in a "smart bubble" with my boss. We had a great deal of mutual respect and complementary skill sets, and we accomplished a great deal in an enjoyable, rewarding way. I went from fearing that I had pickled my brain to deep-seated pride in my work and what I had to offer to my company, too much pride.

It was scary and icky outside the smart bubble. People from other departments had different goals and priorities. They weren't interested in what I was tasked to accomplish. They were threatened by my presence in their domains. You could even say that I was calling their baby ugly.

Using my MBA skillset, I was confident of my direction and goals and assumed everyone would step in line and follow. To my shock and eventual horror, they did not. In fact, their responses ranged from apathy to outright sabotage. Some didn't care about my project, and the ones who did wanted to derail it.

These responses did not deter me from continuing on a path that I thought was best, despite messages from the outside world that my way was not going to work. My reaction was to try harder. Sir Ego was once again wielding the negative edge of the stubbornness sword. I believed my ideas were brilliant and rational, my *special* contribution to the organization, and Sir Ego could not see that I was alone in this assessment.

Except for my boss. He agreed with me. I complained to him repeatedly about the lack of cooperation from certain coworkers, hoping he would wield his mighty scepter of power and make them behave. Again and again, he did not dominate my adversaries into submission. My frustration evoked childhood VVs, where I threatened my brothers, "I'm going to tell Daddy. And he's going to get the wooden spoon, and you'll be sorry that you disobeyed me." In his powerlessness, Sir Ego wanted to enlist other knights with bigger weapons to fight his battles for him.

The wise one did not subscribe to this immature thinking, expecting my boss to solve problems the way my dad solved problems, by forcing people into submission. I wondered if other people replay their childhood dynamics in the workplace with their boss representing parents and coworkers representing siblings. That would explain a lot.

Organizational authority only gets you so far, and I was disappointed in my boss until I realized this. Only daddies with wooden spoons and dictators with armed militia can force compliance through fear. Sir Ego does not willingly bow down to and serve another knight. I still remember my first day of business school in the organizational behavior lecture. Punishment motivates two behaviors: conceal the crime so you don't get caught and avoid punishment if you do get caught. It does not motivate the intended behavior. I learned this lesson again in jail as each of us tried to minimize the consequences we faced. I was one of the few people in jail who was learning from punishment and didn't intend to resume my old ways the moment I was released.

Whether it was Don's angry demands or my intervention friend's loving demands, I was not going to quit drinking until I was damn good and ready. I had to hit bottom. Their momentary influence was nothing compared to the minute-to-minute battle I had to fight to maintain sobriety. I might try to appease these people for a short time, like when I hid my drinking, but long-term behavior changes must be motivated from within. This was a lesson I had to learn for myself, a way to influence and lead without organizational authority. I had to get people to want to follow me. This is servant leadership.

Some of my coworkers triggered my VVs. There were still things in the chest, popping out at inopportune times. I realized that the current situation might have triggered my VVs, but these VVs were old energy and attitudes that I had learned were not helpful or relevant to the present situation. Although the way I felt around an uncooperative coworker reminded me of Don and triggered some old VVs, this coworker was not about to take me to court and lie about me. Maybe he just didn't like my project, perhaps he had a fight with his wife this morning, or possibly I only imagined a scowling countenance. Sir Ego was still fighting a battle that was over, trying to prove himself. Sir Ego had a hair trigger and was quick to reach for the lance or the sword, seeing attacks everywhere and misunderstanding what was actually happening in the present moment causing him to overreact.

As time went on, I grew more and more frustrated. The project was not progressing as my boss and I had hoped. I became the victim and engaged in my old defenses—blaming, rationalizing, excusing, and denying. The situation became more and more negative over time. I clashed with a couple people in glaring ways.

I had thought I was beyond this. Hadn't I already slain that dragon? I found the dragon had many heads, each with a slightly different profile, each arousing a slightly different fear. It didn't matter if his bully behavior triggered me because he reminded me of my brother or my ex-husband. He wasn't either of those people, and those memories and energetic patterns did not belong here now. By now, I knew that this feeling could be released, and I knew how. I had learned the benefit of forgiveness. I was learning how to release these knots of energy, these VVs, though the process was slow, arduous, and imprecise. I allowed the volcano to erupt and the VVs' energy to flow everywhere like molten lava in private.

At this time, I came upon *The Untethered Soul* by Michael Singer. His book showed me a very powerful, efficient, and effective way to liberate the contents of the chest. It showed me how to guide the missile to liberate a stuck VV. I was accustomed to offering up my pain and fear to the Creator. I was willing to feel the pain and see a higher truth in my circumstances, but I hadn't understood the dynamics of inner energy and magnetism.

Honing the energy dynamics of the VV purification process, which had been haphazard for so long, became faster and more effective. Yoga opened a doorway for me to view the inner workings of my consciousness and its relationship to the inner energies of emotions. It enabled me to stop the runaway train of automatically living from Sir Ego's perspective and choose whether to be coached and counseled by the wise one. Heeding his counsel revealed many insights into the nature of the higher reality, so I was learning as well as moving the stuck energy.

Singer explains that the VV is a ball of stuck energy, actual energy. In a quantum view of reality, the world is a sea of energy and intelligence that vibrates at different levels. The vibration takes the form of stars, planets, moons, forests, houses, grasshoppers, ladybugs, slugs, palm trees, grapevines, rocks, and all the organs of our bodies. There are other vibrations of thoughts and emotions that do not have solid forms, yet we can feel and react to them just as strongly as running into a wall.

Creation is continually vibrating. It is always moving, evolving, and expanding. It transforms and, in so doing, causes the constant and eternal nature of change that so confounds us. Just when we get the universe the way we like it, it moves. We are ever pushing Jell-O uphill.

These vibrations pass through us at all times. Some are received and translated by the eyes as sight. Some are received and translated by the ears as sound. Some are received and translated by the skin as touch. Others, like Wi-Fi, ultraviolet rays, and radio signals, pass through us unperceived because we have no receiver.

The thoughts and emotional energy of other knights around us are received, depending on our level of awareness, at some conscious or unconscious level. For example, we may or may not be aware when their energy contradicts their words, as I was with Don. We may feel the hurt in their words, but we may not be aware that their attack stems from their inner pain rather than our failure. Either one or both of us may be triggered by some past unrelated event and not even know it. We are dueling with each other and some unseen and unacknowledged shadows. This doesn't end well.

Throughout this lifetime and many before it, we have experiences that we really like. Sir Ego adopts these as his grail and believes they will make him feel happy, secure, and loved. He shuts down and closes around the vibration of those precious moments. He holds it. He clings to it, as I clung to my marriage and house long after it was clear that it was toxic for me. And the energy becomes blocked. This is how a VV comes to be. We want to relive the moment we fell in love, won the promotion, savored the sunset, or moved into our dream home. And Sir Ego is frustrated that these moments are fleeting. He chases these grails, tries to hold onto them, and craves more of them, believing they will make him feel happy, secure, and loved.

Alternately, Sir Ego remembers times of great fear and is vigilant for threats in the environment comparing the current circumstance to the fears he holds. After feeling the humiliation of the courtroom, the despair of jail, and the agony of betrayal, Sir Ego is hypervigilant guarding against similar threats, attacking with his lance or guarding with his shield without consulting the wise one.

So these items in our chest are actually real bundles of energy, like tiny tornados, stuck in our energy bodies. Energy is not good or bad. It is either flowing or not. Energy has the vibration, memory, and emotions of the situation in which it was stored. This is how we are able to relive events that we really loved or feared. Something in our environment triggers the VV to open, and it releases its energy. This flood of energy causes us to become lost in the energy and memory of the event. We feel the emotions of the event. In strong cases, we call this *post-traumatic stress disorder*. But no matter how overwhelming a VV is, it is the same thing, stuck energy becoming unstuck.

When a VV opens, the emotions flood the heart, and the mind becomes active, similar to the way a teakettle whistles when energy from heated water rises. Once the VV is open, the natural course is for energy to flow until it is completely released. This is very good news.

Now for the bad news. Until he is trained to consult the wise one, Sir Ego has habitual responses to this energy release. Based on his assessment of the battleground, he is a fight-or-flight kind of guy, wielding the lance or the shield. Without consultation with the wise one, he temporarily loses sight of the quest and concentrates on the present threat. Any grail can become a hill to die on.

Rather than allowing the energy to release, taking the path of least resistance, we have a developed tendency to close down around the energy—to close our hearts and to not feel the pain. This is the moment of choice between the wise one's or Sir Ego's response. We must become alert to this moment.

Neuroscientists have found that our repetitive responses to these stimuli carve neural networks in our brains, which reinforce the response. The response is often to express the emotions and thoughts or to use our thoughts (or wine) to suppress the emotions and thoughts. We want the world to be in a state that does not trigger our VVs. We get angry and shout, punishing or attacking in order to manipulate others so they don't trigger our VVs. Or our minds get busy trying to figure out how to fix it, devising various battle strategies to cope with the current threat. This helps to sooth us and shove the energy back down, deep into our subconscious and our hearts.

I had maxed out on these two options. I had maxed out on my lonely tirades of screaming, crying, and fighting Don and my circumstances during my years of isolation. Though the tirades provided a great release, I was spent. When I went into fight mode at work, I painted my world with my toxic stuff, discrediting people behind their backs. Who really wants to be on the other side of that explosion? Beyond the hurt it causes and the bad karma it creates, it is almost always completely ineffective. I noticed that when I was defensive at work, I was challenging to deal with. I was not open to cooperation and collaboration. I needed to be right. I forced my will on people. I was using Don's strategy of trying to get me to love him more by being meaner to me. It doesn't work. A VV is like plutonium. Expressing the energy detonates a bomb in our vicinity.

A VV is also like plutonium when it is suppressed; it is a deadly toxin when we keep it deep inside ourselves. I had also maxed out on suppressing the demons. They were just too big and too numerous to be shoved back into my chest. No amount of fearful, neurotic thinking could get the energy to stop erupting. The slightest perceived threat in my environment put me into hypervigilant, overreactive defense mode. My mind became cluttered and clouded with a constant barrage of justification, rationalization, excuses, and blame. The wine, by shutting down my frontal lobe, quieted the cacophony, but wine was no longer a viable option. I hadn't really found anything else as effective before I read Singer.

We are generally not aware of a third option, to allow the energy of the VV to be released, to transcend and transmute this energy. If we don't intervene, the natural path of the energy is to rise and release. Now the VV is the plutonium used as rocket fuel to ignite our spiritual transformation and lift our consciousness higher. That is the yogic path to enlightenment. Patanjali's yoga sutras are some of the most revered scriptures on yoga. The second sentence (sutra) is that yoga is the neutralization of these energy vortices. The remaining sutras describe this ancient and time-tested path to enlightenment.

Following that path takes the energy of the VV that was stuck in a vortex and releases it to fuel our exalted quest, lifting us to higher realms of understanding. Great teachers, such as Jesus, Buddha, and Yogananda, tell us that they are free from these VVs and live in constant awareness of the higher reality. They came to earth to show us the way to attain this state.

Although this state is often presented in esoteric texts and veiled, abstruse language, *The Untethered Soul* helped me find a very practical and effective way to engage in the process of purifying the VVs. This process is available anytime the VV is triggered and reveals the lesson that is present in the unfolding challenge or obstacle. As the VVs result from Sir Ego being attached to a desire or fear and therefore chasing a false grail, the lesson involves a redirection back to the exalted quest.

The teachings of yoga refer to Sir Ego's quest for false grails as *delusion*. Sir Ego is deluded into thinking the attainment of his desires or the banishment of his fears will satisfy his divine thirst and forsakes the exalted quest for truth. I have come to find that each VV defends one of Sir Ego's false beliefs about the nature of reality, a fear that he's afraid to behold, a limitation that binds us to our negativity. On the other side of each VV is a lesson. The wise one embraces a diamond of understanding, a truth we hadn't seen before. Delusion becomes dispelled.

This Socratic method of learning is a one-way street. The student is changed by the discourse, unlike other forms of learning that yield information but do not necessarily change underlying attitudes and beliefs. I could feel that I embodied each particular aspect of truth once I had tested it this way. It is no longer a belief subject to debate.

From the depths of my being, Sir Ego has fully surrendered this particular topic of the day to the wise one. Once I had become aware of the truth beyond my defenses, I couldn't go back to my prior ignorance and see the world in the same limited way anymore. Once I understood that forgiveness was the key to healing my family, I could no longer have a place for unforgiveness in other situations. That isn't to say that I never felt judgment again. I could watch Sir Ego go into judgement, but I didn't give my energy to his imaginary jousting. I would seek the wise one to help me find the truth and release the delusion about each unfolding situation.

While simple in theory, the process of letting the energy follow its natural path of release involves confronting the reasons we are holding the VV and enduring the original emotion stored in the vibration of the energy. In order to experience true forgiveness with Don, I had to come to a higher understanding of the situation and the errors in my judgements. I was very willing. I was convinced that I needed to let these things go and was willing to revise my perception of reality to gain deeper understanding. I was no stranger to pain and fear. I understood they were part of the purification process, which was better than the pain and fear of holding on to that stuff. My attitude was, *Bring it on.*

I immediately discovered two great challenges. First, I needed to recognize when a VV release was happening in time to make the conscious choice, to disengage Sir Ego's autopilot that fought or fled, expressed, or suppressed. I had been accustomed to unconsciously passing over this point without realizing I was now in a VV.

The other challenge was to deny Sir Ego's compulsions to speak or act long enough to seek the wise one. All of my being resisted. My thoughts ran along their old lines: *This isn't right … This isn't fair … They are wrong … This shouldn't have happened … I need to fix this … I need to teach them a lesson so they won't do this again.*

Every thought seemed an imperative, a compulsion to act. I needed to bring determination and willpower to bear on this matter. And I did. Doing so rapidly increased the rate at which I released the tormentors within. Moreover, watching Sir Ego wage this cosmic battle of good and evil in my consciousness was illuminating, fascinating, and often hilarious.

I had to take responsibility for my internal state. I had to distinguish between what others did and my reaction to it. *You did not make me do it, feel it, or say it.* This focused me on that moment of choice, the instant when I could see the VV firing and Sir Ego's default responses, posturing the shield or the lance in preparation to launch and say *stop*.

this is the moment of free will. All the forces in the cosmos this moment: the laws of physics, biology, karma, magnetism, psychology, and sociology have brought us to these circumstances. our choice in this present moment to choose the wise one, love, and and to advance on our spiritual path or choose Sir Ego, delusion, and fear and then retreat and face the lesson again.

How we used our free will in the past got us to this point, and our choice in the current moment determines our future. The present is the only moment there is that we can choose, we can't change the past, and we can't control the future leap frogging ahead. Each good choice moves us ahead on the exalted quest and advances our soul.

We choose our birth circumstances, and now we must play the hand we have dealt ourselves. Positive choices in each moment will lead to good circumstances as my story shows. Negative choices in each moment lead to messy circumstances, as my story shows.

I called it "the year of forgiveness." As I had learned with Don, Sir Ego will always find fault with our fellow knights. Forgiveness sets aside the prosecution of Sir Ego and transfers control to the wise one for a higher outcome. Forgiveness is the denial of the delusion, which has Sir Ego spellbound and affirmed the truth that we are both perfect, holy, and divine. This was based on my recognition that anytime someone triggered me, I needed to take responsibility for that and offer them love and gratitude in exchange for the opportunity to purge something from my chest. There was not something wrong with the present moment, and no one was to blame. There was a lesson.

These VVs are the vehicle for karma. Say a VV was created in a past life when I persecuted others. Unable to learn from my mistake at the time, this energy is stored in a VV. This VV magnetizes a situation to us that will trigger this VV so it can be released. I had magnetized Don with my unacknowledged need to be persecuted. Experiencing how persecution feels was the only way I could learn to develop compassion and forsake the desire to persecute others. Similarly, I realized that I could never show Don his errors and lessons. He wouldn't listen to me. Karma creates the experience that we will listen to and learn from.

I vowed to treat every person I spoke with at work as a divine companion and have a *holy relationship* with them, no matter how much

he or she irritated me. Using every interaction to free VVs
little techniques and reminders to facilitate this endeavor.

I learned to become aware that I had been VVed. I
shocked at how unaware I was. I was often VVed, but not a\
been hijacked. Over time, I came to recognize the signs. The first sign was tightness in my chest—a closed heart—or tight shoulders and neck. This was the VV starting to open its lotus-like petals and release energy and my habitual response to stop it.

The second sign was my mind chatter going into high gear, offering a million fix-it solutions. *I am going to tell him off. I will do it myself. I will tell his boss. I will send him an email explaining his errors.* And so on. Sir Ego was trying to fix the situation outside to stop the uncomfortable feeling inside, which suppresses but doesn't eliminate the VV. In fact, the opposite is true. Every time we focus on a VV, creating fix-it thought clouds, we are adding energy to it. The solution does not lie in the suppressing of the fix-it response, which would not allow the VV energy to release. The way out is to allow the wise one to take his seat in silent witness and watch Sir Ego mentally jousting, allowing the release of the energy and experiencing the heart expanding beyond its comfort zone.

As I engaged the wise one to watch the activity in my heart and mind, I would do the opposite of shutting down this process: I would allow it. I would allow my heart to open, expand my chest, take a deep breath, and put my shoulders back. In the same way I relax a tight muscle in yoga postures, I relax deeply in the heart muscle, expanding and softening it. I learned to maintain this posture, to not allow my shoulders to cave forward, my chest to tighten, or my breathing to grow shallow. These physical expressions corresponded to the emotional expressions of remaining open, nonjudgmental, accepting, flexible, forgiving, and compassionate.

As for my mind, I learned to disengage from the fix-it energy. I watched it. I became mindful, watching, but not judging what was happening in my mind. I did not fight with Sir Ego. I did not act on his battle plans or engage in strategizing. I removed my focus from his combat plans. I cut off his source of power. My mantras became "Feel it; don't fix it," "Open heart good; closed heart bad," and "It's only energy; releasing it doesn't hurt me, but holding it in does." Now I could consciously control the deep release of VVs more efficiently and effectively than before.

As I explored this phenomena more, I came to see the difference between being *in* the fix-it energy and watching it. When I was in it, I felt compelled to act or decide on a course of action. Sir Ego has low impulse control and high need for immediate gratification. When I was watching, I was amused, amazed, shocked, and dismayed about the mess in there. It was as if I were watching someone else go through it. Sir Ego became further from my center of awareness, and the wise one became closer to my center of awareness.

The first few times, I didn't make much, if any, progress. I was absorbed in my thoughts and deciding which course of action to choose. It was as if I had taken a chair overlooking the mind for a split second and was seeing another perspective. Yet I kept falling off the chair into the mud puddle of Sir Ego's fix-it thoughts. In our multiplayer online video game analogy, this is the difference between wearing virtual reality gear and experiencing the game in first person, Sir Ego, versus using an Xbox controller and experiencing the game from an observer perspective, the wise one.

I became acutely aware of how often I was triggered by a particular person who I used to think was uncooperative and difficult. I had to accept that he did not "make" me mad. His action and my response were independent, not dependent. It was not a mandatory chain reaction. I could step in just after their action and choose my reaction, obeying Sir Ego or the wise one. I could evaluate why I had been triggered and choose to release that energy before responding.

The first thing I came to understand was the difference between what was mine and what was not mine, in terms of ownership, authorship, and control, setting right the upside-down thoughts of Sir Ego. I owned the VV firing and my tendency to attack or defend. I authored this situation for my education and expansion. I controlled my inner energy and response to the situation. I could not change the past, the present circumstance, or the person in front of me.

When Sir Ego diverts us, things we can't control become the targets of our controlling behaviors, and our inner state that we can control are defended in his fortress of VVs. This is a crucial distinction when choosing where to exert your will. Over time, understanding this distinction became the foundation for acceptance, equanimity, peace, and harmony in my life.

A key insight was that most, if not all, of my pain and suffering were a result of this confusion. I tried to control and change things that were not mine to control (other people and the world in general), and I resisted controlling my inner state and responses. Once I focused on the right objective, I had a way to purify my energy.

Most importantly, once I purified my VVs and troublesome energy, the wise one was free to execute a better, more effective, more loving response, which benefited everyone. The wise one speaks through an open heart. He cannot be heard with a closed heart. He speaks silently into our intuition. He cannot be heard over Sir Ego's battle cries. The wise one sees the highest solution for *all* parties involved. This was the leap of faith I needed to make to enable myself to sit still while the energy ran its course.

Soon my experience validated this premise. My response was always more effective when the energy had passed and I was calm, in a place of love rather than fear. The right words flowed from my mouth, in just the right tone of voice at the right time with the right body language. I could be light, loving, kind, compassionate, accepting, nonjudgmental, and *effective*. I also saw improvement in the response: people accepted what I had to say, cooperated with my requests, and were kind in return. Humor would show up where frustration had been, on both sides. My relationships with everyone were markedly improved. You mean to say that they didn't like being blamed and treated with superiority? That's weird. I thought I was the only one who didn't like that.

Truly, I was shocked how often nothing needed to be done or said once I had released the energy. I just needed to release the VV. It was an old wound triggered by the current situation, a ghost of Christmas past, nothing more. Wow. I had been filling the world with my defenses against wounds that were bygone shadows and had nothing to do with the present. I mistook an innocent email about company sick time as an assault on my timekeeping integrity triggering the *I'm-in-trouble* VV. I saw someone else repeatedly leaving work early and felt a compulsion to report it. I was angry when someone walked into my meeting late and missed my opening monologue. If karma did not need my help teaching Don lessons, it did not need me to be the attendance police either.

This is not to discount that there are many situations that do require our attention, words, and actions. There are things that are extremely unpleasant, unjust, and criminal. Yet even these things, though problems for Sir Ego, are not so for the wise one, who knows what will be effective in all situations. If I purified the energy of the VV first, free of the cacophony, I could hear the wise one, and a higher solution would be revealed.

Brilliant solutions appeared to seemingly intractable problems, solutions I had no access to in the midst of a VV, when my consciousness was in the lower realms. Beautiful words spontaneously came out of my mouth, not the well-thought-out, politically correct, and painstakingly chiseled words of Sir Ego, uttered with a fake smile after a ferocious inner debate. I fired the committee in my mind and stilled the monkey mind. I promoted the wise one to be my inner authority.

I learned that the defenses that held the VVs in place were the source of my ineffectiveness, dysfunction, and suffering. These defenses proved to be a difficult fortress to break through in order to allow the energy of the VV to release.

Sir Ego is also prone to disproportionate response, making a mountain out of a molehill. While it may have been true that the person who triggered my old wounds was incorrect, incompetent, unethical, or whatever, I noticed that my interactions with that person bothered me more than true crises such as sex trafficking or world hunger—*real* problems. Those interactions bothered me more because they pushed my buttons. If I could process my eruption first, then I could deal with the situation in a calm, intuitive, loving manner. This was offering forgiveness and denying Sir Ego's lies at the point of the infraction, not later. With Don, I had a million VVs to purify long after the war was over. It would have been easier to purify them as they occurred.

By the end of this year, I had developed some mastery in key areas. I became aware of the state of my heart and mind on a consistent basis, alert to VVs. When I noticed my heart closed or my mind chattering, the moment of choice, I was able to discriminate between the raucous battle cries of Sir Ego and the silent intuition of the wise one. I made a solid effort to choose the wise one over Sir Ego. And I began to develop the patience to not speak or act until the energy was released, my heart was open, and my mind was clear to hear the silent whispers and gently intuition of the wise one. I had sufficient success to trust the process and the wise one.

Based on a year of observing this phenomenon, I became very curious about Sir Ego. *Why did he want the things he wanted? Why did he behave so ineffectively, often in self-defeating ways? Why did he keep closing my heart? Why was he so conflicted?*

12

Why Do I Care?

Gradually I developed the ability to go deeper into these questions and the inner realms, using my mind at a higher level. I could intentionally open the lotus petals of the VV and dig deeper into the energy for a more profound release. I could investigate the defenses surrounding the energy and what lay beneath at the root. I was studying the underlying fears and desires that were driving all of Sir Ego's thoughts and actions. While we think that attaining our desires and avoiding our fears will make us happy, I was learning that my attachment to particular desires and fears was the source of the problem. All the destructive energy of my VVs centered around something I *really wanted* that I wasn't getting or something I *really feared* that I was getting.

What I was trying to do was to go down the layers of defenses that Sir Ego had built. I was continually asking, "Why do I care?" Asking the question allowed me to go deeper, to see what Sir Ego's unmet need appeared to be. I stayed open in my heart and used my mind to dig. This hurt. But it really did release my stubborn issues forever. This is where the magic is. This is where the wise one lovingly helps Sir Ego to unravel the Gordian knot and dispel the erroneous beliefs.

Here is an example of how the process worked. I asked the fleet manager at our company to prepare an analysis for my boss and the bank. He was accustomed to thinking in terms of VIN numbers and truck repairs, and we needed to prepare a financial analysis of the value of the fleet for our bank. I prepared a format and asked him to provide various pieces of information for each vehicle, such as the original cost and current market value. What he prepared was woefully incomplete and my intended format. I was furious. My warning signs flashed get this junk out of the chest and liberate it.

Here is how that went. First, I accepted that I felt this way. I didn't resist it. I allowed it to be. An injection hurts more if you tense against it. I opened my heart, my shoulders, and my mind. Over time, I came to cherish this feeling, glad to have the opportunity for purification, to be rid of more stuff from my chest.

Second, I chose. I had to have willingness. Even if it were only a tiny bit of willingness, it allowed me to access the wise one. I affirmed silently, *I wish to purify and release this energy. I wish to learn the lesson. I am willing to see this differently. Show me. I offer myself for purification, guidance, and counsel. Show me the truth that dispels this delusion.*

Third, I began a cognitive investigation with the wise one. The more fearless and ruthless this investigation became, the better. Sir Ego wants to hide information because he wants to get his way, although he is confused about the nature of the quest and the true grail.

That is how I would excavate the tomb of fear my ego had created. I kept asking, "Why do I care about this?" In the whole universe of things that weren't going well, why was I freaked out about this one insignificant incident? Here is my internal dialogue from the poor presentation scenario.

"I'm furious about what he prepared."

"Why do I care?"

"It is important to complete this fleet inventory for the bank, and I can't do it without information on each vehicle that only he has."

"Why do I care?"

"He manages a million-dollar fleet, and he should understand the financial aspects of his job."

"Why do I care?"

"Because this work product is going to be a bad reflection on me if we present it to my boss and I am dependent on him to complete it."

(I begin to see that it is about me, my ego. I am finally getting somewhere! The problem is *not* out there.)

"Why do I care?"

"It is obviously important to me what my boss thinks of me and my job performance."

"Why do I care?"

"If I continue to give him shoddy work, I will be given a poor performance review, demoted, or fired."

"Why do I care?"

"If he fired me, I am not sure I could get another job. I might end up homeless."

"Why do I care?"

"It would hurt my ego. I am not that person."

(Well, actually I was.)

"Why do I care?"

"I wouldn't be able to care for my kids, and they would go to Don's."

"Why do I care?"

"I would be a terrible and unworthy mother again."

"Why do I care?"

"I feel like I'm just plain bad, unworthy, and unlovable."

"Does the Creator see me as anything other than divine because of a fleet valuation report?"

That was the bottom, the crux of the issue. I had peeled the fear onion and confronted each layer. This took me to the core of my fears, the core of my being, and the core of my faith. It required fearless dedication to find the truth and dispel Sir Ego's fears. Those fears are like the monsters in the closet: fearful when the light is off and the shadows flicker. As I had already discovered in rehab, acknowledging these fears did not bring them to me. I would probably not end up homeless over this fleet report. Rather keeping them inside was more likely to magnetize and manifest them. I had certainly manifested every fear I had!

And if I end up at the homeless shelter with a smile on my face, a helping hand, and love in my heart, things will work out. I had unlocked the truth that only I determined whether I was a victim of my circumstances. Once I saw the core fear at the heart and was able to say "I could handle that," the fear lost all its power over me. Like a parent holding a child's hand to peer into the monster-less closet, the wise one attends Sir Ego to dispel this fear composed of nothingness.

I held these fears and untruths in my mind, alongside the truth: *I ne, holy, and eternally loved.* This was the moment when one a light in the closet and revealed that, in fact, there was *never* a monster there. The lie only needed a moment in front of the consciousness of the wise one, and it was revealed as a lie. Overnight, my energy shifted.

The next day, walking down the hallway, I met the fleet manager who had sent me the presentation I was critical of. I heard myself say, "I looked at the schedule you sent. Thanks for working on that. Do you think we could get together and go over it so I understand it before we give it to my boss?"

Wow, where had that come from?

He came to my desk, and we looked at the report.

"I appreciate your help with this. I am hoping the bank will give us a better financing rate if we can show the value of the fleet exceeds the book value," I said tentatively, checking to see if he shared my view of the importance of this report.

He nodded, and I continued. We are starting with a common goal. That's a good start.

"It's very good that you grouped each of the vehicles into categories and included the make, model, and year." I affirmed what he had completed and continued, "How can we get a current value for each of these? I think the bank should lend on the true value of the fleet if it's higher than the book value."

The light bulb went on. "Yes, I can get a current value. I have access to Kelly Blue Book for cars and trucks, and I could add that here next to the original cost. Some of them will be higher than the book value, but these might be lower." He was connecting my request to his expertise.

"Do you think you would be able to get this completed this week so I can show it to my boss on Friday? Or do we need additional help to get it done?" I was leaving it up to his choice, not my demands.

"Oh, yes, I think I can get this done this week. I will have to fill in a few details before I can look them up. Some of the add-ons increase the value of a vehicle, and others don't. But I know exactly what you are looking for. No problem." He was won over.

As I asked questions with an open heart and without judgment, he realized things he needed to do to make the schedule complete. It was *his* idea to make it better. He felt really good about that and quickly updated the schedule. We had a better result, and we both felt good about the process. He walked away with a better understanding of the important financial aspects of his job responsibilities. I walked away with deep appreciation for him and the lesson we had shared.

I had resisted the urge to judge, blame, and attack him. I accepted that he needed more help to complete the information I requested. Holding the idea that he was incompetent and should know how to analyze the financial implications of his fleet was a denial of reality and would have been totally ineffective. He simply didn't know how to do what I asked. He needed coaching, not judgement.

A couple days later, the fleet manager brought me a box of fudge-striped cookies. That wouldn't have happened if I had given him my initial scathing review of his work product or got locked in a blame game.

I had learned that no matter how loud my inner fears screamed, they couldn't obliterate me. They couldn't affect my essential divine nature. They could only obscure my awareness of it. The Creator is still the Creator. The earth still spins. These fears are nothingness. When we hold the eternal perspective of the wise one, there is nothing that could be at the bottom of this query that would have eternal consequences.

This fearless inquiry allowed me to face the underlying fears that powered the VVs. Over time, I came to see the core of every VV was an untruth about the nature of my relationship with the Creator. Repeatedly, the bottom of this chain revealed the thoughts, *I am not worthy. I am not lovable. I am not good enough. I am ashamed. I am going to be rejected. I am guilty. I am going to be punished. I am going to be abandoned by the Creator.*

The energy doesn't move all at once, but with repeated experiences, Sir Ego eventually embraces this truth, forsaking a shred of the armor concealing his divinity. Sir Ego became more aligned with the wise one and more open to his counsel. The same way I helped the fleet manager, the wise one helps Sir Ego. He doesn't fight with Sir Ego. He shows him what works better.

This is harder to do than it might appear because Sir Ego has hidden these fears deeply in the dark recesses of my mind, the keep of the castle, with layer upon layer of defenses protecting them. Sir Ego has wily ways of twisting our thoughts in circles to defend the keep. Sir Ego wanted to attack the fleet manager rather than face his fear for his job and financial security. My life reveals many places where I was lost fighting outward battles to avoid looking at the deeper, inner fears.

I tried to change Don rather than admit our relationship was not worth saving. I tried to cover up my drinking rather than admit I needed to quit. In the same way, these layers of defenses kept me focused on the outer manifestations of the problem rather than the source of the problem. As long as you are not working at the root of the problem, you will have limited success at long-term healing.

By continuous study of these defenses, I came to understand how Sir Ego behaves when he is chasing a false grail, the object of his obsession. I had to learn to observe Sir Ego's battle strategies, weapons, and defenses that he used in pursuit of his false grail quest. Sir Ego does not fight a fair fight. His desperation to obtain and retain the object of his obsession makes him act in ways he normally would not. He is not a bad person; his desperation drives him to do bad things. His morality is conditional on the circumstances, and he is willing to do the wrong thing for the right reason. And that right reason might be to continue in my addiction.

I could not deny that both Don and I did what we did out of a desperate hope to love and be loved, however dysfunctional and ineffective it might have been. Sir Ego is capable of these misguided acts out of desperation. The wise one can heal and purify these transgressions. No matter how desperate or despicable the acts of Sir Ego, each one is a call for love from a disenchanted and lost knight, a knight whose inner wise one is ever divine and untouched by the stain of the error. Eventually each of us is returned to our healed and whole state through learning our karmic lessons and purifying the energy of the VVs.

Yet we must be vigilant for Sir Ego has many defenses that keep the mind busy at the outer layer of the onion of his intentions. It is these I learned to peel off in order to redirect my life in a healthy manner. Of course, blame was a favorite of mine. Everything was Don's fault. He had destroyed me, and I could not escape his mental training that led me to self-abuse after he was gone. I also rationalized that I didn't need to do better until he started doing better. I didn't need to quit drinking as long as he was still drinking. I might drink too much, but I wasn't emotionally abusive. I didn't need to get a job until he got a job. All of these outer layers of defenses allowed me to continue my dysfunctional behavior and give the power to heal it to him. He had to change before I would. Wow. That didn't work out well for me.

I also was keen to make excuses for my drinking: it's been a hard day, the kids have been fighting, or the sunset is so beautiful. Any excuse, trouble, or celebration would be reason to pop a cork. I had excuses for not getting a job also. I had been out of the market too long, as if my MBA and CPA had an expiration date. I actually had an excuse to lie about my drinking because I wasn't an alcoholic. Don had just convinced the social workers and therapist that I was.

If none of those were working, then I would start the guilt, shame, and self-loathing of self-immolation. If I had a moment of clarity, when I could not deny the mess I was in, I would surrender to these doubts and accept the shame that I was just broken beyond repair. Nothing could be done to save me. I was doomed to the hell I had created and pour another glass of wine or two.

But the grand defense of all, denial, lay at the heart of my dysfunction. In my mind, I was not an alcoholic. I was in a temporarily troubled spot in my marriage and needed to shield myself and cope until we worked through this rough patch, Don became the husband I wanted, my drinking returned to a socially acceptable level, and they lived happily ever after. When you are living in this state of denial about the truth of your circumstances, you start to believe this alternate reality and act as if it were true. I lied to myself and others to try to make this alternate reality real. Since it isn't true, my actions became more and more absurd relative to the true circumstances I was in.

At this point, I started to see how I was exactly like Don when he projected his demons onto me in his therapy sessions. And then he tried to attack me to kill his demons. This is the insanity of addiction to anything, substance, people, money, and so on.

All these defenses keep Sir Ego distracted from the true quest and engaged in a battle with his fellow knights. His false grails form addiction to people, substances, money, and so forth. Each gives him a taste of the joy he seeks but never satisfies. He needs more and more. Chasing these pursuits, he feels there is a lack, not enough to go around, and therefore a competition with his fellow knights. Thus, he is prone to blame others for his lack. And above all else, he calls out for love because that hole in his heart cannot be filled by these substitutes.

While the wise operates at the higher level where love, light, healing, and energy multiply as they are shared, there is no lack. The wise one knows not of addiction because it knows the true grail and the false grails have no power over him. The wise one operates in the realm of truth and goodness and does not need to lie, deny, blame, excuse, or rationalize.

As we use "Why do I care?" to peel back the layers of defenses guarding a VV, Sir Ego and the wise one are engaged in a conversation where the wise one shows the error of Sir Ego's thought process, revealing the defense mechanisms and dispelling the power they held. Once Sir Ego sees the light, he does not return to his former state of ignorance. I came to understand that I my problem was my addiction to Don and alcohol, that it had been hidden behind a web of denial and lies and they were destroying my life. To heal them at their core, I had to dismantle the fortress that held them outside my awareness. At the core of the onion, I started to see that I had a choice to make: this toxic relationship (with money, Don, or wine) over the love of the Creator. I chose more wisely and more permanently.

On my recovery journey, I realized that I needed to call upon the power of the Creator to heal my life. I was sure that it was greater than the power of Don (and the army of self-persecutors he cultivated in my mind) to break me. I also realized that I needed to clean up my act if I were to have access to this power. I had to have pure intentions and best behavior (no jaywalking) to satisfy the courts, probation, counselors, and so on.

More importantly, I now understood the karmic ramifications. I knew I had a lot of karmic payments due, and I would face those situations and VVs with courage. And I became vigilant about the karma I was creating right this moment, always trying to be truthful, to do the right thing, and to be merciful, generous, and compassionate. Aligning myself with the ideals of the Creator was a powerful first step in turning my life around.

Sometimes when I couldn't seem to unravel a particularly thorny issue, I would ask the simple questions. Who did I need to forgive to turn the fear to love? Who did I need to love more? What delusion did I fear? My answers were always surprising, things I never would have guessed. Well, things my ego wouldn't have let me guess. Answering these questions consistently sparked profound insights. The answers flipped the problems over, revealing such effective and gentle solutions that I was stunned.

As we shift the weight of our consciousness toward the wise one and away from Sir Ego, we will attract teachers and guides along the way. When the student is ready, the teacher appears. It helps to seek the insight of a teacher, such as Christ or Buddha, one who sees through Sir Ego's tricks, confusions, and false grails. About this time, I read *Autobiography of a Yogi* by Paramhansa Yogananda. I felt a deep connection to him and often felt his guidance. These teachers came to Earth to help us, and they can always be called upon for wisdom, protection, and comfort. However, they speak gently to our intuition and cannot be heard while our attention is on Sir Ego's battle cries. They speak directly to our heart and the mind of the wise one and cannot penetrate a heart that is closed.

Many times, profound insights came to me during this why-do-I-care process. They were distinctive in that they were out of line with my current thought pattern. They were over "there," while I was spinning around over "here." And frankly, they were beyond my current state of consciousness. I couldn't have gotten there from here without help.

We surrender all of our power when we buy into this; we are no longer co-creating with spirit. We are no longer at the front of the train, on the leading edge of the script of creation, totally present to what is in front of us. We are at the back of the train, holding on to the caboose and trying to get it to go the other way to embark on Sir Ego's futile quest.

This is Sir Ego's dilemma: seek but do not find. Give away a million precious instants to fear, regret about the past, or worry about the future. Meanwhile, the magnificence of our ride through the universe and the boundless love in every atom of creation passes by unnoticed and unappreciated.

Before, my habitual response to a VV had been to tighten my chest around the energy and go into fight-or-flight mode. Over time, my habitual response became to release the energy and mine the VV for the diamond. Now as soon as I feel my chest tighten, I relax and release it. My mind doesn't even get started. Sir Ego knows this works better and doesn't complain. Can you imagine? Something happens that once would have sent me off the deep end, and I just relax and release. I have 90 percent less neurotic thoughts about the past and the future swarming in my mind, and I am free to be present to this moment.

The gold is found in digging deep. After several years of slogging as deep as I could go at the time, I am free of many fears. They are gone, uprooted, never to return. It is painful to look at these fears. But they are nothing. Not only is looking at them not going to make them happen, it is going to make them less likely to happen. Holding fears lowers our vibration and attracts the object that we fear. As you have seen, I was very good at this. I manifested every single thing that I feared. What? I got it backwards? If I had read *The Secret*, I would not have been surprised when this happened.

The Secret tells us that focusing our powerful thoughts on something we would like to manifest magnetizes these people and things toward us. We can attract what we concentrate our attention on and bring it into being. This works with fear as well as desire. I manifested everything I feared so that I would learn lessons. Before we can manifest other thoughts, they must be purified. For the good of humanity, we don't have enough power to manifest the darkest thoughts that we obsess over; I would not be allowed to manifest revenge fantasies. Before we can harness the power of manifestation, we must purify our thoughts.

Over time, dramatic improvements in my relationships rewarded the behavior and encouraged me to repeat it. I was getting softer, humbler, less prideful, more open to suggestion, and more thoughtful. Even if the words were the same, my attitude, demeanor, tone of voice, facial expression, and body language were different. I was more approachable, flexible, and tolerant.

Now that I had tamed the DEFCON one alerts and tuned into my heart energies, I was beginning to notice that there were VVs on a subtler level. I wasn't triggered into fight-or-flight mode; however, I had a closed heart and was unconsciously judging everyone and everything. I had so many *opinions* about things. Everything. All the time.

Sir Ego spent a great deal of thought energy thinking how every moment could be better than it was, and he was secretly engaged in covert operations to change people and things around me to match these opinions.

Previously I wasn't even aware of this, and Sir Ego was free to operate without consulting the wise one. Sir Ego had lessor weapons than the lance and the shield, like a pocketknife and ear plugs, that he could use when he didn't like what was happening. He would gently resist the unfolding reality in front of him. He would be passive-aggressive. I was pushing things away that I didn't want to hear, do, or acknowledge. I avoided a coworker who was prone to scolding. I procrastinated meeting with a coworker who complained about being overworked.

The more I became aware of this, the more I realized it was as destructive as the big VVs, and the same release process would be useful to purify these lessor VVs. I called it unacknowledged resistance, and I was trying to bring it into my awareness so I could release it. So the next year, I inaugurated "the year of nonresistance."

13

Acknowledging Unacknowledged Resistance

I realized that when these lesser VVs escaped my awareness, Sir Ego had free reign. I wasn't conscious of the moment of choice. I had to be more vigilant to disarm Sir Ego and learn the subtler lessons the wise one had to offer. As I tuned into these subtler energies and states of my heart, I was shocked to see how prevalent these little VVs were and how often Sir Ego was engaged in a battle that had previously escaped my awareness or conscious choice.

There was this subtle discontent inside that said, *I want to surf the wave I had yesterday. I want to surf the wave Jordan is on. I want this wave to be bigger. I want this wave to be smaller.* This is futile thinking, a waste of time. More importantly, it's dangerous. In surfing, the key is to be one with the wave and moving with it, not responding as if you were on a different wave. That's a recipe for disaster. The same is true with every moment of our lives. I learned to become conscious of these incongruous thoughts and remind myself, *Ride the wave you're on.*

Somewhere in our subconscious, a tiny voice doesn't like what's happening. It would be better if it were different. A little fear or desire triggers a VV, and suddenly we have a preference about the unfolding situation. We get into our heads thinking about what would be better instead of thinking about how to respond in the current circumstances.

No matter how big or small it seemed, whenever I became aware of a tightness in my heart, a resistance, I heard a tiny thought, *I wish he wouldn't do that. I wish she wasn't talking about that. I don't want to deal with this now.* I want to free this VV. This VV purification process becomes the solution for every single problem I have. It works in all cases and at all times. It shows me that I really only have one problem, my identification with Sir Ego. Identifying with the divinity of the wise one always reveals the truth and the highest outcome. Sir Ego's fears, desires, and battle plans take on many forms, but he only has one problem, and there is only one solution.

At first, it was easier to observe unacknowledged resistance in others. It turned out that other people provided mirrors and their "glamour don't" reflections of failed interactions taught me a lot. With great curiosity, I noticed when others were triggered, frustrated, or just a little nippy. I noticed how ineffective they became when they were pushing things away and others resisted them in return. And I noticed that they were unaware that their demeanor made it hard for others to work with them. Sir Ego was tempted to point things out to his fellow knights, but I realized it would only embolden their defenses. As with Don, I am only responsible for my side of the street.

Looking at my own behavior, I noticed that unacknowledged resistance manifested as complaining, gossiping, procrastination, inferior work products, failure to collaborate, and siloed thinking. I didn't like seeing these behaviors in myself, but I couldn't seem to stop them until I connected them to this closed-heart resistance phenomena.

Many times, contemplating the issue showed me that my VV was the result of feeling I wasn't being validated or appreciated. Sir Ego wanted to be seen as smart and to be followed as a visionary. I was stunned and wounded when that did not occur. In the past, that would have caused Sir Ego to go on the warpath to pursue my brilliant idea. But no more. The minute I let it go, I could see the situation far more clearly and peacefully. This allowed the wise one to take control and always led to a more constructive, collaborative, and effective action.

This proverb appeared in my email one day. While I did not understand the power, I was compelled to print it out and post it at my desk. Actually I didn't understand it at all when I posted it. Over the next few years, I would come to live by it, experiencing its power many times. I was guided to nurture humility where there had been pridefulness. The words allowed me to give up Sir Ego's demands and fears and pursue a higher goal.

"Accept disgrace willingly. Accept being unimportant. Surrender yourself humbly; then you can be trusted to care for all things. Love the world as your own self; then you can truly care for all things."

As I looked at these pesky areas of unacknowledged resistance, it felt as if my pride were attacked constantly. People didn't validate my opinion as I wished. They pointed out errors in my thinking. They went off in their own direction. They didn't get it. I told myself over and over to accept being unimportant, to accept humiliation. This became my mantra. Only Sir Ego could feel unimportant or disgraced.

As a remedy, Sir Ego needs to surrender humbly to the wise one. The wise one really cared more about doing the right thing for my company's mission than gaining status, being admired, or getting my own way. More importantly, I learned to differentiate my ego from my work. I learned to go where the energy was flowing and to adapt my ideas to that flow rather than try to change the course of the river.

It was very enlightening as I watched, with either amusement or dismay, the frequency of my resistance and the things that caused it. Often the causes were of no significance whatsoever. Who really cared who set up the next meeting or spoke first or if the presenter used those icky scented markers? Often the causes were part of a script that only I was reading from. In my mind, this had to come first, this had to come second, and this had to come last. Sir Ego needed it to be my way, just because it was mine.

In fact, Sir Ego seemed to have opinions about a million tiny insignificant things that consumed my thought processes. I missed half the meeting because I was still in a closed, unreceptive state about a negative comment a coworker made as we walked into the conference room. I learned to purify my resistance instead of acting on it and to go with the flow.

As I observed Sir Ego's machinations, I realized that getting caught in his storms didn't serve me and blocked the wise one. When I allowed someone else to start the meeting, everything inside me screamed that they were doing it wrong. How had I become so opinionated, and why? It was very liberating to notice small shifts in energy and to release them right on the spot, melting my resistance and opening up new possibilities for my attitude and behavior.

My awakening was that almost everything outside of us is outside our ability to control, despite Sir Ego's tragic and ludicrous attempts to manipulate them. I could not control solar flares, meteor showers, the global economy, the value of the dollar, global warming, the leadership abilities of our government, the integrity of Wall Street executives, the fate of my employer, the attitude of my coworkers, my health issues, my children's steadfastness at school, or even my annoying and unwelcome thoughts. Seriously. I was one person, spinning on a tiny planet in the center of a humongous solar system in an infinite cosmos.

Contrast this with the very few scenarios that Sir Ego finds acceptable. There is almost no region of intersection between these two sets. No wonder I was so busy all the time, trying to get the world to be just right, trying to avoid every inconceivable pain. No wonder it seemed I was pushing Jell-O uphill every day. I was tired of being ineffective, and now I could see that my own resistance was the problem.

The remedy is equanimity. It's that simple. Accept whatever is before you as a gift from the Creator. Open the chest and free any VVs that arise. This is the exalted quest, taking each step in front of us in the highest possible way. It is the next step on the highest journey we could hope to travel.

Sometimes this meant allowing someone to criticize or confront me, perhaps angrily, possibly in front of other people. This was real energy coming toward me and my habitual behavior was to fight or flight. In martial arts, they say that rather than confronting the momentum of your attacker, you should use it to your advantage. I have a visual of an attacker coming at me with a kick. Rather than go toward them to kick back or block, I step aside and let them fall. I wield neither the lance nor the shield. This has been a powerful metaphor for me. I have learned to stay centered in the wise one, accept my fellow knight is temporarily triggered, and allow the energy blast to blow by me.

Many judged me when I wore the scarlet A for alcoholic. When I defended myself, it encouraged them to attack more, to make themselves right, and to make me wrong. When we move into one corner of the ring, it tempts our fellow knight to move into the opposing corner of the ring. When we ferociously defend our position, it encourages our fellow knight to defend his position. Collaboration and cooperation vanish. When I acknowledged my errors in humility, it took the wind right out of their sails. For a punch to hurt, there has to be resistance. If you relax into the punch, allow it to turn your head. Its power is lost.

When we choose the wise one, we speak to the wise one in our brother. He feels our open heart. It creates a space for him to step up into his own higher self. When I stopped judging Don, I stopped polarizing our interactions. I left a space for him to meet me halfway, and he did.

Our desires and fears, the things in the chest, are the source of all these opinions. We want to manipulate the world so it satisfies our desires and doesn't trigger our VVs. We don't have enough control to manipulate the world to conform to all these opinions. At work, I couldn't control the executive decisions, the information technology adopted, the operating unit's performance, or the personnel decisions. I was fighting an unwinnable battle, attempting to gratify my wishes and intentions without regard to the million other forces at play.

The spiritual principle of equanimity is the sword of truth that cuts through these fears and desires. It is futile to use our will and efforts to create a world in which nothing in our chests is ever triggered. It is impossible, even though we resist this truth. There is too much stuff in there. Rather we should use our will to empty the chest of these desires and fears. They become our liberators rather than our anchors. Fears are something to be transcended, not accommodated.

Desires are trickier to navigate because they appear to light the way to happiness and satisfaction. Yet I had seen how destructive my attachments became and could look at smaller attachments and see their downside as well. My desire for a happy marriage and a nice lifestyle chained me to the toxic relationship.

When I looked deeply into my Sir Ego's inner workings, I saw that he needed to have a certain position to make a certain amount of money to have certain material things. These needs became the motivating force behind my actions, and frankly, no one else was on board. I had linked my project being done, my way, with a promotion and more money. That is why I was so attached to the outcome. I thought I needed it. In faith, I freed these captives, knowing the wise one had something better for me on the other side. I was freed to do the right thing without these needs.

As long as I was trying to make the world accommodate my fears and desires, I was resisting the actual world that was happening in front of me. So I was not present to reality. I was trying to change reality, denying it. I had it backward. I needed to stop using my will in futile attempts to change the world and start using my will to release my resistance to the world. Then my higher self would lead the way to the highest outcome for all concerned. Freed of my inner constraints, I opened up many new, more effective possibilities for my participation in the world.

Obviously this paved the way for dramatic increases in cooperation. I was starting to learn how to influence and lead without having to control and direct. I was just easier to be around, to invite to a meeting, and to negotiate with. Again, each little success increased my willingness to go further and deeper. By the end of the year, I felt competent in identifying my resistance and allowing it to release so I was open to what was actually happening in that moment.

Heck, it sure is a lot easier swimming with the current, and you actually get somewhere. But you have to be willing to go somewhere a little different from where you intended. Since I had unconditional love for everyone, I was willing to allow them to have input into the destination. I wasn't so superior anymore, not so critical. I could take feedback and criticism. Before, I had thought there were only As and Fs, perfection or failure. I would beat myself up for all the non-As. Acceptance was the fruit of my purification, a virtue I could not have won by fighting with VVs, but by surrendering them.

***

According to Singer, all these thoughts, fears, desires, and VVs that I was studying and releasing are the building blocks of the psyche, Sir Ego's identity. As I delved deeper, I got to more fundamental beliefs about myself that also needed to be transcended. By now, I was a ninja at this type of mindful introspection. I was willing to confront and examine anything that I held sacred, knowing it was the highest path for my life, bar none. There was nothing I was willing to keep in the chest anymore—no cow too sacred, no fear too terrifying, no desire too intoxicating, or no pain too penetrating. Final sale! Everything must go.

As I investigated the roots buried deepest in the bottom of the chest, I found the "sacred shoulds," the roles I identified with. These were the firmly held but unconsciously developed ideas I had about myself that limited my options, choices, and responses. I wanted to shed these layers of defenses that were hiding my authentic self, which was divine, boundless, sexless, religionless, professionless, casteless, familyless, eternal, and infinite.

I was affluent and *should* have a certain standard of living.

I was a person of integrity and *should* be treated as a professional.

I was smart and well educated, and my coworkers *should* revere me as their leader.

I *should* hold a position of power and decision making.

I *should* be a good mom whom my intervention friends would approve of.

I *should* submit to others to keep myself in everyone's good graces, codependently.

Don't should on yourself.

After two years of work, these ideas had already started to crumble. My defenses and my resistance had been the glue holding them in place. I had cut through the superficial layers of defenses, revealing the deeper core of the onion. I was getting good at watching my thoughts and emotions. Like Luke Skywalker, I was alert to disturbances in the Force. I curiously listened to my mind telling me what I should do. Then I challenged each notion: Was it real? Was it eternal? If not, I could consciously release that requirement. It wasn't real, it wasn't me, it was self-defeating, and it must go!

The shoulds had defined a finite set of decision criteria and possible actions, but they were based on nothingness. A good mom does this. An affluent person needs that. I went off the rails when my shoulds got clobbered. *My mother shouldn't die. My husband shouldn't treat me this way. I shouldn't be an alcoholic. I shouldn't be in jail. I shouldn't have lost custody of my children.* Without shoulds, I had an infinite number of ways to respond to the current reality, not the one I thought *should* happen. I had more choice. I could change the things that weren't working, that had always just seemed to be on autopilot. I could break the mold and think outside of the box.

When I put these three ideas together, I saw the futile nature of the "my way or the highway" attitude. But I no longer knew what I "should" do. So I listened to what the world was telling me. I started becoming very present in meetings. I could see patterns and currents that I had overlooked before. I could bless each person and create an opening for his or her input. I could give honest and genuine compliments, and I could take criticism.

One particularly stressful meeting involved my former nemesis, who had prejudiced all the others against my objective in his pregame warm-up. He had triggered their fears suggesting that my proposal threatened the security of our corporate databases. I had expected the others to receive my proposal openly and objectively, but they did not. I sat with my heart pounding (the sign it was time for purification), facing five angry men with metaphorical guns drawn. The walls of the conference room seemed to be closing in.

It seemed that I shouldn't show my vulnerability in this position. Sir Ego would like to puff himself up and prepare for battle. But the wise one engaged, and I got real. Breathing deeply, opening my heart consciously, and relaxing my shoulders, I released enough energy to speak calmly without counterattack.

"I think there is a misunderstanding. It is not my intention to put our corporate data at risk. You are the experts and can help me see if it is possible to meet the user's needs without jeopardizing the security and integrity of our databases. I would appreciate your honest and open review and appraisal of this proposal to see if you can find a safe way to meet the objective."

It was a gentle, kind way to call attention to the real problem, the resistance in the room, and dispel it. If one could see the color of energy, the room would have turned from dismal dark grey to a silvery-white light. They too had all been ambushed in the past and, in compassion, holstered their weapons. Each one objectively reviewed the portions of the proposal within his or her expertise and concluded it was doable. I had been fighting this invisible fight for over a year and had won in one meeting. I had replayed this scenario many times in the past, and it had resulted in total annihilation of my self-esteem and a major obstacle to my project. I had learned to open my heart in the face of a potential attack, accept any attack that might be forthcoming, and continue to advance centered in the wise one. This made my invulnerable to attack. This is the power of the wise one, which transcends the power of Sir Ego.

***

The next thing that needed to go was Sir Ego's attachment to results, his false grails. It simply wasn't part of the paradigm I had shifted into. It didn't work to hold well-formed pictures of the process and the outcome when I was going with the flow. So I began to focus on attuning to and choosing the wise one's will over Sir Ego's will. I could see that ego-defined outcomes weren't attainable in my new organic leadership style, outside of the hierarchy of control that I had abandoned.

At first, I was perplexed about how to maintain a passionate commitment to creating something useful at work without being direct and authoritative. I sensed that letting go of authoritativeness would bring me to a position of apathy and ineffectiveness and not allow me to accomplish great things. But only Sir Ego sees the world in these black-or-white, all-or-nothing bipolar terms.

I searched for the middle way, a place in between without the downside of either extreme. Bouncing off these two boundaries, I started to find the Tao, the middle way, at work. I discovered that Sir Ego operated in a world or duality, hot versus cold, feminine versus masculine, controlling versus apathetic, and aggressive versus submissive. I saw these as the opposite ends of the fear spectrum. The Tao is in the middle, the neutral position where fear is not, the place of love without fear, action without attachment, and awareness without judgment.

The Tao was the path upon which I was passionately present, but with equanimity, finding alignment with what was happening at the moment. I was neither commanding, resisting, nor apathetic. I was more effective because I was contributing in the highest way to the flow that was beyond my control. Every time I noticed that Sir Ego was mentally ping-ponging back and forth between two polar opposites, I would go purify those fears, and the middle way would be revealed.

This was a natural evolution resulting from releasing the VVs and being receptive to the people and issues in front of me. I was releasing the dreams, goals, constraints, shoulds, objectives, hierarchical or linear process, and milestones. I became more open, receptive, and attuned with those around me.

Even though I completed my project, it was put on the shelf. Despite my newfound interpersonal skills and years of work all of my brilliant ideas had been in vain. I realized that Sir Ego often just keeps pushing at something that is not meant to be. While Sir Ego can create it, he cannot enliven it. Only the Creator's purpose can do that. Maybe the only purpose was to develop interpersonal skills.

I used to think it was my job to put on my thinking cap, develop a project plan, and spend all day defying gravity to make it happen. Steamrolling the obstacles (often my coworkers) in my way was an accepted part of the process because "I knew best." In my new way of being, it became my job to see what was trying to happen and determine how I could best contribute. This approach honored everyone around me and their contributions. I had the shocking revelation that two or more heads really were better than one—even mine. Humility was becoming my friend.

I learned two things. First, Sir Ego is capable of creating things that don't matter, that don't serve the Creator. I did not ever want to repeat that. Perhaps the Creator's will for me in this project had been learning to "be" better. The true gold was in the process, not the result. Imagine that. I needed to learn relational skills that would allow me to be of service.

Second, I learned that the Creator puts you right where he wants you. People are in the jobs because of the lessons they can learn and their karma, not their competence or fit with the job. You might have an overbearing boss so you will learn humility. With this awareness, I understood what had not made sense before, how so many people could seem to have trouble with their job. It isn't a rationale algorithm that places people in jobs; it is the wheel of karma. With this, I released everyone from my judgments about his or her competence or lack thereof and understood that he or she was just where he or she needed to be. And so was I.

The same is true for all aspects of our lives. Our relationships are not perfect fits because they are not meant to be. They are meant to bring up our issues and set the stage for our lessons. When I began to view my relationships this way, they slowly started to make sense. I stopped trying to make them something they are not. I allowed the lesson to be revealed and transcended. Relationships offer us the opportunity to empty our chests. I realized each person wears mirrored glasses that would show me something about myself.

Traditional wisdom states that we are offended by seeing qualities in others that we deny in ourselves. Often what it revealed was more than that. Sometimes we are offended by a quality in others that we take *pride* in for ourselves. Or it may be a quality that we have felt victimized by in the past. Sir Ego's distortions are many. I look deeply into these relationships and found they were lighting the path for me.

It is no longer about what Sir Ego wants to do or create. It never was. Now I understand that and have relinquished my attachment to Sir Ego's goal, dreams, and objectives. I offered myself to the Creator's will. His divine plan for me would be my celestial navigation. I accepted my commission. I allowed the plan to unfold. I offered unconditional love. I accepted the Creator's will for my work, my mothering and my children, and my growth and transformation.

It is hard to take your hands off the steering wheel until you realize that it was not connected to anything. It was not connected to the power source. It was only an illusion. Surrender is not your enemy. We surrender to the source of all power and intelligence. Then anything is possible.

About this time, my church offered a Thanksgiving gift. We received beautiful thank-you cards—not for us, but to give to others. I wrote on several of these cards and gave them to my coworkers, expressing my appreciation for their help and support. Tiny tears ran down my cheeks as I wrote out these cards. Gratitude and appreciation felt good. The wise one smiled. I got the same heart-opening, warm, and fuzzy feeling when I gave them the cards. Years later, these cards are still prominently displayed at their desks. I learned that day the value of giving without the expectation of anything in return, of heartfelt gratitude and acknowledging others.

From this lesson sprang other behaviors. Things I resisted in the past, I would run toward. In the past, it had been very difficult for me to give genuine compliments and sincere appreciation. Now it was beautiful. This one lesson encouraged me to do this more—more often, more deeply, and more broadly. This was another gift of the purification process. Formerly I had held minor grievances against everyone. Even those with whom I worked well had some chink in their armor that I was all too willing to judge. Now we were both liberated from this bond, and my thankfulness could flow freely.

I silently blessed people in the elevator, the lunchroom, the board room, and the grocery store line. While Sir Ego felt diminished by giving gratitude and compliments, the wise one and my heart expanded. I thought of it as having a million golden blessings with one catch. I could only receive each blessing as I gave it away. Now the wise one gave blessings, gratitude, and compliments freely.

My virtues became stronger: releasing vengeance uncovered compassion, releasing pride uncovered humility, releasing judgement uncovered acceptance, and releasing insecurity brought contentment. My purification process turned anxiety into peacefulness.

As I studied VVs and defenses in myself and others, I became attuned to conversations in a deeper way. The wise one, who was on duty much more than Sir Ego by this point, was aware of the energy dynamics that Sir Ego had overlooked or disregarded. My awareness showed me the moment the other person became triggered. The wise one knew how to handle this with love and compassion, retiring Sir Ego from the field. We cannot collaborate and compromise when our brother is triggered. When he has entered the *need-to-be-right* frame of mind, defending his keep, I learned to relax and allow this energy to flow. I did not resist this energy. I did not engage with this energy. I did not confront this energy.

In fact, when I had to have a difficult conversation about a problem, I faced it in a new way. I would start with taking the blame for the situation. "I must have misunderstood." "I think I made a mistake." "I guess I wasn't clear when I explained this." This accomplished two purposes: It immediately shifted me from Sir Ego to the wise one. (Sir Ego still has a little problem saying those words.) And it takes the blame game off the table. My coworker is less likely to go into a defensive posture when I have accepted the blame. More effective, cooperative conversations were immediately possible.

With compassion, I sought to understand and comfort my friend when he needed it. In tense conversations, I learned to seek common ground above all. I thought of it as *finding a yes*, sincerely searching for any topics that we could agree on and complimenting anything I could. The wise one isn't manipulative, like Don's false flattery. He has an open heart and connects with our fellow knight at the highest level, seeking communion and collaboration and affirming our mutual divinity.

Instead of preparing my project plan and presenting it to a conference room full of managers, I met with each one individually beforehand. This allowed me to gain his or her perspective, recommendations, and response to his or her resistance privately. It completely changed the meetings I conducted. The proposal was better because it incorporated everyone's perspective and corrected for the flaws others had revealed to me. Everyone was in general agreement with the plan prior to the meeting. No time was wasted debating superficial points, and so deeper issues could be discussed.

This was a whole new way of being. And it was more important than getting any project done. This was the holy instant, a moment shared with our brother in the eternal now, filled with truth and love. Nothing we could accomplish in the material world was more important. It was transient. It was busy work. My true work was to share love with my brother and remind him of his divinity.

My great learning and transformation were about to be put to the test when my children began to experience challenges. Testing these techniques and hypotheses in my workplace allowed me to gain confidence and faith, which I would need when the tests got more personal and delved into deeper fears.

14

Double Trouble

Throughout these years, my daughters had bounced back and forth between two environments that were becoming increasingly dissimilar. Once Don and I had wrestled in the same mud puddle, but no more. There was a lot of drama at their dad's house, and my children would occasionally discuss it with me. This wouldn't have happened if I still harbored the guilt and rage. Instead I honored our past as a profound growth and learning experience. I was grateful that I was in a better place to be positive, helpful, and supportive.

For two years each Friday night, I drove Nicole to dance class. This was a unique opportunity for time alone with her. Despite my many years of asking for separate time with each of the girls, this was the only way it actually occurred. Don would not let me have equal alone time with Chris. (I never said things were perfect.)

Often when I picked Nicole up, she would be upset. With an open heart and few words, I allowed her to open up.

"Dad wouldn't buy goldfish. He knows that's my favorite snack."

"Dad forgot to put money on my school lunch account, and I had to borrow it from Megan."

"Dad wouldn't stop at the store to pick up notebooks that I needed for my history project."

"Can we pick up some food? Dad made the casserole with cream cheese. He knows I don't like cream cheese, but he won't leave it off my serving."

According to *The Five Love Languages* by Gary Chapman, there are five ways to express and experience love, and each of us resonates with one more than the others. The five languages are gifts, quality time, words of affirmation, acts of service, and physical touch. Nicole's love language is acts of service. She feels loved when you take special care to meet her needs. These slights were more than inconveniences to her. She equated the lack of these loving gestures with being uncared for and unloved. This was outside of Dad's awareness and caused a great divide between them. Worse, this tension between them caused her to get angry with frustration.

"I got so angry at Dad that I threw the remote at him, stormed to my room, and slammed the door." She confessed, "He does that on purpose. He wants to make me mad."

Although she realized her anger fed him, that he liked it when she lost control, she was unable to resist his provocation. She didn't have an anger problem at my house, but remembering my own interactions with Don, I had no problem imagining how this occurred.

I had long contemplated the notion that there was a definite problem in the interactions between Don and me, and I always came to the codependent's conclusion that it must be me. I must be the problem. This was a very destructive conclusion and the foundation of my addiction to his approval.

Nicole looked at the problematic interactions between her father and herself and concluded, "It must be you, Dad." This allowed her to see things more clearly and wish to detach from the dance.

I allowed her to process these emotions and thoughts, gently offering comfort and reassurance that it was "not about her." The old me would have cherished this opportunity to bash Daddy. But I did not. My forgiveness allowed me to get beyond this temptation and support Nicole in a loving and kind way. A couple times, she called me to pick her up from his house late at night because she could not tolerate the conflict. Finally it was her choice to stay at my house full time.

"I'm unhappy when I'm there, and my friends at school can always tell when I've been staying at Dad's. They see how miserable I am," she whispered dejectedly.

This was a true test of my ability to have a rational conversation with Don, something that had never happened during my marriage. But I had changed the dance between us, and it was much more productive. I presented her decision as a "teenage girl thing" and didn't imply any problem with him or his house. He was furious and demanded that she confront him and her issues with a therapist. Home court advantage: he knew just how to make any therapist see her as the bad kid and him as the good dad. I politely offered to go to any therapist he chose to discuss this, but I would not force her to go. At her age, the court would allow her to choose where she stayed, so he never presented any legal custody complaints to me.

He always had the advantage when our knights sparred because he was more cunning and devious. Now he sparred with the wise one. The wise one did not fall into his traps. The wise one brings the conversation off the battlefield and into a higher octave, the highest good for both parties.

Several months later, the fruit of this became apparent when Chris went into the hospital for a week of undiagnosed abdominal pain, perhaps appendicitis. She was on morphine for a week. As the test results continued to puzzle the doctors, we vacillated between thinking it was nothing and fearing it was everything.

Don and I were a perfect team, negotiating hospital shifts, bringing each other food, and sharing our conversations with the hospital staff. We were co-parenting for real. We could never have done this when we were married. Even in this time of great stress, I was peaceful, calm, and loving. I established a new dance now, and he could not help but follow. The old dance was gone. It was so obviously the right dance, the one that our children required. My heart sang with joy to be free of the bondage that had once held it. Eventually the symptoms disappeared, and Chris came home.

Chris's love language was physical touch and affection, an easy one for Dad to speak to his daughter. She had an open heart and easygoing personality, and she was more flexible at accommodating others, sometimes too much. She continued to play softball and played with commitment and dedication, no matter how poorly her team performed. I admired her persistence. She was more adaptable to her environments, both at my house and Dad's.

Chris's mood took a dark and hopeless turn. She stopped caring about schoolwork and friends. I would sit with her for an hour or more, and she would sob heartbreaking tears, but the pain was too great or buried to deeply for any words. I would just sit with an open heart and love her.

A wise counselor told me not to try to guess what was going on because it might not be right. "No mind reading," she admonished when I started to speculate by looking over *my past* experiences. I easily could have made the conversation about my issues with her dad if I had continued to try to "fix" her. It would be years before I understood she was in a gender-identity crisis. This was not even a concept in my worldview then.

Sitting in her room, painted with happy sky blue and sunset orange walls, I assured her she was perfect and divine inside. There were just some dark thoughts that needed to come out. Any loving, positive, affirming comments I made, she turned against me. She said things like "Not this … this is not fixable," "You like Nicole more," "I am not fixable," or "Don't say those things." She could not see the reflection of love in my glasses because hers were so warped.

Then Chris started cutting. Cutting is an addictive, maladaptive coping mechanism. The physical pain causes the brain to release endorphins and temporarily eases the emotional pain. I learned that Chris had been drinking during her friend's parents' party. She was spending most of her time at her dad's house. She was distancing herself from Nicole and me. She would come over to my house or go out to dinner with me, but if I tried to talk about school or her mental and emotional state, she would get in her car and go back to her dad's. Although I felt rejected, I did not make demands. I could not force her to confide in me.

Finally she grudgingly agreed to go to counseling. I was grateful that she had someone to talk to since she wasn't talking to me. Meanwhile, I had work to do of my own.

I had VVs exploding all over the place: VVs about Chris's welfare and her suffering; VVs about addictive behaviors, hers and mine; VVs about being rejected; VVs about failing as a mother; VVs about her choosing to stay at Dad's; and VVs about my VVs.

And I knew how much damage I could do to our relationship if I let any of those VVs explode in her direction. I couldn't make her trust me. I couldn't make her confide in me. I couldn't make her pain go away. I couldn't make her confide in Nicole. I couldn't make her stay at my house under my watchful eye. I couldn't make her well. I couldn't fix this. Not even the absolute authority of the wooden spoon would fix this. As I had learned a new way to lead, I needed to learn a new way to parent.

Sir Ego wanted to use his lance or shield. He reasoned that his parental obligations required him to act. He strategized guilt trips, addiction lectures, bribes, demands, and punishments. He was so loud. I couldn't find the wise one, but I did not let him act on these misguided manipulation strategies. I faced the pain of rejection, helplessness or suffering, and fear and let the VVs release, knowing that they were *just energy*, energetic attachments to desires and fears.

I had learned enough about fear to know it was not serving me. Heck, everything I had feared, I had manifested. I had attracted my fears to me. More importantly, my fear would not serve Chris. My fears were a cloud of darkness between us. She could not open her heart to me because she did not want to let those fears in. She could not confide in me when she saw fear in my eyes. She didn't need my problems on top of hers. I had to show her something else in the unspoken realm of the energetic bond between us, love and only love.

ACIM says that love cannot be present when there is fear. Although I had trouble understanding this, I knew I wanted to transcend the fear. Sir Ego thought I could have a combo platter: some love and some fear at the same time. How could I fulfill my parental obligations without fear? His fix-it thoughts were surely born of caring and love. Weren't they? I was on the next step of my quest to discover if there was a kind of love that had no fear.

One gloomy afternoon, I tearfully sat alone, pondering this question, and I felt the Creator say, "She's mine. She's in my hands. Fear not."

Yes, I thought. *I am her guardian and teacher, but she is not mine to direct, control, or fix. The Creator has no grandchildren.*

A great revelation was that *my* fears had no place in our relationship. My fears were between me and the Creator, who could and would help me transcend them. I spent many, many hours working with the wise one on purifying my fears. I came to believe that this was the purpose of teenagers, to bring up our unresolved stuff for purification and release. Teenagers trigger the fears in our chests. Problem arise when we litter VVs all over the relationship. In the same way we set up the lessons for our children, they set up our lessons when they become teens, returning the favor.

Me being okay was the wise one's concern, not Chris's. Period. How Chris needed to be was something that I did not know. Honestly, her wise one knew her path, lessons, and needs. It was not my place to legislate how she needed to be. As a parent, Sir Ego believed it was his job to legislate how his kids need to be. I had to find the line between what legislation my children needed for their safety versus what legislations I wanted for my own emotional comfort.

I had a poignant dream that helped me to deepen my understanding about the consequences of fearful thoughts. In my dream, I was walking in a magnificent paradise—let's call it Eden—with the Creator. It was an extraordinary feast for the senses, a jungle of trees, animals, flowers, and vibrant scents and sounds. As we walked, I noticed some monkeys fighting. Their screeches reminded me of my brothers' roughhousing and assaulted my senses. I wished they would stop. Instantly my thought became reality, and they stopped. I guessed that walking with the Creator had a few perks. My wishes were instantly granted.

Equally instantaneously, I saw the domino effect of chain reactions play out. First those monkeys stopped fighting; then all monkeys stopped fighting. The fighting was part of the monkeys' mating ritual. As soon as they all stopped fighting, they stopped mating. One thing led to another, and bam, the monkeys were extinct. Wow, I hadn't intended that.

Next, we came upon a lion feasting on a newly deceased gazelle, and the grisly sight repulsed me. Again, I wished it weren't so, and again, it immediately stopped. Once more, the domino effect became astonishingly evident to me. All lions stopped eating gazelles. The lions all starved and died, going extinct. Without predators, the gazelles overpopulated and ate everything green. The land became barren, and the gazelles went extinct also. Paradise was dead and barren.

Oh my, this omnipotence thing was quite a responsibility. Everything had to be orchestrated in a precise manner. Every character had to play his or her part. Every domino effect had to be foreseen.

When I awoke, the lesson for me was quite clear. Every time Sir Ego acts in fear, even a little resistance, he sets into motion an entire sequence of consequences and side effects. The ultimate outcome of these is unknown. When we judge that the Creator's plan is flawed and attempt to fix it, we do not have the appropriate perspective to act wisely and consider all the consequences. When we act selfishly or fearfully, we unknowingly birth an entire sequence of events, each inheriting the fear in which it was born.

This awareness had a great impact on me, and I contemplated it deeply. I understood it to mean that even the most insignificant thought or act of hate, anger, or greed sets ablaze a chain reaction of events. And conversely, even the tiniest acts of love, grace, mercy, and kindness echo throughout the universe. These reverberations touch people we may never meet and affect situations beyond time, as I would learn later.

I realized that every time I had an interaction with my children when I was holding this fearful or resistant energy, there was a domino effect in a bad direction. I could see them walk back into their room more dejected than before. I imagined this went onto social media and started spreading the hurt and encouraging their friends to witness their victimhood. Then their friends would continue to witness to this darkness and affirm it in their in own reality and on and on.

In the future, when I was tempted to say a judgmental or negative comment, the wise one would remind me gently, *You made the monkeys extinct*. This taught Sir Ego to hold his tongue and holster his weapons. In the place where I had wanted to express negativity, I prayed a silent prayer for my children instead, turning the tide of the energy exchange.

Taking these fears off the table, I was able to offer Chris unconditional love and acceptance, even when she was rejecting me. This was a very demanding parenting assignment. But this turned out to be the perfect posture to keep from alienating her. I realized how fast I could have pushed her away by getting in her face about all kinds of things, many of which were my fears. There was a big difference between talking to her with fear in my eyes and talking to her with unconditional love and acceptance in my eyes. I had learned how we sense this in others even if it is not revealed in their words. One was quite disagreeable; the other was quite irresistible.

Choosing my battles wisely, I was open to many changes that were happening. Chris cut her hair short, dyed it pink, got a tattoo, started binding her chest, pierced her nose, and gauged her ears. She had transformed into a new someone, and I wanted to allow her to experiment with her identity. I resisted the temptation to resist. I had to release many VVs to be okay with the rapidly unfolding changes. I had to stay in the wise one and resist Sir Ego's battle cries and opinions. These were not dangerous or criminal activities, and I kept an eye open for those.

Chris began a romantic relationship with Madison, and she began improving in every way. Being gay was way better than being depressed, pun intended. I was so grateful that she found someone to confide in. Their love deepened, and Chris came out of the darkness. Her mood and confidence seemed to soar. She opened up to Nicole and me again. I was grateful for all the restraint Sir Ego had shown since there was no trash littered in our relationship that had to be taken out. A moment of Sir Ego's harsh words can be difficult to forgive, forget, and let go of.

Soon she was comfortable again at my house and didn't run to Dad's house to hide. Both girls often went to their dad's and had a wonderful relationship with their little sister. It was perfect. They made frequent appearances, which made Don happy. I encouraged their relationship with their dad, but Nicole responded that all her dad wanted was "access to her emotions." *How insightful*, I thought.

But the girls were nonetheless establishing boundaries. They were becoming aware of what to expect from their dad and stepmom and to accept that. They did not have to play Don and Barb's games on a regular basis. From the bottom of my heart, I was overjoyed that the situation did not end up in complete alienation from either parent, which would have prohibited the resolution of unfinished business.

Occasionally I spoke with my grown stepchildren, Lauren and Bob, as our relationship resumed after the custody war. I could hear my own victim cries echoing in their assessment of their own conflicts with Don. They sang the broken record victim's song, reciting Don's crimes and misdemeanors, egoic foibles, alcoholic behaviors, and emotional manipulations, as if they could want him to change enough for him to actually change. They demanded that he become the father they wanted, to undo the past and to heal their wounds. Sadly, even if he did repent and make amends, he could not heal their wounds and undo the VVs. Our VVs become our own lesson guides, and each of us needs to find our own path to release them.

Nicole and Chris did not have this open and raw anger. Although they saw their dad's weaknesses and were beginning to recognize the impact this had on them, they did not demand that their dad change. They had more acceptance. As they had accepted and forgiven me, they were forgiving him. The Course explains that our wise ones are all interconnected in the universal consciousness and we were all sharing in these beautiful lessons of love, compassion, acceptance, and forgiveness. And as we shared them, they became stronger for all of us, drawing us closer to the truth, higher in our consciousness, and deeper into our hearts. This is the power of *holy relationships*.

At Christmastime, the volatile relationships at Dad's house erupted. The girls' half-brother, Bob, was visiting their dad's house for the holiday. An eruption over dirty dishes resulted in a fiery exchange between Barb and Bob, and Nicole got caught in the cross fire. Somehow this ended up with Barb demanding that Nicole leave and telling Nicole that she was not welcome at Don's house anymore. While there may be situations in which excommunication is appropriate—for example, drug addicts who are destroying their families—first-offense dirty dishes was not such a situation.

When Nicole got home, she was very upset and conveyed this story to me. Given my newfound ability to smooth things over with Don, I called him to discuss this. I felt confident that he could see that this was an overreaction and smooth things over with Nicole and Barb. Long story short, he could not. He affirmed Barb's eviction order. I couldn't believe it.

Nicole was done. She did not go over there for four months. Again, she stood strong in her boundaries. She was not unkind in return; she simply abided by the order. On several occasions, I implored them to work this out, but they were resolute. They were waiting for Nicole to apologize and come crawling back on her knees. *For what?* I wondered. The dishes hadn't even been hers. Nicole was up to this test of wills.

The old me would have loved this opportunity to go on a bashing spree, but the new me rejoiced with Nicole. I emphasized that this was not any kind of reflection on Nicole. It was about Barb and Don. I applauded Nicole's calm and kind way of teaching them that they could not treat her this way. They had exploded, but she did not counter. They were not the ones pulling her strings anymore. She had found her power. I affirmed that this would allow her to have a new relationship with them, one in which inappropriate behavior would not be tolerated.

Nicole began having severe and debilitating headaches and tummy troubles, causing her to lose weight and to experience panic attacks. She finally became immobilized and could not attend high school for most of junior year. Nicole is a classic type-A personality: overachiever, perfectionist, and prone to anxiety. This looked really good for a long time. She never had a B grade. She did her schoolwork and chores before fun stuff and maintained my linen closet meticulously like a Bed, Bath and Beyond shelf. She was top scorer on the lacrosse team, managed her money, and spent hours playing *Little Mermaid* with her four-year-old sister. She wanted to go to Stanford and become a surgeon. She had watched surgeries on TV and YouTube since fifth grade.

As soon as the doctors heard the symptoms combined with information about her overachiever personality, they concluded she had an anxiety disorder and prescribed medications. Her situation was not improving. For months, they threw more and more meds at her, increasing her zombie-like state. She hardly left her bedroom or even her bed. She felt there were physical causes that the doctors were overlooking. We went to appointments with many more doctors, seeking a treatable diagnosis, but we never got one. The downward spiral was devastating.

I had learned enough from Chris to take my fears out of this equation, to make this not about my concerns, my expectations. But unlike Chris, who pushed me away, Nicole sucked me in. She wanted me to fix it. She wanted me to save her. She wanted me to share her pain. It took me a long time to understand that I was going to have to face my codependence.

Every suggestion that I could come up with were what I would do if I were in her shoes. They related to my VVs, my past experiences, my spiritual journey, my health concerns, and so forth. I didn't know what the present problem was or where her journey would lead her for healing.

After my evening bath, I was in wind-down mode for the evening. All my work and housework were done, and I cherished an hour or two of peaceful contemplation outside under the stars.

As I passed Nicole's room on my way to the patio, she called out, "Mom."

I came to her door and felt the sadness. Sometimes she slept all day. The room that was darkened both night and day, the bed that was never empty long enough to get made, and the abandoned schoolbooks becoming dusty on the unused desk were stark reminders of her challenges.

"What's up, lovebug?"

"I have three lessons to complete for history that I need to turn in tomorrow, but I can't concentrate enough to get it done. I only have one class, once a week now, and I can't even keep up with that. Will you call my teacher and tell him I can't make it to our weekly meeting tomorrow?" She had given up on attending school full time and had transferred to the home study program due to her health problems.

"Do you think you could do one lesson and meet with him to turn that in tomorrow?" I inquired hopefully, thinking one lesson would give her some sense of accomplishment.

"No, I can't even read. My mind is so fuzzy. How will I ever finish school? I'll never get into a good college, much less Stanford. I am ruining my life. And worrying about this makes me feel ten times worse. I haven't felt good in two months. What is wrong with me? When is this going to get better? I can't live like this." She was very dejected and hopeless.

The pressure on high school students to build a strong college application, be awarded the Nobel Prize, win an Olympic medal, and fund a not-for-profit for impoverished children weighed on her, as she lay helpless in bed. Her noble Sir Ego was overwhelmed with the expectations and her complete inability to fulfill them. Guilt and anxiety flourished.

"Did you go to the chiropractor today?" I asked.

"No," she responded. And then there was more guilt that she was not doing the right thing or doing something wrong and was to blame for her situation.

"Why not?" I added hopefully. "I thought that was helping."

"No, it's not helping. What am I going to do?" she retorted without any details.

"Well, let's try the acupuncture the doctor suggested. I can call for an appointment tomorrow," I offered.

"I am not doing that. That is not going to help. I need to feel better now. I need to get back to school now. I am ruining my life. These doctors don't know what they are doing. What am I going to do? I need to be at school. I need to be president of a club. I need to make the varsity lacrosse team. What will I put on my college applications, that I laid in bed for my junior year?" Her pitch and frustration were rising.

"Yoga would really help. Maybe you could come to class with me tomorrow," I suggested, thinking, *Here we go again.*

"You don't get it. I can't do that. I can't even get out of bed. That isn't going to help. That is the last thing I need," she hissed at me.

"It would feel good to do some volunteer work, and that would help your college applications. Let's look online. There's a website called Volunteers of America that has all kinds of volunteer opportunities," I offered feebly.

"Are you crazy? I'm not going to make another commitment to something so I will fail again. I feel bad enough about myself now. You're not helping," she exclaimed.

"I'm trying to help. You need to *do* something. Anything. To help yourself. I have ideas, but you don't like any of them. I don't think the prescriptions are helping you. They are making you worse. I'm going to call the doctor tomorrow and tell them to figure something else out. I can't fix this for you. I don't know what else to do."

Exasperated, Sir Ego's VV exploded in full force. And I saw by the look on her face and the tears on her cheeks that I had made things worse. I was making the monkeys extinct.

"I'm sorry. I just can't handle this now." And I stormed off to my room, leaving her worse than I had found her. I hated myself after these conversations. I wanted so much to help, and I was making it worse. I apologized later, but I could see that no apology could undo the damage. She desperately wanted something from me, and not only was I failing to give it to her, I was causing her more pain and anguish.

I am sorry to say we played this same conversation many times before I could understand how to change it. I was so frustrated from making suggestions that were dismissed. She wanted me to *fix it, but not that way.* She had an excuse for every suggestion that I offered. Sir Ego fell for the fix-it trap. Something was different with her than with my coworkers.

There was an added dimension here, a gravitational force that was pulling me in that was stronger than the one I had handled before. Unlike my coworkers, Nicole's pain was my pain. I could feel it viscerally. The mother-child bond made it nearly impossible for me to not resonate with her pain, for my heart to stay open and allow her pain to be shared. Sir Ego would do anything to make it stop.

When I watched Sir Ego's response to this situation, I noticed a repeating theme: *This is how you need to be for me to be okay.* Sir Ego wanted my children to be in a happy place, so I would feel happy. He was not okay when they were not okay. His VVs were triggered. I needed to learn to be okay no matter what place my children were in.

I was missing the moment of choice. I crossed right over it into an exploding VV. I had to learn where I was missing the cue. Eventually I realized my signal was the thought, *Here we go again.* At this moment, Sir Ego recognized that she was triggered and I was about to be triggered and I could choose whether I would *go* with my own VV and repeat the same interaction for the zillionth time or seek the wise one.

In that thought, I intuitively realized that she was *gone*. I could not control that. But I didn't have to *go* with her. This was my reminder that I needed to stay centered, without expressing or suppressing my VVs, and weather the storm. I needed to open my heart to her pain and allow a portal for it to be purified.

Upon contemplation, I realized that she was triggered and wanted to express the energy. I was uncomfortable with her pain, and I was resisting her expression of the energy. I was energetically pushing back at her with fix-it ideas. I was too enmeshed in her emotions. I couldn't distinguish between her pain and my pain. I just wanted it to stop.

At that moment, she didn't want a solution. She wanted to vent. She wanted to feel loved and secure. She wanted her pain to be witnessed. And I was resisting it because it didn't want to feel it. When I resisted, she felt invalidated and unheard and got louder. I had to stop falling for the same trap. I was resisting her emotions, but she felt that I was resisting her.

I recognized this as codependent behavior. I had read books about codependence, so I had information in my head, but the information hadn't travelled the distance to my heart. I couldn't incorporate the information into my behavior. Until now. I had a tried-and-true way to work with my VVs, so I used that to study my dysfunctional and ineffective efforts to help Nicole with her struggles.

The frustration became overwhelming because I had solutions that I would use to make the pain stop if it were mine. But she rejected those solutions. I was condemned to feel *her* pain and unable to implement *my* solutions to fix it. I was frustrated because I had no control. I was feeling the pain but couldn't execute any of my remedies to stop it. I realized that this enmeshment was not serving either one of us and it must be purified.

In my mind, I saw that she was in a mud puddle and I would jump in with her. This never had a good ending. I needed to learn to stand on the edge of the mud puddle and offer my hand, my empathy, and assistance without getting in the mud. I learned to allow her anger, pain, and fear while staying centered in the wise one with an open heart.

It took me a while to master the higher response in the moment of choice. At one point, all I could do was stop the imminent explosion of my VV. As soon as I realized that I was triggered, I needed to stop. I needed to stop midsentence and go to my room. I learned that if I let my mouth open for one more word, even to say "we'll talk about this later," the word vomit would start. My VVs were so strong, and Sir Ego wanted to make the pain stop, have the last word, and be right.

I was changing the dance, and she didn't like that at first. She was still insistent that I could save her and was very offended when I walked away. Was I saying "I don't care?" Yet I had to remain strong and stop these bad interactions until I could recognize the VV in time to choose the wise one and stay steady. I knew some part of her understood that it was actually an improvement. At least I wasn't making things worse anymore. I only had to walk away abruptly a few times before I learned to recognize my cue—*here we go again*—and have the strength to stay centered in the wise one.

I needed to have a new strategy, a way of showing that I cared without the fix-it energy. From the bottom of my heart, I wanted to help. I realized I needed to put the burden on her to tell me how to help. And if I offered help and she didn't accept, she couldn't think I didn't care. The wise one suggested a new way of being.

"How can I help?"

"I'm sorry that's happening."

"Is there anything I can do?"

"I have faith that you will figure it out."

"You have slain bigger dragons than this."

At first I had to memorize these phrases so I would not say the wrong things. Over time, I came to embody this loving, but unattached, attitude.

Dispassion is the yogic term. *I cannot help you with your VV when I am having my own VV meltdown* is the English terminology.

Eventually this new pattern created a safe place for her to explode and a strong place for me to stand. Now she could move through the energy. Instead of being stuck on a carousel trying to get me to understand the first layer of her pain, she could go to deeper layers. Over time, I could see her movements into solution thinking on her own. My open-heart energy was helping to allow the river of energy to flow when before I was an obstacle that had dammed it up.

In case there wasn't enough going on in my life, our golden retriever, Sierra, was dying. She was my beloved and trusted friend, the only one who had been there for me for the dark nights of excruciating loneliness during the custody battle. Everyone loves his or her dog, but this relationship was on a different level. Somehow her kind, loving energy and soulful brown eyes consoled me when nothing else could and when there was no wine to numb the pain. We enjoyed many healing walks through the woods and by the lake near our house. The water soothed me, and Sierra loved it. I had to spell the word L-A-K-E because, if I said it, she would go crazy.

I feared most for the girls—that they couldn't handle the news in their delicate state. But truth be told, it was the girls who told me that we had to take Sierra for that one-way trip to the vet. Sierra had so much innocence and purity. There could never be a better dog. My love for her was great and my anguish penetrating.

My dearest friend, in great sympathy, allowed me to distinguish between love and the object of love, a profound lesson. Love is everywhere, but we only see it in a few beloved objects, and we are inconsolable when they depart. I reflected on her wisdom, appreciated the gift of her love, and accepted the knowledge that her death did not, in fact, diminish the amount of love in the universe.

On Christmas Eve, Nicole said to me, "You are going to be shocked when you see what Chris's friend, Brianna, gave her for Christmas."

Shocked, hmmm? What did that mean? Imagine my astonishment when Chris walked in the door with a tiny pit bull puppy snuggled up in her arms, an ear-to-ear grin on her face, and the sparkle of puppy love in her eyes. My immediate reaction was total resistance. *This has got to go.*

Take it back. No way. But those were not the words that came out of my mouth.

Somehow I saw the Creator's love in this picture, and I could not snatch that puppy out of my daughter's arms. Obviously my daughters needed some puppy love, and that was why Sunny came to us. I simply told Chris that puppies were *a lot* of work and, if she didn't step up, Sunny would be looking for a new home.

I dealt with my resistance, which continued for several days, with the Creator. Then I fell in love and found myself shampooing the carpet and buying a pen for Sunny. Since I had been a complete dog training failure with Sierra, way too permissive, I invited Don to participate. He too fell in love. We had our first happily shared custody and financial arrangement. And the Creator smiled.

I searched again for the middle way in my parenting role. This year had taught me to allow my daughters to have their process, life, and lessons, despite how hard it was to watch. I had the courage to continue to look at them with love, not fear. I had the wisdom to look at them as divinely perfect, not broken. I was holding a spot for them to step into their perfection, and I would continue to hold it, as long as it took.

15

The One Truly Serious Philosophical Problem

Sir Ego and the wise one had in-depth conversations about parenting as I worked hard to be in the highest consciousness for my children. I could see the dysfunctional ways that Sir Ego wanted to speak and act, and I wanted to know why he was often self-defeating so I could release his fears and judgements. I wrestled with the question of how to fulfill my parenting responsibilities without fear. It seemed like "good parenting" was protecting children from the things I feared. Isn't that why I kept my toddlers away from the stove? So they wouldn't get burned? Wasn't it a parent's job to create rules, boundaries, and curfews, using car keys and cell phones as rewards and punishments? I was frustrated because every Sir Ego parenting thought would make the monkeys extinct. There was an imperative for me to understand and integrate what it means to parent from a place of love without fear. I had to have such a deep knowing that I would be able to *be* this way in even the most demanding circumstances.

One morning, I awoke, and the answer was there. The wise one revealed *unconditional love means that you hold the eternal perspective of your children, that they are perfect and divine, ever safe in the hands of the Creator. You do not know what their lessons are, so you cannot understand or evaluate their current circumstances. It doesn't matter if they appear to be failing the midterm. Everyone passes the final exam in his or her own time. This is the way the Creator loves you. And as you open your heart to offer unconditional love, you open your heart to receive it, in the same way you received the forgiveness that you offered.*

I was grateful to have such a clear answer to my prayer that was filled with truth, grace, and love. My heart melted at this thought of the Creator loving me throughout my toughest circumstances and greatest failures. In jail, my circumstances looked the worst, but it was really a crucial and positive turning point in my understanding. As I had received self-forgiveness by offering forgiveness, I understood that offering unconditional love to my children would open my heart to receiving it. How exquisite.

I remembered the unconditional love that patiently teaches a toddler how to walk down the stairs, cross the street, and safely roast marshmallows, no matter how many repetitions are required. Over and over, we are willing to show them, with love and no judgement. Yet Sir Ego was very frustrated with my teenagers' lessons and didn't want to have the same acceptance and patience. Why? Because Sir Ego is blossoming in our teenagers. He is individuating from us. And our Sir Ego is threatened by this and wants to control it. He spars with them. But this blocks our relationship and obstructs the wise one when we need him most.

This awakened the realization that I could continue to enforce boundaries, but with love, not judgement, no matter how many times it was required. My mother exhibited this when she held me as I cried over being grounded. This was not resorting to my father's guilt, shame, and punishment.

The goal is total equanimity about what they choose, whether they prefer the reward or the consequence. *Either is fine. I love you no matter what. Take as long as you like to get this lesson. I have time. I will still be here. I will enforce the boundary, but with love, not anger, which arises from fear. You want to work hard and get good grades? Great! You reap the benefit. You don't? Oh well, you pay the price. I love you either way. I will be okay either way.*

Their resistance to our controlling parenting behaviors reveals that they are done with that part of the lesson plan. When the children are young, we teach through exposition, telling them what to do, explaining why it's important, sharing our values, and using rewards and punishment for reinforcement. By the time they are in middle school, they know everything we are going to say before we say it. Now they experiment with various behaviors, and the world—teachers, coaches, friends, and teammates—gives them feedback so they learn. We are done telling them how to get their homework done and be a loyal friend. They must test everything we have taught them, experience the consequences, and decide how they will be. This explains how it seems that the good values and behaviors they had seem to disappear. They have not lost the values, manners, and information. They are just stress testing them.

They know how to clean their room, and they will decide if they want to live in a big mess or not. It does not mean that they will be messy as adults. They are just trying it out. They have different priorities now. We don't need to demand they clean their room or think we have failed when they don't do it. I realized that if I continued to try to enforce my will on these individuating teens, I would force them into one of two coping strategies: the rebel or the pleaser. Sir Ego either favors the lance or the shield.

I was under a lot of pressure both at work and at home, constantly in learning mode, releasing VVs. I longed for a vacation, and then it appeared. I got an email about cheap airfare to Maui on the same day I realized I was getting an unexpected tax return. I booked the trip the same day. We planned wonderful adventures for the three of us: scuba diving, shark diving, and hang gliding.

The trip was blissful. We had all learned to let it be, to come together when there was mutual interest and go solo when there was not. No judgement and no expectations. We all got to have exactly the vacation we wanted. My children went shopping for souvenirs, and I found a tour guide to take me around the sacred sites of the island. She was extraordinarily knowledgeable for a *haole* (non-Hawaiian), as she had taken classes and attended presentations offered by the Hawaiian shamans, the *kahuna*. It was interesting to see the similarities between the Hawaiian and the yogic traditions.

The girls did the shark dive at the Maui Ocean Center while I watched from the spectator's gallery. There were twenty-three sharks, ranging in size up to seven feet long, and five stingrays, but no great whites. We went hang gliding over Hana. The equipment we used was an ultralight craft, like a motorcycle with wings. The motor was used to take off, and then the operator shut off the motor and glided. We went one at a time with the instructor. I experienced the freedom of flying and a stunning view of the rainforest and waterfalls below, including George Harrison's estate. And our GoPro camera caught it all.

But when we returned to California, several relatively minor teenage dramas turned into a crisis for Chris. Two separate incidents happened where she was tangentially involved with a squabble between a friend and her parents. These messy dramas spilled over onto her and caused great angst. Don was taking the parent's side in one of the dramas and giving Chris a rough time. I was unaware of the hurricane forming offshore.

The next day, both girls were at their dad's when he pushed the "let me get control over this situation" button. Nicole came home and told me that he had exploded at Chris. He had taken away her car keys and her cell phone and told her she was throwing her life away. She would have had a chance to go to a University of California college, but no more since her grades had fallen so much. (The only problem with her grades had been caused by missed work due to our trip. As soon as she made all the work up, she had a 3.75 GPA.)

Later Chris arrived, quite forlorn. I offered my mantra of "This isn't about you." Don was stressed and had taken it out on her; none of these things were that big a deal.

Chris wailed, "This is taking me back to last year." Her despair was palpable.

I called Don and negotiated a return of the car keys once Chris made up all the work, which we expected would be the next day. But like a moth to the flame, she needed to get him to make her feel better. She went back into the emotional torture chamber to try to persuade him to be reasonable, and she sustained another blow. He was stuck in a "have to be right" place and could not see the extent of her pain or the amount of his overreaction. She came home again, even worse than before.

The next morning when I got up for work, she came and told me that she had been vomiting. I told her to go back to bed and to stay home from school. I went to work. In the afternoon, I texted her to see how she was feeling, and she asked when I would be home.

I asked, "Why? Do you need something?"

"I just want you to be home."

I dropped everything and got in my car and went home. When I arrived, Nicole was on the couch in the living room.

Sitting down next to her, I asked her, "How's Chris?"

"I tried to talk to Chris earlier, and she seemed incoherent." She mentioned that her hands were numb. Nicole suggested that there was something of a neurological nature going on. Yikes. Maybe somebody should have called me sooner?

I went into Chris's room and sat with her for an hour. She wouldn't talk. She sobbed and cried, but as before, there were no words. Careful not to put something out there that wasn't already there, I said little except to offer the comfort, "Everything is fixable."

"Not this," she whimpered.

I was connecting the dots in an alarming way. Chris said her legs were numb. I asked if she had eaten, drunk, or taken something that had made her sick that morning. She did not deny it.

"Did you take something to try to hurt yourself?" I pressed.

"Yes."

In a very calm and delicate manner, VVs in check, I questioned her about what had happened. It took some time to learn that she had taken more than thirty-five of Nicole's migraine pills. She was feeling numb all over—dazed, confused, and terrified. She said that she wanted to die or get better. Either was fine, but this zombie state was horrible.

By this time, it had been twelve hours since she took the pills. I suggested that we go to the urgent care for some kind of antidote. I took her there, and they sent us to the adjacent emergency room for a suicide evaluation.

I remained completely calm and focused, completely present to Chris, VVs in check. I had been there myself. She was too foggy to uphold her usual defenses. She told me more about what happened in the car.

She referenced me saying, "When the Creator decides it's your day to die, you die. No matter what the cause, no one is to blame."

She wanted to see if today were her day. She told the ER mental health evaluator that was how she'd decided how many pills to take—enough, but not too many. The Creator would decide.

I sat in the waiting room while they took her for an examination. My heart was pounding, and I was laser-focused on her needs, denying Sir Ego's temptation to explode. The wise one could see Sir Ego storming about. *Why did you this? Are you crazy? I'm furious. How could you do this to me, Sunny, Nicole, and Teresa? This is Don's fault. He caused this. Did I do this? My heart is exploding. Stop this! Undo this.*

I took all my strength to resist the temptation to follow Sir Ego into this VV pit. If I went there, I knew I would get lost there. I wouldn't have been able to support Chris. I couldn't think of me right now. I couldn't catastrophize about the future right now.

Many hours passed as we waited for the lab results that would tell us if she would live or die. Chris was quiet and in and out of sleep. I was alone with the Creator, praying for strength, and the Creator's grace was abundant as the fears were kept at bay.

Eventually we learned that she was okay and there was no permanent damage. The ER doctor warned her that brain damage was a common result of suicide attempts to discourage a repeat. In the morning, she would be transferred to the psychiatric hospital on a three-day hold. Again, a million fears rose up, and it took all my strength to stay in the consciousness of the wise one. I was shockingly aware of how powerless I was to guarantee my daughter's safety even though I would lay down my life to do so. She was going to have to walk this scary road alone, but not without my love.

Despite her resistance to counseling in the past, she showed some interest now. I hoped group therapy would help her to have a new willingness to look at the pain in her life, as I had in rehab. This would be new for her, a place where people could share their secrets, problems, and dysfunctional family life. She wasn't the only one. When she was released from the seventy-two-hour hold, she wanted to stay longer. But they sent her home.

She was required to attend a partial hospitalization program for two weeks—every day, all day—and more group therapy sessions. She was processing the event and receiving the support of experienced counselors and other comrades, suicide survivors. She alternated between resistance and resignation as well as optimism and hopelessness.

The counselors gave us a safety plan. Lock up the sharps and the pills, sign a contract to not self-harm, and empower parents as vigilant watchmen. I executed these safety precautions with love and without judgement. As Chris and several other people pointed out, if she really wanted to kill herself, nothing could stop her. In fact, I told her that I understood her pain and fear, and no matter what happened, I would love her for all of eternity with all my heart. My heart wanted to close, to not feel the pain and fear, but the wise one knew better. I allowed my heart to stay open so the fear would pass through me, unabated. The wise one watched the fear and watched Sir Ego and did not get involved with either of them.

Using all the muscles and skills I had developed, I coped with the ever-present threat of another incident for months. Every day, clinging to the wise one, forsaking Sir Ego and purifying VVs, I had one firm rule. Fears are for the wise one, and love is for the children. Don't make the monkey extinct. As long as I obeyed this rule, things worked. The wise one was teaching me constantly, and the children were loved and not subjected to my fears.

Death, my old friend, was knocking at the door. In my own time of despair, I hadn't wanted to commit the act, but I would have graciously and gratefully accepted—in fact I longed for—a terminal release from my suffering. I could empathize with Chris's struggle in a way that she could not imagine. From my early sobriety, I understood the moment-by-moment nature of the struggle. An instant of weakness or an uncontrollable impulse, and the fight would be lost. I also understood this was why no one else could do it for you. No one else can want it enough. No one can take your place in the existential battle.

I already knew this battle would rage until Chris made a decision, as I had made one in that holding cell in jail. I had made the decision that I was willing to face any amount of fear, pain, humiliation, despair, trauma, punishment, and suffering for the love of my children because the love was stronger. Love made me more than those threats.

Likewise, Chris needed to make a decision, a commitment, a choice in the days and months to come. In all, there would be four suicide attempts, four trips to the psychiatric hospital, and a year of counseling for Chris and myself. My level of fear or love was the only way I would be able to influence this choice. I knew that releasing my fear allowed me to offer unconditional love to her in this hour of her need. I could offer nonjudgment and total acceptance of her and her reality, right where she was, not where I wished she were.

From the world's perspective, Chris had everything going for her, no Achilles heel. But I recalled vividly how malevolent the inner voices can be. I was familiar with the tormentor within who could deliver a constant barrage of self-loathing and self-flagellation, a cacophony that would not stop. Great compassion opened my heart to her suffering.

I noticed that Chris's bad mood days were tied to interactions with certain people who treated her badly and manipulated her wounds. More than anyone, I understood how she must learn these lessons herself. If I attempted to pull her away from this exploration of the dark side, she would return later. If I refused to allow her to see one person, she would just find another. We must all explore the dark in order to choose the light. Her half-brother, Bob, texted me a link to her Tumblr social media page, and I was forlorn to see how bleak and tortured it was. Yet I knew any outlet was better than none, so I didn't say anything about it and accepted her desolate screams into cyberspace.

Toxic, dysfunctional relationships involve a triangle of three roles: perpetrator, victim, and rescuer. While a person may play one role more often than others, all people play each of the roles at various times. After being the victim long enough, we become the perpetrator. A rescuer gets frustrated at his or her failure to rescue others and becomes a victim. Being ostracized, the perpetrator becomes a victim. I chose to step off this merry-go-round.

If I had gone to Chris's rescue, that would have affirmed her victimhood and her inability to be whole herself. If I had played the victim of her rejection, that would have made her a perpetrator. Or I could have affirmed our joint victimization by Don. Any of these would have kept us all on the merry-go-round. I stepped off and refuse to rescue, to be a victim, or to be a perpetrator. That stopped the merry-go-round. I stood firm in the center of the storm, in unconditional love, unwilling to witness to these archetypes.

The wise one allowed VVs to be released, and it seemed like a thousand puzzle pieces were dumped out of my chest, leaving all my issues swirling in my mind. Sir Ego was standing on the sidelines, healed of his reactive behaviors. I started writing and wrote for twelve days, the first draft of this book, to organize, synthesize, integrate, and purify the pieces into a perfect, divine, beautiful puzzle. At the end of that time, I saw the perfection in my quest and how each step had to happen to provide for the next step. I couldn't be coping with this if I hadn't had all the lessons that came before. It was a premature life review, seeing my struggles, lessons, and failures with understanding and without judgement. Many times, in the coming days of darkness and confusion, I would rely on this one truth. It would all make sense one day. I was sure of it.

Over the course of seven months, there would be four suicide attempts, which required all of the wise one's wisdom, compassion, and strength to navigate. Thankfully, my employer had a flexible family leave program, so I could work part time and take as much time off as I needed to care for both children, which was a lot, a day or two a week. Living with two children in crisis was demanding, spiritually, emotionally, intellectually, and physically.

I needed to stave off the school administrators who treated my children as if they had an attendance and disciplinary problem rather than a health problem. I had to navigate the myriad of doctors, counselors, and pharmaceuticals for both children. I had to be in two places at once, at the ER with Chris and bringing dinner to Nicole in bed. I went each evening after work for visiting hours at the psychiatric hospital even if Chris didn't seem interested in my company. The wise one guided me to go and show her my love and support were ever-present, regardless of how she treated me.

When the third attempt happened, Don mentioned feeling manipulated, and he didn't want to *encourage* this behavior, so he stopped visiting Chris at the hospital. Nicole and I were in the car driving to the hospital, and she also mentioned feeling manipulated. I resonated with this and could feel of flash of angry energy rise up from my stomach, Sir Ego wailed, *How could you do this to me after all I have done for you. Really? How could I? How could I make this about me?* I could see Sir Ego's barter system in its naked, ugly essence.

Instantly the wise one regained control, the energy was purified, my heart opened, and I thought, *If this is how loudly you have to scream to get my attention, then I better listen to you.* It didn't become a second-degree cry for help because she might not be seriously suicidal anymore. It was still the resonating cry of desolation, reverberating out into the void, compelling unconditional love to respond. My heart was filled with compassion and love for her.

Her actions were saying, *Listen to me! I need you. I need you to love me. I need you to pay attention to me. I need you to hear me. I need you to accept me as I am.*

I created a sacred place between us where her pain was allowed. There would be no repercussions, no repayment, and no debt incurred. I was learning the essence of impersonal love. I loved her without any ego involvement, without any expectation of reciprocation. I was expanding beyond her mother. I was channeling the divine love that falls equally on every being, despite their level of awareness, receptiveness, or reciprocity.

Both my daughters were like caterpillars in the cocoon, awaiting their emergence as magnificent butterflies. I knew understanding lay on the other side of the darkness, and I allowed their journey and process. All the darkness must pass by the lens of our awareness so it may be dispelled. Society might tell a parent to get involved in this process, control it, legislate it, establish boundaries, fix it, and deny it. But I learned to allow it, to hold a place for the light while they could not see it. As I write this, as I feel and process this energy, they unknowingly do as well. Our wise ones communicate constantly, despite our silent alliance.

Our children's struggles are a gift to us because they inspire an increasingly wholehearted search for unconditional love and surrender. My daughters are my greatest teachers. For them, I am willing to go to any dark place, confront any ego stronghold, release any false identity, and surrender completely to divine wisdom and will. This is what it takes to help them. Because I cannot fix it, I cannot live their journey for them. I cannot feel their pain in their place, find the right words to make it all disappear, or give them a God to save them. This is the futile wish of every parent watching his or her child suffer. But I must not fear that they can't do it. They can. They will.

I made a daily, even hourly, commitment to do my part, to confront my demons and to take my fears off the table of our communion. It purifies the mirror that I reflect to them. As I move to a solitary message of unconditional love, void of any fear, judgment, or demand, I allow them their process in a sacred place. The wise one shines through me, ever faithful of their eventual triumph.

One evening as I sat on the patio contemplating the cosmos, C came out and sat next to me. Tears flowed down her cheeks, her p and exposed. Her only words were "I don't want to live anymore." There was nothing to work with, validate, fix, or solve. My hands were tied. There were no words to be said.

I kissed her and whispered, "I love you, infinity, infinity, infinity."

I don't want to hear these words. I don't know what to do. I need this to stop. Sir Ego was exasperated. I realized that when I closed my heart so I wouldn't feel the pain, she felt I was closing my heart to her, resisting her, judging her, invalidating her, and not accepting her. The wise one said we must do the opposite. We must open our heart as wide as we can and summon all the love we can, no matter how great the pain of the VVs, which wanted to be released and purified.

So I learned to sit with her, opening my heart a mile wide to allow the wise one's love to come through, feeling eternal, unconditional love for Chris and praying for her, knowing that this was more real and more effective than any amounts of words. I was present to her pain to bear witness to it. I did not resist it because I knew she would feel resisted and invalidated.

I did not pray that she that she would get back to school or that her despair would vanish. These were not prayers that would disrupt her process, abort her mission, or short-circuit her lesson so I might feel better about the situation. My prayer was always the same in all circumstances because Sir Ego does not know what is best. *Please protect, guide, and bless Chris. Fill her heart with light and love.* She asked me to lay down with her until she fell asleep, and I knew she felt my unspoken prayer and the depth of my love. It had broken through the wall she had erected between us.

I had dispelled the *Brady Bunch* sitcom myth in Sir Ego's mind. Although Alice could solve any of the Brady children's problems in a thirty-minute episode, life doesn't work this way. I had learned that Sir Ego's talking did not help. It was not true that I should deliver a lecture and solve each problem my children had. It was a *should* that I had surrendered. And I came to rely on the wise one's inner communion and shared energy ⁓ to understand the distinction between fear, caring, and to *be* that were beyond fear.

nothing Sir Ego could do that would help her ght that she fought. In fact, his judgements and her feel invalidated, unheard, and unworthy. The only way I could effectively contribute to her struggle was to shine the light of unconditional love into her heart. I held a place for her divinity and perfection when she could not see or experience it. I looked past the present problem into the eternal perfection of her soul. This was the only thing I could control or contribute. Yet it is the most powerful thing. Feeling that unconditional love is the only thing that is so attractive that she would want to continue to live. It is the breath of life that sustains us. And it is the only thing that could heal the emotional wounds caused by our family's struggles.

Later I would come to understand that moments, like those on the patio, taught her how great my love was for her. I taught her that I accepted every part of her, no matter how dark or scary. I held her hand while we turned the light on in the closet to see and reveal the nothingness of the monster that lurked there. There was nowhere that she could run or fall that was beyond the reach of my love. This is how the Creator loves each one of us.

16

Love, Heroically

It was one thing to endure my own years of pain and suffering. It was quite another thing to endure my children's. Now the wise one and Sir Ego had regular meetings about the unfolding events and how to work together in the highest way. Each time I had chosen the wise one with his open heart and surrendered Sir Ego's defenses and fears, a new habit pattern was formed that made it easier to choose wisely the next time. And the balance shifted between the mind share devoted to each. In the past, Sir Ego consumed most of my mind. Now the balance of power had shifted, and the wise one consumed most of my mind. Before it seemed Sir Ego was me and the wise one was outside me, and now it seemed that the wise one was me and Sir Ego was outside me, moving further away and becoming quieter. I could sit in the witness and watch Sir Ego, allowing VVs to release without taking action.

Sir Ego would speak first because he couldn't contain himself when he was triggered and the wise one would watch and listen. The wise one would ask "Why do you care?" and the Socratic conversation would commence. Sir Ego was gently guided to greater understanding and a knowingness, testing spiritual principles in the inner laboratory of the heart and mind results in unshakable conviction and faith.

As I accepted divine love as my one and only grail, I aligned my will with it. The only thing that I could control that was effective in every situation was my state of consciousness. Yogananda tells us that when we become self-realized, it elevates our ancestors and descendants for generations. It works in both directions in the realm that transcends time.

Our families rise with us as we expand our consciousness because they are bound to our energy forever. I accepted this as truth and knew it was the highest thing I could do for my children. Again, staying in the path of love and forsaking fear. This faith allowed me to have the Creator's eye view, the satellite perspective of the tornado, when Sir Ego felt really lost and unsure. He was willing to surrender to the wise one's equanimity, acceptance, and nonattachment, which seemed previously impossible, as it pertained to my children. I adopted the eternal perspective that this trouble would pass and my children were perfect, divine, and secure in the arms of eternity.

Again I learned about the Tao, the middle way, the path of unconditional love that lay between the fearful extremes of Sir Ego. At this point, I had developed enough awareness about what was going on between my ears that I could see the ping-pong game. In response to all the crazy teenage "things" that were transpiring at my house, my fix-it thoughts vacillated between extremes: permissive versus controlling, codependent versus apathetic, no boundaries versus too many boundaries, no enforcement versus angry enforcement, powerless defeat versus anxiety, and no expectations versus overly engineered expectations.

I came to know this problem as the "this is how you have to be for me to be okay" problem. In other words, the way you are right now triggers my VVs, and I need you to be different so you don't trigger them. Those are two different things: how you are and how my internal state are not dependent, de facto. I had learned to separate them, to have a moment between the realization of how you are and the realization of my choice of how to be. This was a critical distinction. This was the antidote to my codependence. Now I knew how to navigate this: first, equanimity, nonattachment, and acceptance of the unfolding situation; next processing the explosion inside; and finally responding in a fully present, loving, calm manner.

The first thing I acknowledged was that Sir Ego had an illusion of control over my children. This illusion begins the moment we get pregnant, when we believe we can do pregnancy yoga, listen to Mozart, breastfeed, do time-outs, take them to Montessori, eat whole grain bread, read Dr. Seuss, watch *Sesame Street*, go to ballet and piano lessons, take them to soccer, and enroll them in advanced placement literature, turning them into perfect adults with no dysfunctions and no damage, going on to have perfect, trouble-free lives.

For a long time, we parents ignore the fact that we do not have a big enough lock to keep out childhood cancer, car accidents, autism, foreclosure, poor academic performance, football championship defeats, and first-love heartbreaks. Although my delusion was dispelled earlier than most parents, at some point this realization must occur to all parents, and the sooner, the better. It is not our job to create a perfect eighteen-year-old who will be the perfect ball player, have perfect grades, go to the perfect college, have the perfect career, marry the perfect spouse, and have perfect healthy habits and finances, living happily ever after. And it is outside our power to do so.

Every time I heard the inner whisper "don't make the monkeys extinct," I stopped and explored Sir Ego's desires and intentions. In stillness and silence, I looked directly into his inner workings. Investigating this desire of Sir Ego, I found that he is willing to invalidate, reject, manipulate, extort, and overrule his children, a little bit, in a socially acceptable way, kind of. Many times, I felt him tend toward a behavior that was very similar to Don's methods, maybe lower in volume, but the same in intent. I felt the burning desire to do something to stop or redirect the unfolding events.

In a flash, I saw the reason. I saw the loving eyes of my toddler shining into my heart with angelic love, and I saw the angry, tearful, disgusted eye roll of my teenager. Sir Ego thinks if he creates this heaven on earth in his child's life, he will once again see the angel eyes and never again suffer the evil eye. Let me get this straight. Sir Ego is willing to try to shield his child from his or her invaluable, divinely inspired life lessons so he doesn't have to experience the ups and downs of his or her journey and feel like a parenting failure. The wise one looks at both the newborn and teenager with awestruck wonder. Sir Ego looks at the teenager as a home improvement project: leaky roof, broken windows, bad attitude, poor grades, and messy bedroom.

It was more heart wrenching, but having already slayed this demon at work, I was able to stand in the wise one while my children looked at me with pain in their eyes and disgust in their voices. I knew it was not a reflection of me, but of their inner state. Sir Ego demurred, and the compassion of the wise one flowed freely.

I recalled a demonstration in a sermon that stuck with me. The pastor invited a member onto the stage and gave him a class of water. He bumped him, and he spilled the water.

He asked, "Why did the water spill out of the glass?"

"Because you bumped me," the member responded.

"No, why did the water spill out of the glass?" the pastor asked again.

"Because I couldn't hold it steady when you bumped me," he tried again.

"No. *Water* spilled out of the glass because *water* is what was inside the glass when it got bumped. When we are bumped by outside forces, whatever is in our heart comes out."

The lesson was revealed. My children could have disrespectful or confrontational demeanors because there was disrespect and conflict inside, not because I was a bad mom. With this understanding, my response went from defensive to compassionate. The Course says that every uttering is either a call for love or an offering of love. When someone calls for love, Sir Ego is tempted to respond with his own call for love. *Don't disrespect me, don't talk back, and don't treat me that way.* But the wise one knows to respond with love, that shift of consciousness changing everything about the interaction. We communed in a holy instant where it could have been an unholy mess.

As I looked at Sir Ego's fears, I started to notice that he was primarily concerned with his own past disappointments and failures. Most of all, I worried for my children about the possibility of addiction and abusive relationships. I did not worry about leukemia and teenage pregnancy. Naturally I did not want them to experience the pain I had experienced, and other kinds of pain weren't really on my radar. This made me curious, and I looked more deeply into it. Let's take addiction. Sir Ego wanted to get it right this time and make sure they didn't suffer my same fate. It seemed like a reasonable fear, and I had trouble releasing it.

Until I realized that I was trying to use the present situation, which stimulated my addiction VV, to heal my past. If I could just get it right this time ... This made me assume that I understood what they were thinking and going through when in fact I was going through my past and trying to fix it. No wonder they rejected Sir Ego's words. I was coming from a way different place and assuming they were in that same place, with the same problem, the same feelings, and the same solution. Their situation brought up this VV for me to release, not for me to project onto them and then try to undo it.

My counselor noted that even if I did understand exactly what my daughter was going through, those were the last words she wanted to hear. She didn't want to be like me; she wanted to be *not me* and try that out for a while. I even saw my daughters go through this individuation between themselves, judging each other mercilessly. It seemed like, *I don't know who I am, but I know I am not you.* So they changed sports, hair colors, glasses, and friends to distinguish themselves from each other.

Recognizing that their lessons and quest was unknown to me and most certainly different from mine, allowed me to exit fix-it mode, saving the monkeys from extinction. This is another narcissistic trap for parents, thinking that we even know what is best for our children. We have no idea of their past, karma, lessons, inner worlds, or current scorecard. When I looked the worst in that jail cell, I was actually having a profound awakening.

A parent has a lot of power over his or her children, physically, mentally, and emotionally. It is a sacred responsibility and is best offered to the ways of the wise one. Sir Ego is willing to abuse this power, calling controlling, manipulative, and misguided behaviors parenting. Trying to stop Chris's gay relationship would have been going in the absolute wrong direction.

Chris and I patriated in a nine-month counseling program of Dialectic Behavior Therapy, the gold standard for impulse control issues such as suicide attempts. I resonated with the program as it was developed by a Buddhist psychologist and embodied the kinds of mindfulness that I was learning to practice. A key construct was developing the ability to hold dualistic thoughts at the same time: I have a weakness now, and I am working to improve it. I feel that I can't go on, and I know how to cope with this feeling so it will pass. This replaces self-negating black-and-white, all-or-nothing thinking and impulsive behaviors.

The counselor made an excellent point that was a great polestar for me when I lacked clarity. Sir Ego is prone to normalizing abnormal behavior and overreacting to normal behavior. It is normal for a teenager to experiment with swearing, drinking, smoking, and so on. These are battles that often do not need to be fought and detract from the overall relationship. On the other hand, one must not normalize extreme behaviors, ignoring these cries for help. The trick is to determine when it crosses the line and becomes dangerous. The wise one is sensitive to this, yet Sir Ego is quick to judge and react blindly.

I walked on this razor's edge for a long time with both children and had to constantly remind myself that *I made the monkeys extinct*. Choosing moment after moment, love over fear, helped me navigate this treacherous territory. The wise one knew that I could not force them to get up, get their act together, get back to school, and make it work. I could never push hard enough to get them through the daily rigors of classes and homework. It would have been like pushing a wet noodle. They had to find this inspiration and determination within themselves.

They both reached a point where they had to withdraw from high school and do independent study. They both resisted this. For each one, there came 1 day when I had to say, "The school counselor called, and you will receive an F in several classes if you do not transfer into the independent school program tomorrow. I accept whatever choice you make."

Despite Sir Ego's screeches that an F was surely the end of the world and destroyed any hope for their future, I said, "I am more interested in your health and well-being than school. I don't care if you take an extra year. I don't care if you want to accept a bad grade. These are not important to me. You are important to me. I have faith in you and know things will work out no matter which decision you make." And I had to mean it when I said it, from a totally purified state. And I did.

Vehemently, both initially resisted transferring out of their school. But both did. It worked out well for them, and both eventually returned to their high school. If I had forced them to transfer, they might have been inclined to rebel and resist, causing this to fail. Sir Ego has been known to cut off his nose to spite his face.

Sir Ego is blossoming in teenagers. They are constantly comparing themselves to everyone around them and seeking to judge themselves superior. They find fault with everyone—their parents, siblings, teachers, coaches, friends, and teammates. And all those people are judging them in return with grades, scoreboards, Facebook likes, and groundings. This is an important process for Sir Ego, trying things out, trying to understand who he is apart from the forces that have molded him this far. But he needs a safe port in the storm, an unconditionally loving parent, cheerleader, support, helper, and polestar. I needed to be the calm center of the cyclone, like my mother before me. This was everything the wise one had groomed me for. I could do it.

I needed to accept their depression and know that it would pass. The wise one helped me understand that something was happening in those darkened bedrooms deep within their soul that was not for me to know. I stopped resisting and allowed the depression to go its course. It serves a purpose. It is a sacred hibernation, a break from the monotonous treadmill of life where deep truths can be pondered and integrated. I honored this time-out and knew it was better to happen in the safety of my nest than in a college dorm. Fear asked, *Would this ever pass?* Love knows of the temporal nature of all things and asked, *How can I support your process?*

In my quest to be only love and transcend fear, I found that it was a question of attaining a high enough perspective. If I still felt fear in a situation, the wise one needed to draw my consciousness up higher and expanded wider. When the issue of suicide was before me, the fear seemed to go out to infinity. Eventually I went higher enough to see the Creator's eye viewpoint, the eternal viewpoint.

Chris and I were both eternal beings and bound by a love greater than my human love, infinitely and eternally. We both had a quest that extended beyond human lifetimes that was magnificent and extraordinary and always ends back in the heart of the divine, from whence we came. This is the truth—the truth that set me free, the truth that allowed be to release my fear and VVs and to keep my heart open wide and love free-flowing. This sustained me for the seven months between the first and the last suicide attempt, when her life hung precariously by a thread.

I was not ignorant of the enormity of the grief I would feel if she succeeded at suicide or experienced permanent brain damage. I had lived through it with my own mother. I had survived, yet I had suffered in Sir Ego's victim consciousness. Never again. If it were to be, this time I would make my grief a sacred offering to the Creator, allowing him to feel the illusionary pain of separation through me. I would experience the most excruciating, agonizing, unbearable pain that a mother could know, expanding my grief to all mothers who had lost their children. As each person purifies his or her fear, the entire body of human fear decreases. In this way, Christ's passion consumed and transformed a vast universe of fear into an even larger universe of love.

Reflecting back on what she had said to me during those conversations about why she did took the pills, I was struck by how profound her reasoning was. She had challenged the Creator with the ultimate question, "If there is a purpose to this life, let me live. If not, let my suffering end." She had thrown herself on his mercy. Most of us are unwilling to even look at that question, the only one worth asking. Would we stake our lives on it? Were we that sure there was someone there to answer? Sir Ego wants to hide behind his shield on this issue. But the wise one does not fear it.

This was not an absolute denial of the Creator's power or an affirmation of the hopeless, pointless nature of life. This was a very legitimate question. According to Albert Camus' essay *The Myth of Sisyphus*, "There is but one truly serious philosophical problem, and that is suicide. Judging whether life is or is not worth living amounts to answering the fundamental question of philosophy."

I had asked it myself on many occasions. In fact, Chris and Nicole were my answer to that question. Love could provide the will to live that fear, and guilt could not. I could not use guilt to stop Chris's suicidal ideation.

I felt that Chris would be all right. But I also knew our bond of love was eternal and was not dependent on our bodies. I would love Chris for all of eternity. So I was able to release "me" from the equation. This would not be about my fear, my pain, or "How could you do this to me?" If I had to bear the pain of every mother who had ever lost her child, I would not have that moment of pain until it was happening. I would not dwell in that fear of the possibility of future pain. And the Creator's grace enveloped me in a shield of protection and peace.

I learned about selfless service because my children needed so much maintenance and support, and they temporarily had so little to offer in return. I needed to go to every doctor appointment, drive to counselor appointments, pick up the one food Nicole's tummy could handle at eleven o'clock, go to the psychiatric hospital and sit in silence, and advocate for my children at a school where the administrators were prone to treat them as attendance and discipline problems rather than health issues. I worked all day, served all evening, and collapsed like a zombie for sleepless nights.

I noticed that Sir Ego was having VVs of resentfulness. The wise one inquired about this and found that Sir Ego was feeling that his heroic service was unappreciated and, not only was he not getting kudos for it, he was getting dumped on. Sir Ego revealed the scorecard he had been secretly keeping just outside of my awareness. I began to study Sir Ego's need for compensation for his efforts in order to free myself of these VVs.

In return for my efforts, I got teenage attitude, eye rolls, angry outbursts, tearful panic attacks, little domestic help, doctor bills, judgement from my employer, invalidated, uncompensated, and so on and so on. Each time, Sir Ego, no longer a victim, bowed to these calls for love. I learned what my mother had taught so long ago: only I determined if they are laughing *with me* or *at me*. If I'm laughing at my own humanness, my own quirks, and my own uncoolness, then it's *with me*.

I continued to serve and do whatever was necessary, finding the love in the act of serving and forsaking expectation of result. It wasn't about me; it was about what was required of me, and I learned to comply joyfully, grateful for the opportunity to serve my daughters in this way. It glorified our love when I stopped getting *payment* for my services.

It was painfully obvious that my children couldn't possibly repay my efforts in the current circumstances. They couldn't even care for themselves, much less my wounded ego. Nor should they have to, I realized. The wise one did not see these relationships in the same barter system that Sir Ego did.

Releasing VVs, I deconstructed this barter system. It was based on fear or being invalidated and having a lack of love. In its place, the wise one's love flourished and flowed freely without attachment to a particular response. I gave because they needed my service, and I gave with a full and open heart abundantly. Then I cherished each eye roll because it underscored the importance of the love I was giving and the empty cup I was filling.

Another person might have looked at my behavior and termed it permissive. The wise one and Sir Ego had many conversations about this. In the end, it came down to fear or the absence of it. Permissive parenting results from the parent's fear of the child's rejection or noncompliance. The permissive parent gives and serves as a means to an end, to get the child to have a nicer interaction or to comply with his or her requests. A submissive person surrenders out of fear, also to manipulate the other person into a more pleasant interaction. Abandoning fear took me out of these consciousnesses. These are attachments to results, Sir Ego's scorecard. This is fear disguised as love in the codependent's mind. I learned to surrender these attachments to results and serve from a fully open heart, without fear or expectations.

In all these ways, my heart was opening, expanding, and releasing. It was more important than any material pursuit. I was modelling this to my children. Sir Ego thinks we can teach our children to serve by forcing them to do chores or volunteer work. I came to believe that my selfless service spoke louder than this into their hearts. I asked them to choose a few chores they would do each week, and I was grateful if they did them. So the reward was inner gratification. And I accepted any effort with gratitude, not judgement. Our relationship is more important than loading the dishwasher in my perfect way. Fighting with them over chores would have built resistance and increased their guilt and resistance. I would rather have one act of service, willingly given, than ten acts of coerced service.

Instead of love with a lowercase *l*, filled with insecurity, controlling tendencies, and randomly generated expectations for them, I found love with a capital *L*. I no longer saw them as achievements or possessions to enhance my own stature. My love for my children became expansive, boundless, luminous, infinite, and eternal. I saw them as goddesses of light, equals on the spiritual path, bound to me in joy for all eternity. Even in the bleak times, the highest love shone through, yielding a greater high than any alcohol-induced intoxication, and this affirmed my trajectory. Another beautiful affirmation came when Nicole gave me this tribute on Mother's Day.

Forty-Six Reasons You're the Greatest Mom

1. You always make things work.
2. You put up with my fits about school.
3. You are my biggest supporter.
4. You see the best in me.
5. You do everything I ask, no matter how inconvenient.
6. You have complete faith in me.
7. You trust me implicitly.
8. You guide my decisions but ultimately let me decide.
9. You are determined to help me even when I won't help myself.
10. You know and accept all my idiosyncrasies.
11. You are totally hilarious.
12. You expose me to new places and things.
13. You are a phenomenal cook.
14. You taught me how to be a good person.
15. You give me everything I want and need.
16. You treat me with complete respect.
17. You like all of the shows I watch.
18. You rarely get mad at me, even when I really deserve it.
19. You attend my games, school events, and so forth.
20. You are impressed by everything I do.
21. You give me the praise I need.
22. You treat Chris and me equally.
23. You are always fair.
24. You fight for me.
25. You are my number-one fan.
26. You always put me before yourself.
27. You help me achieve my goals.
28. You encourage me constantly.
29. You never criticize me.
30. You laugh at all my jokes, even if they aren't funny.
31. You have shown me that everything will be all right in the end.
32. You always assist me, even when I act stubborn.
33. You give the best gifts.
34. You are the strongest person I know.
35. You let me work things out for myself.
36. You have intellectual conversations with me
37. You inspire me.
38. You understand me.
39. You are always there for me.
40. You remind me to just relax sometimes.
41. You never give up on me.
42. You always know exactly what to do.
43. You tolerate my terrible attitude when I am sick.
44. You have stuck with me through all my issues.
45. You and I have countless inside jokes.
46. You love me unconditionally.

Nicole threw this at me and ran out of the room so she would be spared my tears. Was this description really me? It wasn't who I used to be. No, this accolade was not for Sir Ego. It was for the Creator flowing through the wise one and upon my daughter. This is how our Creator loves us. How does that compare to controlling, legislating, directing, manipulating, nagging, and fretting about your teen?

There couldn't have been anything more exquisite. Equally exquisite was the author. These were profound insights and awareness from a teenager in the midst of an emotional breakdown. When this passed, as all things must, she was going to be an emotional powerhouse. Whatever she was learning in this hibernation was an essential step to her growth and development. I saluted her.

Take a moment to reread this list. This is what the Creator is offering each of us throughout all eternity. No matter how far we run or fall or how long we wait to look upon the divine, the Creator waits for us. Offer this like a prayer and give thanks.

17

Breaking Up the Band

November 30 was a beehive of activity at our house. College applications were due, and both of my daughters were submitting multiple online applications. I knew Nicole was preparing for this and had been working on essays for some time. However, I hadn't seen much interest from Chris. It was gratifying, rewarding, and a bit shocking to see them burst into high gear. It seemed impossible to believe that either of them would be able to move away to college in ten months, yet my intuition told me they would. It was both miraculous and terrifying.

In fact, as time went on, I *knew* that they were going to. Yet I didn't know how we would get to a place where they were strong enough to live on their own. I noticed that I was able to stay strong in faith and love. Anxiety and worry were no longer a part of me. It felt weird—in a good way.

Things were moving, but in fits and starts. Chris was enrolled in a senior-year work study class where she spent fifteen hours per week at the local hospital shadowing nurses, and this gave her inspiration and motivation. Sometimes it was the only thing she would do during the week and had dropped most of her other classes. It was powerful to see this pursuit pulling her out of the darkness. The nurses loved her, and she was fascinated by the things she learned and experienced. She started talking about a career in nursing. Her personal experiences helped her to develop both courage and compassion, the perfect Tao. A nurse without courage can't stay centered in an emergency. A nurse without compassion has a poor bedside manner. She had developed both.

Nicole returned to school and was making it work, although I knew her symptoms still made it a challenge. She was nocturnal, and so her waking and sleeping hours were very irregular. But she was determined to succeed and go on to college. She had been steadfastly working on college applications, parlaying her junior-year sabbatical into an inspiring essay.

By spring, acceptance letters started to flow in. Both girls were accepted to their top-choice schools, among others. Overnight, they transformed into rocket ships preparing to launch. As if nothing had ever happened, they moved into warp speed, graduating with honors. I couldn't believe my eyes. It was an affirmation of my faith. Evidence to the contrary, I had known all along they would be fine in the end, and they were. They were more than fine. They were soon to be passionate, inspired college freshmen.

Although no one can say with certainty, my belief is that this miracle is the result of the healing power of unconditional love. Healing was happening in that cocoon; my role was to support it, to create a safe place for it, and to resist interfering with it, something about not making the monkeys extinct. Being loved when you are at your worst is a powerful experience, and I imagine it allowed them to go deep into their pain to release it. Power, confidence, and maturity were gained.

Chris completed an emergency medical technician program during the summer and was soon certified. She obtained a part-time job as an EMT and would be able to work during summer, school breaks, and weekends. She went from being the emergency room patient to being the emergency technician. She went from being the psych hospital patient to transporting patients to psych hospitals. She had great emotional and psychological strength; that was what had been happening during that hibernation. The butterfly emerged from the cocoon. I was astounded, inspired, grateful, and euphoric.

To pursue her lifelong interest in surgery, Nicole enrolled in a summer surgery program, filled with cadavers, blood, and scalpels, at UCLA prior to her matriculation in the fall. With great anticipation, she prepared to move into an apartment in July, where she would live throughout her freshman year. Awestruck, I watched her dark and gloomy path yield to a flower-lined yellow brick road. She was off to become the wizard.

As they flourished, the toll the past two years had taken on me began to be revealed. I had run out of time-off options at work, and they graciously offered me a six-month severance package. Now there were times that I needed Don to pay the children's car loan or insurance payments.

Still, before each phone call I made, asking for financial assistance, I spent time purifying my energy, opening my heart to him, humbling my pride, and achieving equanimity. If he didn't pay the car payment or car insurance, he could tell the kids why they couldn't drive and face the holy-hell consequences. I accepted that possible outcome and had no intention to persuade him to do anything. I was merely making a request. He had all the power to agree or not—no judgement. My nonattachment to the result of the conversation changed the dynamic entirely. I had learned that it only takes one party to stop a power struggle.

Each call followed the same general agenda. I would open with a sincere statement of appreciation for all he had done to help the children when I was unable to and an affirmation of our mutual interest in their success and well-being. This was difficult for Sir Ego to say, which ensured that he was surrendered to the wise one from the start of the conversation.

That was usually followed by his verbal assault on me about my failings and weaknesses, to which I reiterated my remorse and regret. "I know. I'm sorry. I screwed up. I'm glad you're there to make sure the kids have what they need. Now, about the car payment. It's due on Thursday. Would you like to pay by cash, check, or charge?" In my defenseless state, he would stop attacking and make reasonable arrangements. This was infinitely more effective than anything that had ever happened during our marriage.

I started a consulting project for another nonprofit, and it turned into a permanent position, but it was an hour and a half from our house, so I had to move. It was challenging to find a rental property that allowed a dog and two cats, so I settled on a house that would accept the cats. Sunny would have to go to Dad's. But Don and Barb had gotten another dog in the meantime, and they were resistant to taking Sunny. Like it or not, Sunny showed up on Don's doorstep on August 15 when I moved to my new house. By then, Nicole was in her new apartment in LA. Chris moved to Chico on August 20. And they all lived happily ever after.

Not.

While I had come to accept the Creator's will for *my* life, I was happy, relieved, and grateful that my children appeared to be set up for success in worldly ways. The eighteen-year marathon was over, and we had made it to the finish line—or so I thought naïvely.

The first rumblings of the next storm started after Nicole's summer program ended. She was very lonely and homesick in LA. We had hoped she would make friends when school started, but she did not. We developed a nightly FaceTime ritual. She would call me to utter every fear, pain, frustration, and despair that consumed her. Absolved of fix-it thinking, I allowed her to vent her energy and witnessed her pain, holding my center. I was strong enough to stay centered, but not untouched by her pain. It was heartbreaking. Unattached to her remaining at LA, I allowed her to mentally explore options. "It's all about the right fit. If it isn't right, try something else."

Chris was blossoming at college. She loved school, enjoying her apartment-like dorm and five roommates. She came home one weekend, and we sat on the deck of my new home, enjoying the sunshine and talking.

Just before it was time for her to leave, she said, "I have an appointment in two weeks with a doctor in San Francisco to begin hormone replacement therapy."

Faster than the speed of light, my thoughts flashed on the screen of my mind. I thought that meant Chris was changing her gender, but I wasn't even sure. I knew absolutely nothing about this. The wise one observed Sir Ego frantically deliberating. *Who would pay? Was this a good idea? How had I not seen this coming? This could mean a challenging life.*

Well, I hadn't been asked my opinion, and this train was clearly leaving the station. I would either be on it or left standing on the platform. I was getting on board. Whatever life challenges this brought to **HIM** were life lessons, not something I could control. There was no resistance.

"That's going to be an interesting journey," the wise one said in a calm, accepting, humorous, light tone with a gentle, loving smile.

I gave not an ounce of resistance. There was perfect peace and acceptance. After suicide attempts, this was a walk in the park. I didn't even have the urge to pry because I had no need to control this. His relief was palpable, and the bond of love strengthened between our hearts. There was a shared knowing that we would walk this path together wherever it led. Later, I would look back on this moment and know that a mother's love and acceptance give one courage and stability to become whatever species of blossom is planted in one's heart.

He invited me to attend the doctor's appointment. The doctor, in the Castro district of course, specialized in gender reassignment and seemed compassionate, competent, and confident. I winced when he mentioned that the hormone therapy would almost certainly make Chris sterile.

I whispered, "No kids? Are you okay with that?"

"I don't want to pass on these faulty genes anyway," he replied.

"Do you think your [five female] roommates will be okay with this?" I wondered out loud.

"Oh yes." He brightened up. "I'm a rainbow potato."

I didn't really know what this meant, but it was clear that his roommates were more than okay with this. I loved his contagious enthusiasm. My heart burst open seeing how accepting young people are and how much his roommates supported him. An invisible tear of joy fell down my face as I saw a higher truth about who he was and how boldly he was willing to pursue his truth.

I confided my concerns about Chris's emotional stability to the doctor privately outside the examination room. He assured me that there would be sufficient psychological counseling and that cutting and suicide attempts were common precursors to realization about one's gender-identity matter. He said the medical procedure would transpire at a safe pace. I took comfort that it would give us time to process this and ensure he was psychologically prepared for what he was going to face.

But he moved forward full speed ahead. He was filled with inspiration. He researched the doctors and procedures and fought the insurance battles, with the efficiency and competence that his EMT training afforded him. Normally there is a compulsory twelve months of counseling before any actions can be taken. However, Chris' DBT counselor was happy and willing to sign off on his emotional readiness and stability. Apparently, outside of my purview, they had delved deeply into this topic. Although it was a surprise to me, he was working through this for a long time.

Within eighteen months, Christine was re-christened as Christopher legally, completely transformed and even more powerful and secure in himself. Soon he was the lead teaching assistant in his anatomy studies, performing cadaver dissections in lab and acting as a peer mentor. What an inspiration. What courage. I salute him.

Releasing and purifying resistance had become a habit for me, and I flowed through this with minimal angst. I had to break habits of gender language, which was awkward at first. But I committed to it as soon as Nicole explained to me the proper etiquette and how important it was. I was delighted to see that she was his greatest supporter and partner in gay pride activities.

On occasion, I wondered if I needed to grieve a loss of my expectations for my child. But it never came. It would be understandable for Sir Ego who had expectations for his children. However, the wise one did not see any change in the sexless soul that I loved so dearly, and I was free to celebrate this next step on his quest without hesitation.

Thankfully, no one in our immediate family resisted it. And most of his classmates and friends celebrate this kind of diversity. In California, this generation is open and receptive to all expressions of gender and sexual identity. Prejudice of all kinds is just another lance in Sir Ego's arsenal. It is a product of his ignorance about the divine brotherhood he shares with all his fellow knights. This is a hopeful sign that younger generations are more accepting and have higher perspectives.

LGBT, the movement of lesbian, gay, bisexual, and transgender identities, is a result of the masculine and feminine energies of humanity coming into greater harmony and balance. The old energy was polarized into strong masculine and strong feminine opposites with little in between. Now there is a rainbow of variations in between that encompass the best aspects of both masculine and feminine natures. In this way, I see Chris as beacon of this emerging reality. I believe his ability to tap into both the yin and the yang, depending on the situation, will help him to live from a deep and powerful position. This will certainly empower him in his nursing career. He graduates in a few months with a major in women and gender studies before heading off to nursing school. He's the quintessential renaissance man.

There wasn't even a moment after that initial conversation that I felt any negative feeling, not once. During the challenging times, I had come to see his inner light, looking beyond his body to his divine perfection. I almost hadn't noticed it when his wardrobe had become more and more masculine in the prior two years. I pray for his journey to be safe and smooth, but I know there will be difficulties, his karmic lessons, nothing more.

Now I could understand the unspoken pain of those silent tears. I could understand how wrong and broken he had felt inside. And I realized that I never could have had the right words or fix-it ideas in the past because I didn't understand the struggle he was facing at all. I also understood that my unconditional love showed him that I would love him no matter what. Not judging his dark moods and suicidal tendencies showed him that even the most terrifying aspect of his inner world were not judged, were not eternal damnation, and were not him.

Please pray with me that he will always be accepted and escape persecution for his brave adventure. I had experienced persecution as the alcoholic mother doomed to supervised visits, and I had to face that it was not about me. Persecution comes from the closed heart of the persecutor and reflects his consciousness. It says nothing of the target, the persecuted. Purifying my own heart expunged this demon of shame and saturated my consciousness with love. Then this is the energy I shared with my children and my persecutors.

On another occasion when Chris came to visit, we were out taking a walk and having a great conversation. He was talking about a discussion is his *Freshman Year Experience* class where the topic was "How do know who you are?"

He chuckled as he recalled his classmates' answers related to hobbies and travel experiences. Boldly, he said "You find out who you are when you go through the dark place."

He had spoken a deep and great truth and the class was silenced until the professor restored a light mood, saying "This, coming from the person who has *Outrageously Happy* tattooed on his forearm!" This beautiful vignette describes his profound transformation. He boldly went to the darkest places, discovered truths about himself and the world and chooses to be outrageously happy. I have great admiration for him.

We were interrupted when he got a call from his dad. Sunny and the other dog had gotten into a fight, and Barb was threatening to call the pound to pick Sunny up right away.

I couldn't blame her. You can't have two pit bull puppies fighting when you have a five-year-old child in the house. Bringing some calm to this storm, I agreed to pick Sunny up and take her to my house until we could find a better solution. I had hoped to return her after a few day cooldown period, but Don and Barb refused to take Sunny back under any circumstances.

My lease prohibited dogs, and it had some teeth in it, a three-day eviction clause for violation of lease terms. As I pondered this problem for several weeks, I channeled Anne Frank, fearful that at any moment my landlord would appear with a lightning bolt that ejected me from the universe. Whoa. This VV was overwhelming. It is a primal fear of Sir Ego. He doesn't trust the Creator to provide security for him, thus his many false idols in the material world.

My landlord must have realized I had the dog there. He sent me a letter saying that he would be doing a standard maintenance walk-through of the house sometime in the upcoming week during work hours. I had to make this dog disappear immediately. It seemed hopeless. I couldn't even find a short-term place for a pit bull, much less a new rental house.

As I received rejections from kennels, friends, and Don, my fear neared breaking point. Yet I spent the entire day affirming that I had faith in the Creator to solve this problem, to provide for my material needs, and I would not succumb to the fear but allow it to release. My faith had grown and solidified during the dark trials of the past. I was sure the Creator had a solution, and it would become apparent once I had purified the fear.

The next day, I shuffled Sunny around to a friend's house and then to a kennel. A friend at work mentioned a house in her neighborhood that was for rent. I immediately went to see it and inquired about their pet policy. He was open to negotiation and even agreed to put in a dog door and dog run. I was ready to move in a week and gave my notice to my landlord. It was an answered prayer in a swift and perfect way. The new house was even nicer and had a third bedroom so my son and daughter would not have to share a room. Perfect. I was marching in tune with the script of creation.

By Thanksgiving, Nicole had decided that she would complete the term and wouldn't return to UCLA next semester after Christmas. A few days after she returned to LA from Thanksgiving break, I was having lunch with a friend who was an admissions counselor at a college. I realized that November 30 was once again upon us.

If Nicole were going to submit a transfer application, it would need to be done in thirty-six hours. Again, the wise one's timing to alert my intuition was uncanny. Nicole was overwhelmed when I reminded her of the deadline but succeeded in dusting off the old application and submitting it to one university, UCSF. She had been accepted there the previous year, which predicted success for a transfer. I was proud that she had had the strength to overcome her failure and make a good decision for herself.

At Christmas, Nicole moved into my newer-new house with me. Although she was in a place of low energy and self-esteem, she didn't fall into a deep depression ... until she received notice that she had been waitlisted at UCSF. It seemed hard to believe that she would get another curve ball, yet here it was. I surrendered all my fear and didn't even start offering ideas. Nicole was adamant that she would not go to a junior college and try again to transfer for junior year. She looked like she was at risk for a downward spiral, but I had faith.

Within a week or so, she did surrender. She got a job at Target and conceded to the junior college plan. Within days, her acceptance letter arrived. I have come to believe that when we are tested by the possibility of a difficult impending challenge, if we surrender our fear and purify our energy around this difficulty, we get the lesson and do not have to face the actual challenge in our material circumstances. The material circumstances are magnetized to us when we hold onto the fear and need to learn the lesson in a more visceral way, like me landing in a jail cell.

She was getting a late start, so registering for classes and obtaining an apartment caused her some consternation. I held steady, affirming that the perfection of the situation would be revealed, and it was. She loved UCSF.

I learned that it never ends with children. They will always have bumps and bends in the road. Both of them will graduate from college with honors this year and plan to go on to pursue careers in medicine. What an accomplishment given where they were! Even though they will sometimes have struggles, I know they have the power to overcome them. I have come to an entirely new place of understanding and acceptance about my role in their lives. I am not the fixer. I am the lover. I have faith in my children and their ability to manage the challenges in their lives. I am the supporter. I am the stability when the ground shifts. I have grown into this role by consistently choosing love and transcending fear.

Centered in the wise one, I am not at the mercy of the winds of fortune in their lives. I achieved the state of caring more about their spiritual, emotional, and psychological development than their egos' comfort. Knowing they will encounter karmic tests, I am there to support them in their highest eternal quest, showing them their divinity and denying the delusions of Sir Ego. I can be okay while they have a karmic test, enduring watching their pain, when I know it's for their long-term growth and expansion. I have to choose growth over comfort for them as well as myself. That's how the Creator parents us.

18

A Higher Octave

By now, I could see that each lesson I learned prepared me for the next lesson. Each VV, each stepping stone was building on the one before. With my children, I had learned some powerful truths about divine and unconditional love. It naturally blossomed into an investigation into my other significant relationships and an ability to see them in a new light of understanding and eternal truth, the higher octave of love. My next lesson was to apply what I had learned to my relationship with my own parents.

There was a woman, Lynn, in my yoga fellowship who was terminally ill. Yogis approach this with a different philosophy than in most worldly thinking. Yogis embrace the cycle of reincarnation and see peace in the next step in their evolution. It is very sacred to spend time with someone on the cusp of transition, facing it with great introspection and without fear. Although I didn't personally know Lynn, I understood and appreciated the process I was observing in which community members cared for her spiritual and physical needs. I could feel the sacred bond that was honored and the lack of resistance or fear.

I reflected back on my mother's passing and how different it would have been if I had had this much understanding. Driving to work one Friday, I had the realization that time isn't real. I could go back and relive that period with my current understanding. Tearfully, I made a U-turn and returned home for a three-day seclusion to transmute that pain and fear into love and understanding.

I dredged up the old VVs of abandonment and despair and saw that they had resulted from my misunderstanding of bodies, death, souls, and self-realization. I talked to my mom the entire weekend and explained how I now understood that it had been her time to go. It must have been so difficult for her to see the pain and fear in my eyes. I told her that I wished to release the part of me that had held her locked in my pain and see both of us fly freely toward our ultimate reunification with each other. I cried, ached, loved, and changed. While none of the facts changed, my energy around them changed into peaceful acceptance, unconditional love, and confident anticipation of our future meeting.

Feeling the wise one's presence on a Palm Sunday weekend, I continued in that peace throughout Easter week, culminating in a spiritual resurrection for me on Easter. I was whole again. I no longer had the gaping hole in my heart. For thirty years, I had paid tribute to that grand canyon, forsaking all the beautiful memories of my mother. All that was finished.

I spoke to her about how I had grown to become so much like her and how my parenting was a result of hers. I thanked her for protecting the children when I could not and acknowledged that she was very much a part of their lives, even if they didn't know it. I spoke of how hard it must have been to see me flounder like I did and how it was good that she had had the Creator's perspective while she was watching that horror show. I could feel her presence, love, and gladness at seeing how much we all had grown from our troubles.

In Sir Ego's script, my relationship with my mom was special because she provided the nurturing of my body, mind, emotions, and spirit throughout my childhood. In her soulful eyes, I saw my beauty and perfection reflected, which I had not yet claimed as my own. In her lifeless eyes, I saw the death of my concept of being lovable. Grieving for this loss blinded me to the truth this love embodied.

When I surrendered this relationship to the wise one and prayed for a *holy relationship*, I had no idea how or when the transformation would occur. When the time was right, it did, thirty years later. The wise one showed me that my mother's death did not signify the death of anything eternal, such as my lovability or our bond. As the seasons change, so the nature of our relationships change, ebbing and flowing, coming and going.

Our shining moments basking in the warmth of these loving relationships are not diminished by the fewness of those moments. This love had been lost to me all these years because I was grieving an illusion and refusing to look at the truth. In reliving my mother's death, I discovered that it was not her death, but my misunderstanding of love that caused my pain.

When I looked at the truth of our eternal love bond, the pain was liberated, and the good memories were freed. I could now cherish the revelations of how my motherhood was modeled after hers and affirm the joy that I was becoming more like her every day. Embracing the knowledge that she watched over my children and me, I realized that we had shared this journey longer than her body walked this earth and that her comfort was never absent.

This revealed the eternal nature of love, the Creator, and who I am. It could not be otherwise. It could not be that a love so strong could be extinguished by an energy transfer from form to spirit. The part of my heart that had been so long closed and dormant hopefully opened and allowed the anguish to be released.

The love continued, but I had looked away because I could not bear the sight of my perceived abandonment. While I had lost an affirmation of my lovability and worth, those qualities were beyond uncertainty. Confronting the pain of the abandonment showed me there was a reunification beyond it and that true love must lie there in the celebratory reunion, not in the temporary parting. While my emotional body cannot yet experience the blissful reunion, I have faith in the inevitability of it. A quality of love must be ever existing, and I surrendered my delusion that it is temporal.

I understood that this was a necessary step before I could open my heart to love again, to be vulnerable again. I didn't know that this was also a foretaste of what was to come in my relationship with my father.

Sometime later, I went to a workshop for intuitives. I had developed my intuitive abilities to hear guidance from the wise one, and I was seeking expansion in that direction. In the afternoon, we were instructed to pair up and take turns channeling a deceased relative for our partner. As we did not know our partners, we were to spend a few minutes offering details about our deceased relatives to help our partners tune in to their energy. I planned to tell my partner about my mother.

Before I could utter a word, my partner said, "Your dad is here."

My VVs went to red-alert status, but I didn't resist. Opening my heart a little, I said, "Oh."

"He wants to patch things up with you. He says that he let your mom do all the parenting and he could have been more attentive. He is offering a bouquet of flowers."

That made sense. In life, my father's gardens had been dearer to him than I was. He didn't permit me to cut them for flower arrangements. I accepted the peace offering. I don't recall much else about the conversation as I didn't perceive its significance.

Shortly thereafter, the wise spoke through my intuition, *It is time to let this thing with your dad go.*

I thought, *Sure, that's a good idea. I don't know how to do that, but I'm sure you are going to show me.*

Pondering this on the way to work, I thought about how we have expectations that our parents will be perfect and give us exactly what we need. But the Creator is the only parent who can provide perfection. Our earthly parents are just fellow travelers on the journey of self-realization: imperfect in their humanity and perfect in their divinity. I surely learned this lesson in my own role as a parent. Sir Ego was quite flawed and misguided.

I reflected on what I had learned in my own parenting about surrendering the *special relationship* for a *holy relationship* that puts the relationship in the service of the wise one for the highest good of all in place of Sir Ego's selfish service. I realized my disappointment with my father resulted from my "special needs" that he had been unable to meet. I could feel my resentment fading away.

I had a vision that ego love was the attempt to build a bridge between two bodies, throwing favors, compliments, and gifts across the river to each other, expecting something in return. When we don't get what we want in return, our feelings toward that person sour. If that was ego love, then what did real love look like?

I had learned about unconditional love in my relationship with my children. I had learned about forgiveness in my relationship with Don. It was obvious how these could be extended to my dad. I allowed my "dad VV" to start to open. I had swept it under the rug, and it had been dormant for a long time, but no more. The VV was being poked because it was ready to be released.

I arrived at work and still had this energy swirling around. I mentioned this to my intuitive healer friend, Mary. I remembered that another intuitive had told me years ago that I had experienced a significant trauma when I was about three years old. It had stayed with me and affected me still. Although I did not know what it was, my intuition told me that it was my dad's temper scaring me in a profound way. Maybe this was the piece of the puzzle that needed to be exposed to get to the next step in this healing process. Mary said the "egg treatment," whatever that was, would help. I should come over that evening so we could heal and release this.

When I arrived, we started with the egg treatment. It was intended to clear out some of that energy, and then we were going to move on to talking to Yogananda about my dad. The egg treatment consisted of three steps. In the first step, I was given seven red chili peppers to hold and instructed to put all my negative energy and fear into them. I contemplated how I had had this energy before I came into this lifetime. I had chosen my dad to stimulate and cultivate this perpetrator-victim energy.

Because I hadn't released it, I had attracted my ex-husband to trigger it some more. Then I had attracted an entire army of custody governors to trigger it some more. I was ready to release this energy so I wouldn't attract any more perpetrators! They weren't to blame; they were messengers telling me that I needed to relinquish this victim energy. I thanked them for their service, and my friend took the red chilis out of my sight and disposed of them forever.

Next, I was handed seven cloves and instructed to do the same thing. This time I thought about how I had incorporated these oppressors into my own consciousness so they stayed with me always. I was definitely ready to be rid of them. So I put all that energy into the cloves, and they too were taken out of my sight and disposed of.

Finally, a whole raw egg was swept over my aura to remove the VV energy that had been loosened in the previous steps. Finally, the egg was also disposed of. In my purified state, we began the conversation with Yogananda.

Through Mary, Yoganada asked, "Do you want to know exactly what happened when you were three years old? We can proceed either way, with or without your exact knowledge of the event."

Dryly, I said, "No, I don't care what happened. I just wish to be free of it. And I wish for my father and I to go on our own ways in light and love, released from our past."

Although my dad had been an injustice collector, reciting everyone's rap sheet from memory, I had no wish to bring charges involving this mysterious crime. I didn't want to give it more energy or bring it before Sir Ego to judge again.

Mary revealed that both my dad and Yogananda were present and that Yogananda was elbowing my dad to encourage him to speak. I imagined my atheist father standing next to this Indian teacher, who was prodding him affectionately. My father reiterated several of the things that my partner at the workshop had previously conveyed.

He added, "I have been advised to consider our relationship and the unresolved nature of it. I did not participate in the way that I should have in your parenting."

I thought, *Interesting. I wonder what that means.*

He went on, "I will be going through the port in eighteen days to six weeks."

Mary interpreted this to mean that he was being reincarnated. Wow. We were meeting at a moment when he was contemplating his upcoming incarnation and choosing his life lessons. Advised? I guessed you get advisors to help with that sort of thing. That was good to know. I realized the sacred nature of this meeting, although I was too stunned to comprehend my role in it.

I said, "I understand now how difficult parenting is. It must have been really difficult for you to have so many children and so little inclination. Perhaps your life had fallen short of your hopes because of the sacrifices you made for our family. I have made devastating parenting mistakes of my own. I understand how overwhelming and challenging it is." My heart was as open as I could pry it.

Mary described and pantomimed the interaction she was observing in her mind's eye. Yogananda encouraged my dad to continue, despite some resistance. I realized that he was encouraging my dad to apologize. I thought, *I don't need an apology.*

I reflected briefly on how insignificant that would have been in my forgiveness process with Don, even if Don had given one. Then I realize that the apology was for my dad, not for me. Yogananda was encouraging him to have a change of heart for his own benefit, not mine.

Mary motioned that my dad was in tears, as I was.

"I am sorry that I couldn't be the dad you needed me to be," Dad said. "I have watched how you have learned about love and forgiveness in your life and how wonderful that has been for you and your family."

I thought, *Oh my God, he has been watching?* The *I'm-going-to-get-in-trouble* VV was opened and released in almost the same second.

He suggested that he would search for the Creator in this upcoming lifetime because of what he had seen that was beautiful in my journey. He wanted that. And he would come find me.

At that moment, I saw a river with him on the other side. I saw our hearts reach out across the river and explode in love, merging with each other. We joined hands and jumped together, flowing merrily, merrily, merrily down the stream. Life is but a dream. Love filled the room. In that holy instant, the pain of the past was vaporized into a firework's display of love and joy. Mary was visibly moved by this joyful and somewhat unexpected turn of events.

My father asked for the egg treatment. My friend was hesitant to give a treatment to a disembodied spirit.

Yogananda said, "Give him the egg." So my friend got another egg and traced my father's astral aura, purifying seeds of karma. It was finished.

Afterwards Mary and I were both overwhelmed and overjoyed by what had just happened. I realized that I was free from the critical, punitive energy that had plagued my life. Nothing about the past facts had changed, but everything about my energy around them had changed. The pent-up energy of my power struggle with my dad was released. The ominous threat of punishment for some unknowable crime vanished. There was no more bone to pick with me.

But much more had happened. My father's future incarnation had been affected. His entire cosmic journey had been accelerated at the same time as mine. I had had just enough willingness to meet him in this place, without judgment, for my own healing. He had had just enough willingness to meet me in this place, without judgment, for his own benefit. My long-forgotten prayer for a *holy relationship* had invited Yogananda to be there to mediate this miracle. It had been the miracle of which *ACIM* speaks in all its splendor and exemplary testimony. All parties had been healed and benefited in the highest way. It was easy to see how this healing could have domino effects in his next lifetime, his next children's generation, and so forth. It was also easy to see that its release would have positive effects on my journey and my family's.

This was the opposite of making the monkeys extinct. This was sending a flow of unconditional love and higher consciousness in all directions, reverberating for eternity. Everything changed for me. I dug out my pictures of my father and prayed for him, talked to him, and joked with him. My heart overflowed with love and joy. Not only had I not expected that to happen, Sir Ego neither wanted it nor believed it could happen. The power of this sent shock waves through my understanding of what was possible, expanding my consciousness beyond the limits I had submitted to for so long.

For the first time, I truly celebrated with my father on Father's Day and thanked him for the eternal gift we now shared. And I wished him "happy birthday" and "see you soon." It was lovely to see love fill the void that had been in my heart for so long. About a year later, my dad came to me in a dream. Upon seeing him, I instinctively fell to my knees, acknowledging this beautiful divine being. I ran to hug him and my heart was filled with love. I was overjoyed. I awoke and was very grateful to have our hearts still joined in this *holy relationship*.

My childhood response to my father's abuse of his power had become habitual in my adult life and career. I bowed to authority figures as if their knight had donned the royal crown. Now I noticed a change in my relationship with authority and power. As I had learned to channel the Creator's forgiveness and unconditional love, now I learned to channel his power and authority. I came to recognize when someone was keen for a test of wills and I would not engage in the battle of Sir Ego versus Sir Ego.

Tuning into the wise one, I honored my sparring partner and elevated our interaction into a divine communion where the highest results would be found. Truth stands on its own two feet. It does not need Sir Ego to push it upon anyone. Freely, I offered the wise one's love and messages to each that I met and understood that not all would be receptive.

In the special relationship, my dad had the role to protect, empower, and challenge me to become strong and capable. However, he was not suited for this role and dwelled in his own quest failings. These he projected onto me, and I, in a spongelike innocence, absorbed them. I know this resulted from his own parents' failures to empower him. It was never about me. It reveals the intergenerational nature of these lessons. Each generation has the power to transcend the weaknesses and begin a new inheritance for their descendants. This is a power of the exalted quest to extend beyond our own lifetimes.

Again, it was many years before I saw this relationship transformed into an exalted relationship. The wise one is patient and faithful, attuned to signal the appointed time when we are receptive to healing. Then he arranges the circumstances.

My understanding began with the idea that I had expectations of my father that were impossible for him to fulfill. Our parents are only fellow travelers on the quest. They are not perfectly in tune with the wise one. Although my father failed to meet my expectations, it was not an indicator of his (lack of) love, but of his immaturity. He had lessons of his own to learn.

As he and I came to a new understanding of our relationship, a deeper truth was revealed. Again, the pain of the past was washed away in an instant when this revelation inspired our hearts to join in mutual acceptance of our divine nature untouched by our human failings. Everything changed. I reclaimed the power that I had relinquished to the demands of his ego's script for me. And I understood that love cannot be won in a power struggle. It is won by surrendering Sir Ego's expectations and *allowing* this powerful river to come coursing through our lives and beyond the grave.

My forgiveness of my dad would not have been possible if I had not had a practice run with Don. In my special relationship with Don, I sought affirmation, companionship, security, family, material possessions, fascinations, and, of course, love and respect. I was entirely deluded that these could be found in that relationship. The signs were there, but my blind desire and ambition did not look upon them. Over time, each of these delusions exploded into a devastating realization that this relationship was stealing these things from me. The manipulations of my guilt and fear exacerbated the losses, adding loss of my sense of well-being, personal power, and connection to the wise one.

My romantic notions of marriage, committed love, and honor in a mutually beneficent bond were also shattered in favor of a mutually manipulative, self-serving folie à deux. In courtship, Don and I read each other's scripts and auditioned for the roles of savior, setting up expectations that were doomed to fail. We had committed to these ultimately divergent and incompatible ego scripts rather than to love, so it was no surprise that we were disappointed and disillusioned.

Surely love could not be fooled and foolish in this way. It could not require submission and repudiation. Love could not be earned, bartered, or stolen. It must be given freely, without expectation, resentment, condition, and betrayal. This was fear disguised as love: fear of loneliness, fear of emptiness, fear of unworthiness, and fear of isolation. A quality of love must be compassion, charity, and benevolence. Thee aspects were uncovered as VVs released.

Upon surrendering this relationship to the service of the wise one, profoundly beautiful things sprouted. They were tiny at first and eventually bloomed into a family-wide healing. Again, this would affect generations to come. Once more, I understood that Don's cruelty to me started with cruelty to himself. His role in my quest was to show me where not to go, and he surpassed all expectations. Relieving him of his duty as persecutor and seeing his eternal innocence literally allowed me to regain my innocence in light of my crimes and misdemeanors.

The gift of true love was the awareness of our mutual innocence and eternal divinity. While I recognize my freedom and he does not yet, I know his freedom is already secured for him and awaits his acceptance. Love is grace and mercy, and we receive it to the extent we give it.

My special relationship with firefighter Nick was a pleasurable, hedonic vacation from the excruciating pain. However, it ended in even more anguishing torture. I was so openhearted with him, and the love flowed so freely. My cup runneth over. It was a taste of the eternal love and bliss that lies within each of us. My error was ascribing the source of this ecstasy to him instead of its true and eternal source. I studied this heartbreak for years trying to uncover the diamond it possessed. Finally I realized that it was a taste of my true nature, love, and bliss. It was a sneak preview of the true grail so I might have faith that it existed. But first I had to acknowledge that it was within me and not to be found in an external person or thing.

In service to the wise one, my relationship with Nick showed me that this love lies within me. It awaits my willingness to be vulnerable and to open my heart. I must courageously return to this exposed meeting place to find the true beloved, trusting I will not be rejected again. I must confront the truth that I first rejected the Creator and he has never rejected me. He stands ready to fill my hollow heart the moment I yield and grant admittance.

In the special relationship with my children, I sought exaltation through them. Looking into my child's eyes, I could see the eternal and divine that I was seeking. Again, I confused it with their eyes, and when the teenage eye rolls appeared, I realized that I had misunderstood. Parenting young children, we are rewarded with those loving eyes when we nurture, protect, guide, esteem, and honor them. We become addicted to this approval and seek to make their lives perfect so they will look at us this way always. If we do our job well, our children will be loved, successful, healthy, financially secure, college educated, and relationally balanced. In their happily ever after, they will honor us for this perfect life, according to Walt Disney.

The wise one showed me the fear that this engendered: the fear I would fail in my parenting quest and be denied the adoration of my children. Offering this relationship to the wise one redefined the purpose of parenting for me and exposed the truth and nature of unconditional love and selfless service. It couldn't have been more opposite, more unnatural to my ego, and more contrary to my prior understanding. It also couldn't have been more powerful, right, beneficent, respectful, effective, or transformative. My narcissist parenting paradigm exploded into a wave of love that washed over all of us. It purified, sanctified, and healed the unseen wounds.

I learned that love did not come from me, but through me. The wise one could call it down to earth and through my heart. My role was the willingness to call it down and allow my heart to open, despite the pain of breaking through its crusty casing of pride, hurt, and fear. I learned to wield the mighty sword of truth and love in preference to Sir Ego's double-edged weapons of attack and defense. The results stunned my sleepy eyes and awakened a whole new way of being.

Watching Christine blossom into Christopher showed me that love transcends a body and an identity. In a gentle wave, my love flowed through the transformation like the rapids of a river, increasing with admiration and esteem for his courageous and authentic declaration of his essence and his truth. A quality of love is unconditional acceptance of the beloved in all their humanness, evolution, and fragility.

The natural process of aging also revealed important insights about the nature of love. I began to feel resentment and judgement as my body aged and my youthful vigor and fitness faded. I struggled with the knowledge that this was a downhill slide. Inevitably I would lose the battle. I could not go back to my bikini body that could rock a little black dress. I had to face the fact that I was attached to that youthful, vibrant picture frame. Lots of VVs there.

Turning to the *ACIM* for answers, I learned that the body is also a *special relationship* of Sir Ego's, and it can be offered up as a *holy relationship* to transform the illusion. As Sir Ego's home, the body is never good enough to match his script. Much of Sir Ego's efforts are focused on the body's comfort, attractiveness, and pleasures. As the symbol of our separation from the Creator and each other, we adorn the picture frame, use the body to compete with our fellow knights, and fail to look upon the holy altar within. The wise one is disembodied and does not struggle with this, and I wanted to attain his perspective.

The Creator's purpose for the body is different from Sir Ego's and will lead to a *holy relationship* with the body. The higher purpose of the body is to be a communication device for divine love and service. The body is a delivery vehicle. When the body is used in this service, it doesn't matter what the body looks like or how well it functions. When we walk into a room full of people, we can either choose to "look good" and be concerned with the impression we are making or we can radiate divine love through a wide-open heart without saying a word. Ironically, I noticed that I preferred being around people who made me feel good rather than people who were focused on looking good. Sir Ego's ways are often self-defeating. Having surrendered ego-oriented objectives, this is the purpose of every moment of my life, to bring light and love to every situation. Nothing else.

The wise one has shown me what love is and has guided each of these lessons. Only the wise one guides, protects, instructs, empowers, heals, transforms, and inspires without compensation, negotiation, or dilution. The wise one is ever present, unconditionally loving, universally prophetic, impartially beneficent, wholly good, eternally divine, and infinitely expansive. The wise one comforts me in my moments of grief, encourages me in my moments of despair, inspires me in my moments of openness, and instructs me in my moments of receptivity. The wise one is unfailing, although I can fail to seek him. The wise one is all-knowing, although Sir Ego can believe he knows better. The wise one is fair to all, although I can condemn.

The wise one tastes and savors both the sweetness and bitterness of life, free of Sir Ego's preferences. Both were seen as the beauty of the orchestra of the human heart and all the ballads that it can play—the light-spirited melody, the somber bass, the stormy crescendo, the ominous tempo, the playful flute solo, and the dreamy harp pieces. The wise one embraced everyone as a fellow spiritual traveler on his or her own unique quests for the grail and wished each one well.

For the wise one knows that we all share in the universal thoughts and emotions of humanity, and each of us may benefit the whole by our own rising consciousness. This is the higher octave of the heart, which shares the divine love that comes from beyond Sir Ego. Unlike Sir Ego's love, it never judges, dies, fails, covets, fears, forsakes, and betrays.

I have learned what love is not. I have joined in the symphony of human hearts breaking from crushed idols of false loves. I have shed rivers of the sacred tears of the beloved. I have forsaken the romanticized notions of love that Sir Ego used to crucify me over and over again. I have learned of the higher octave of love that comes from beyond and through us and flows in abundance and power to the extent we open our hearts.

19

The Script of Creation

Studying Sir Ego's methods, fears, and desires, I realized that he had created a script for his idealized version of reality. It itemized how everyone and everything *should* be. Sir Ego wrote a script that he believed would make him feel happy, secure, and loved. While the wise one sings the celestial song of the Creator calling to his beloved creations, Sir Ego knows not of the origin of this song and seeks to find it where it is not. He identified false grails that he believed would satisfy the heavenly desire to be peaceful, loved, and joyful. And Sir Ego condoned any means necessary to attain and retain these grails, thinking they would save him and restore him to wholeness. Initially, Sir Ego was idealistic about how he could be good and happy and help others. But over time, Sir Ego built up frustration, resentment, and despair. His methods became more defensive and offensive and less collaborative.

In my moments of despair and terror, I actually wrote down this script and suggestions for how to attain and maintain it. I needed the kids to be happy and well-adjusted, I needed to stay in my house, I needed a job with a certain salary, I needed a boyfriend, I needed Don to be nice to me, I needed to lose ten pounds, I needed to get my hair highlighted, and I needed a good divorce settlement. To do: send out ten résumés, go on a diet, find a new hairdresser, send Don an email, and create a profile on match.com. Somehow this soothed my fears by offering me some tiny feeling of control over my chaotic universe. It suppressed my fears.

Over the years, I had come to realize that my script was either not attainable or sustainable. In fact, it was often the source of my suffering.

There were greater forces in the universe, and I was powerless over them: Don's behavior, my offers of employment, and my divorce settlement, among others. All of my fellow knights were reading from a different script. And I was written into their scripts differently than I was behaving. It dawned on me that this why I had been betrayed and rejected. It wasn't personal. I simply didn't match the other person's script. And then we engaged in a game of mutual manipulation to get others to follow our script. And when they don't, Sir Ego screams, *That's not fair!* or *You're wrong!* Wow, no wonder it is so difficult to get along with others. We are all reading from different scripts with incongruent goals, story lines, and scenery.

And I had come to understand that there was a greater script, the script of creation. All the natural forces in the universe conspire to enliven this script: biology, psychology, chemistry, physics, sociology, astrology, magnetism, and energy dynamics. Sir Ego's power is less than these forces, and he is either not able to make his script happen or maintain what he achieves. He can't make someone love him, he can't make someone hire him, and he can't make someone buy his house. He can't keep the job when the market fails, keep the house when he loses his job, or keep the spouse when she has an affair.

These forces are governed by karma, our lessons, and our need to purify VVs. The energetic vibration of the VVs is magnetically charged, and it either attracts or repels other energies to us. When we have reached a level of consciousness for our next lesson to be undertaken, the VV draws the people and circumstances to us so we may choose to learn the lesson and purify the fears held in the VV. The wise one is tuned into this higher script, and that is why he was more effective, peaceful, loving, kind, and compassionate than Sir Ego.

Sages and teachings around the world describe the exalted states of self-realization, awakening into our true nature as truth, light, and love, communing with the Creator in bliss. This is the destination and grail of the script of creation and the true source of happiness, security, and love. Sir Ego's goals can't compete with this. Along the journey, we are hosted in a splendid garden of Eden on our magnificent planet. We are accompanied by great ones, united in the universal consciousness of wisdom and love. We can enjoy the ride when we are not trying to hijack the plane.

This is a journey of healing from a place of brokenness to a place of wholeness. I experienced this healing in many ways and have enduring faith in the promise. I reflected on my own transformation and testify to the miracles. I have come too far to go back; I cannot unlearn what I have learned. I might be temporarily seduced by Sir Ego's delusions, but I eventually see them for what they are and seek the wise one and the script of creation.

Our exalted quest follows the script of creation, which is the highest path for us and our influence on those around us. This script is where our uniqueness shines, the stars align, the right people appear, our power lies, the doors will open and the circumstances will manifest. I had confirmed this many times in my life experiences. Stress and anxiety are created based on the size of the gap between Sir Ego's script and the script of creation. VVs are triggered as a result of trying to operate in our script when it doesn't match the reality that is before us. This is where I was stuck when my idealized version of my marriage was very far from the truth. The gap created my near-hysterical state of anxiety and stress as Sir Ego tried desperately to pull the script of creation to match his script. I was standing on the caboose, trying to pull the train in the opposite direction.

Depression is the result of this unwinnable war and quest and unquenchable thirst. It is no surprise that Sir Ego is prone to depression. He is constantly engaged in chasing things he can't attain, choosing things that aren't good for him, attaining things he can't retain, and sparring with everyone around him. He feels lost at sea during the shifting tides of the material world. He resists the spiritual path, denying the very thing that would make him feel happy, secure, and loved without any bad side effects.

I knew despair, the desolate place where my darkest fears and my reality met. I screamed the unheard cry as I suffocated in the darkness: a thousand wails, a thousand curses, and a thousand demands without responses. My shattered heart lay, pulsating tears of blood, spilt for what? Somehow my breath continued in the heaviness, and a tiny light flickered in the darkness drawing my forward. In desperation, I sought to leave this anguish behind me and turned toward the divine spark. I would do anything to reach that beacon of hope and avoid returning to that torture chamber.

Once I had these two different scripts firmly established in my mind, the wise one questioned Sir Ego about his attachment to his script, which repeatedly was shown to have failed him. Sir Ego revealed that he did not trust the Creator to know what was best for him and did not think he would like the Creator's script. Sir Ego felt that the Creator would withhold the earthly pleasures and vices that seemed his only solace.

I recall, with clarity, thinking that anyone who didn't drink alcohol was no fun! Sir Ego wants to be free to indulge in his vices. In fact, this is his definition of freedom. Nobody was going to stop me from drinking. Now it had become obvious that my right to continue drinking was not freedom, but bondage. My insistence on staying in my toxic marriage was not freedom, but bondage. Holding on to my material circumstances at the risk of my emotional health was not freedom, but bondage. Our vices are not freedom, but bondage.

And Sir Ego had another reason he was not keen to align with the script of creation. He thought he could provide the love, security, and happiness that he sought, while the script of creation would yield the punishment that was due for his past transgressions. Having peeled away so many layers of defenses and delusions, I looked at the origins of guilt and shame. Many VVs had to be released in order to have the courage to look into the belly of the beast.

Guilt is the erroneous result of our belief that our mistakes are unforgivable sins rather than correctable, healable mistakes. This is a belief of Sir Ego that the wise one does not share. The wise one is in touch with our own perfection and divinity and that of our fellow knights. He sees all mistakes as a call for healing, not condemnation. Forgiveness is the antidote for guilt. We open ourselves to the awareness of the Creator's abundant forgiveness when we offer it to our foes.

Shame is the erroneous belief that we are not divine and are intrinsically flawed, unworthy, and unloved. Yet no matter how strongly Sir Ego believes this lie, he is not able to make it true. We are ever as the Creator created us: perfect, holy, and divine. As I learned to offer unconditional love to my children, I opened myself to the awareness that this is how the Creator loved me. As I loved and accepted every part of them that might seem unlovable or unworthy, I opened myself to that kind of love and acceptance. Unconditional love is the antidote to shame. I truly recognized it as something that was flowing through me and was not of me. It came from beyond me, and I controlled how open my heart was and therefore how much flowed through. The instrument is blessed by what flows through it.

In their unacknowledged state, guilt and shame are dark clouds that hid the ever-present sun from our awareness. When Sir Ego wishes to hide these from himself, he tends to project them onto others. He loves to declare his brother guilty and condemned, especially for the same mistake he himself has made. Sir Ego envisioned a line of people that extended from heaven to hell, and he was ever jockeying for a good position in the line. He is obsessed with either trying to move toward heaven, showing off his superior knowledge at work, or pushing people behind him toward hell, persisting in my accusations that Don was worse than I was. When I began the practice of forgiving and blessing everyone I met, I stopped this projection. I was not in competition with other knights for a good spot in line. The wise one, attuned with the script of creation, joins our brother in the universal consciousness for the highest benefit to all, the *holy relationship*.

I went through a period of feeling these lowest energies pass through me. I had a lot to purify, and it was painful to look at the humiliating things I did during my addictions to alcohol, my marriage, and my material circumstances. I simply allowed this energy to pass through me with great compassion for how hurt and lost I was. My heart was habitually open, so these energies were free to simply flow through me unencumbered. Having profound faith in forgiveness and unconditional love was the sword of truth that allowed me to slay these dementors. From the denial of addiction to the truths of the higher realms, my quest had taken me a very great distance.

I embodied the *ACIM* prayer I had prayed for so many years:

I am here only to be truly helpful.
I am here to represent Him Who sent me.
I do not have to worry about what to say or what to do, because He Who sent me will direct me.
I am content to be wherever He wishes, knowing He goes there with me.
I will be healed as I let Him teach me to heal.

ACIM T-2.V.A.18

Now I understood that each step of the exalted quest would be revealed to me in the moment I was ready. The next VV would show me a fear that was ready to be released and the insight that was ready to be revealed. The magnetic energy of the VV draws the people and circumstances to us at the appointed time. In this blessed moment of choice, choosing the wise one over Sir Ego is the solution to every problem. It becomes the holy instant, the highest step for every moment. It is engaging with the present moment in the highest way possible. It is following the path of creation. Each VV is the next stepping stone on the exalted quest.

The knights have incongruent goals only until they aligned in *holy relationships*. We meet together in the universal consciousness for the betterment of ourselves and our species. Sir Ego may not like the way this plays out in the short term, but he can have faith it will be optimal in the long term. Hitting bottom and being arrested answered my prayers and improved everything in my family, although I didn't appreciate the gift at the time.

Despite Sir Ego's misconception, true freedom is found in the script of creation. We are not bound by our limitations, ignorance, and fear. I reclaimed my power when I seized control over my inner state and aligned with the powerful forces that enliven the script of creation, exerting my will where it was effective. I accepted that I had been dealt this hand and my aspiration was to play it the best way I could, aligning myself with it and forsaking all other desires.

Mine is a sacred quest, and it is unique to me. Ride the wave you're on. Play the cards you're dealt. At the end of my days, I will be satisfied if *I exalted every step as well as I could, and then I will know that the people and situations in my life benefitted in the highest possible way from my contribution. Thy will will be done. Amen.*

The wise one's purpose for Sir Ego is a light bearer whose thoughts, words, hands, and feet bring this love and light to every dark corner of humanity, elevating it to the heavenly realms. When Sir Ego forsakes his individual script of competition and embraces the script of creation, he is fulfilling his exalted purpose. His wounds will be healed. Love and joy will be revealed.

This job is not dependent on his wealth, health, race, creed, age, financial status, marital status, or any other physical manifestation that he might obsess over. We are each born into the circumstances we need for our quest and encounter the opportunities and challenges along the way to fulfill the script. Our free will is to make the right choice in the current moment, to be receptive to the script of creation or to follow Sir Ego's script.

The wise one reclaims the power that Sir Ego had given to the perpetrator when he played the victim. As I looked at the world stage, I saw the same drama being reenacted. Sir Ego rules from his thrown of worldly power, and many may feel victims in this theatrical drama. However, no matter how much worldly power Sir Ego wields, he cannot rule the realm of my heart and my wise one. I became free to rule those realms and follow the highest quest that was individually designed for me. As each of us grows in our spiritual power, strongholds will fall.

Sir Ego had given all his power to Don while I waited for him to undo what he had done and heal my wounds. I had to retrieve that power to heal myself, my life, and my family. And I offered healing to him in the process, whether or not he is currently receptive and aware of it. I came to have an entirely new understanding of who I am and what love is.

One of the great scriptures of yoga, *The Bhagavad Gita*, tells us how Sir Ego becomes disillusioned by his fears and desires and loses sight of the divine. *The Bhagavad Gita* tells us that our true nature is ever existing, ever conscious, and ever new bliss. We exist in a sea of unconditional love from the Creator. But our awareness to this truth is hidden underneath the layers of VVs. The Gita is a conversation between an exalted sage, Lord Krishna, and his student, Arjuna. The story takes place on an allegorical battlefield where Krishna is advising Arjuna how to achieve self-realization and victory over his inner demons and lower qualities.

Krishna describes the fall from awareness of the divine, our true being, true grail, and true journey into the delusion where Sir Ego becomes lost and chases false idols. These are the steps that Sir Ego falls down and the steps that the wise one climbs back up to truth.

- *Desire*: Our true heart's desire is ecstatic communion with our Creator, but the material world also offers a many delight that stimulate desire.

- *Attachment*: A desire is not problematic until we become attached to it.
- *Craving*: The greater the desire and our attachment, the more likely it will result in cravings that stimulate our feelings of lack.
- *Anger When Frustrated Desire*: Instead of seeing our attachment as the problem, we see the obstacle that thwarts the fulfillment of our desire as the problem.
- *Delusion Is Produced*: We create our own quest for this false grail.
- *Loss of Memory of Divine Nature*: We no longer see ourselves or others as divine beings. We only see Sir Ego.
- *Decay in Discrimination*: We cannot discern truth from delusion.
- *Annihilation of Right Understanding*: We forsake right attitude and right action.

The practice of asking "Why do I care?" helps us to climb back up the ladder from our erroneous thinking to clarity. I think of this process as peeling the onion. I peel back the layers of lower consciousness to arrive at the core of the issue. The core is the delusion, which must be dispelled by the truth. When the core is exposed, we can transform our thinking, understanding, and consciousness permanently. This is pulling the weed out by the root.

The reason is that we are addicted to delusions and false gods, which stem from attachment to our desires. The tiny desire itself has no power until we take the next steps down the ladder of ignorance. Each step becomes more compelling and harder for Sir Ego to resist, until we're falling into delusion and away from our true nature and the Creator.

Layer upon layer of defenses wrap around a core desire or fear so we cannot see where we fell, what tiny desire snowballed into a problematic delusion. We use the end to justify the means. We blame others and our circumstances for our suffering. We excuse our behavior because they "made us do it." We rationalize our behavior because we are not as bad as another person.

The wise one knows that love, bliss, and security can only be found in the divine. It is the nature of self-realization. Yogananda describes our self-realized state as the ever conscious, ever new bliss that we experience as direct communion with the divine love and ecstasy of the Creator.

However, Sir Ego feels that these are missing from his life and seeks things in the material world to satisfy these desires. Thus, he formulates his script that will offer him love, happiness, and security. These primary urges are linked to our addictions to romantic love, intoxicants, and material forms of security.

In my case, Sir Ego was addicted to Don, alcohol, and financial circumstances because he believed they offered the love, bliss, and security that he sought. In my ego's script, Don was the source of love, wine was the source of bliss, and money was the source of security. In the following charts, you can see how I feel from feeling those ever-present desires to obsessing over false grails.

The wise one knows the true grail, and as we live from his understanding and power, we forsake these false grails. The wise one is the remedy to addictions. Left to his own devices, Sir Ego goes on substance abuse and toxic relationship merry-go-rounds, failing to release the VVs and learn the karmic lessons. Even if he abstains, he is at risk until he transforms his consciousness around these issues to the perspective of the wise one.

Sir Ego falls from the original desire for divinity to attachment to a false grail. From there, he recognizes lack in the material world, and this stimulates craving for the false grail. In craving, his desperation causes him to blame others when he is thwarted. Delusion is produced, which causes Sir Ego to see the false grail as the means to his salvation instead of the divine path. Now that his whole world view is upside down, he cannot discriminate between right attitude, right thinking, and right action versus unhealthy and ineffective attitudes, thinking, and behaviors. Hence, his worldview losses touch with the divine reality.

My story clearly represents this slippery slope of addiction and how insane, toxic, and ineffective my worldview became. I was lost. Yet my story also shows how purifying VVs caused me to climb back up this ladder to right understanding, right attitude, and right action. It takes courage and faith to surrender Sir Ego's delusions, but is the only permanent solution to his dilemma.

As I came to see divinity in others and then myself, I started to return to the right understanding of reality. From there, I learned to discriminate between what was positive, healing, and helpful versus my old ego desires and to affirm the true savior and grail. Purifying VVs caused me to release many false notions about the delusions that another person could provide divine love, that wine could compete with divine bliss, and that money could buy eternal security. Great faith was required to transcend these old ideas when I wasn't currently experiencing divine love, bliss, or security. But having given up on Sir Ego's ability to provide these, I put faith in the teachers and teachings that these were attainable grails, the only grails worth seeking in my life. Each opening of my heart provided affirmation and assurance that this path was better than the lower path.

Taking control of my inner state, I came to understand that no person was an obstacle to obtaining these higher grails. Only Sir Ego and my closed heart stood in the way. There was no one else to blame and no cause for anger. Understanding that offering unconditional love, forgiveness, generosity, and service were the portals to receiving the divine blessings affirmed that there was no lack in the universe. I was not in competition with my fellow knights. Then the craving turns toward the divine instead of the material satisfaction of the underling desires for love, bliss, and security.

This transformation of my perspective caused the permanent shifts in my inner state, my understanding of reality, my purpose in life, and my choices. I transcended that paradigm of addiction. In early recovery, I fought the persistent thought that I was being denied my basic right to bliss, wine. I was jealous of others who could drink in moderation. I had a mental reservation that there would be one day in the future when I could drink again without repercussions, something like crossing the international date line and skipping a day so it wouldn't count against me. As my lifestyle and understanding changed, this desire melted away. Now I don't drink because I seek a higher goal and wine isn't on this path; I know it would only be an obstacle, a detour that I am not interested in.

I also was jealous of others in seemingly happy romantic relationships. Why was I also denied this basic right? Yet as I was working on my inner state and my host of defenses, I thought, *I really don't want the kind of relationship I would attract at my current level of consciousness*. Like attracts like. I prayed not to have another relationship until I was purified enough to learn through love and not through pain and fear. I don't feel lacking as I have filled the hole in my heart with love for everyone: my children, my parents, Don, my coworkers, my friends, the store clerks, and the guy who cuts me off when driving.

Sir Ego believed Don's money bought me financial security. Turns out, it bought him years of legal services to fight me. Yikes. I had to give up my fight for a divorce settlement because I could not fight for both the children and the money at the same time. I struggled financially as a single parent, providing a home for my children, even while I was still fighting for custody and their bedrooms were unused.

I came to see that I was deluded to think that money bought me financial security. It was swept away. Yet I was never without. Sometimes I was down to a few dollars in my pocket, yet I always had just enough for what I needed. Pay raises and a bankruptcy showed me that the divine had ways of making up what was lost, and I started to see that money was a flow of energy. When I clung to it, it stopped flowing. When I surrendered the money battles with Don, it flowed.

When my faith was in the material world for security, it was an imperative to stay in my marriage. I did not understand that it was not providing eternal security. I was not able to discern that this bondage was the source of my suffering. With money as my false grail, I made poor choices. I was furious when my relationship and thus my financial security was endangered.

When I went through the bankruptcy and subsequently felt threatened by eviction for having Sunny living with me, I had to confront the question of where I found my security. I had learned that the security that Sir Ego thought he found in my marriage was a lie. I realized that jobs, pension funds, and economies change. I wanted to put my security in the hands of the divine. The divine had a job waiting for me before I even left rehab. The divine had a new job waiting when I was severed from that job. The divine had a house waiting for me when I couldn't keep Sunny at the first house. This was more reliable than Don.

So I learned to trust the divine flow of abundance and relinquish my financial battles. I trust that there is no lack and abundance is magnetized to me from my generosity and selfless service. Again I control the flow through my life when I tune into the divine abundance of energy and magnetism.

My shocking transformation is simply the result of operating from the level of the wise one, purifying the VVs that blocked him and teaching Sir Ego that the higher grail and the higher quest satisfy his needs more effectively and permanently without side effects.

The Gita's Descent into Delusion	Sir Ego's Romantic Love Delusion	The Wise One's Truth of Divine Love
Desire	I desire to feel loved.	I desire to feel loved.
Attachment	I want this person.	I receive love as I give it.
Craving	I need to hold onto him.	Love flows freely through my open heart.
Anger When Frustrated Desire	You are not playing your role in my script. Change!	Only I determine how open my heart is and how much love I experience.
Delusion Is Produced	This person is Sir Ego's grail.	Divine love is the grail.
Decay in Discrimination	All's fair in love and war. We misbehave because of our false beliefs.	No one's behavior causes him or her to be anything less than divine.
Annihilation of Right Understanding	This failed relationship reveals I am unloved, unloving, and unlovable.	You, I, and everyone exists in a sea of universal love.

The Gita's Descent into Delusion	Sir Ego's Wine Delusion	The Wise One's Truth of Divine Ecstasy
Desire	I desire ecstasy.	I desire ecstasy.
Attachment	I want this feeling from wine.	I receive joy as I give it.
Craving	I need wine—more wine.	Joy flows freely through my open heart.
Anger When Frustrated Desire	Don't get in between my wine and me.	Only I determine how freely joy flows through my life.
Delusion Is Produced	Wine is Sir Ego's grail.	Divine ecstasy is the grail.
Decay in Discrimination	Addiction caused me to deprioritize my parenting duties.	No one's behavior causes him or her to be anything less than divine.
Annihilation of Right Understanding	I cannot live without wine and with my failures.	You, I, and everyone exists in a sea of ecstasy.

The Gita's Descent into Delusion	Sir Ego's Money Delusion	The Wise One's Truth of Divine Providence
Desire	I desire to feel secure, knowing my needs will be met.	I desire to feel secure, knowing my needs will be met.
Attachment	I am attached to my material forms of security.	You get material abundance when you give generously.
Craving	I'll do anything to maintain this house and lifestyle.	Generosity flows freely through my open heart.
Anger When Frustrated Desire	That's my money and I'm going to sue you.	Only I determine how freely abundance flows through my life.
Delusion Is Produced	Possessions and wealth are Sir Ego's grail.	Divine providence is the grail.
Decay in Discrimination	My things are more important than you are.	People are more important than things are.
Annihilation of Right Understanding	I will never be happy without my material comforts.	You, I, and everyone exists in a sea of abundance.

20

Exalted Quest

The miraculous changes in my inner dimensions, my relationships, and my circumstances are worth infinitely more than the price I have paid, in terms of forsaking Sir Ego's false idols, sacred cows, and other strongholds. And they are just the tip of the iceberg of the true depth and ecstasy of the exalted quest. Every now and then, my faith was rewarded by an experience that validated the authenticity of the teachings.

During a yoga retreat program, I had a profound experience of divine love. For over an hour, I was overwhelmed by a heart-filling experience. Tears streamed down my face as I was immersed in an ocean of love that seemed to appear out of nowhere and everywhere at once. It was as familiar as my mother's love, but bigger, more powerful, more joyful, more playful, more intimate, and beyond any expectations. This wave was overwhelming in power and magnitude in reference to my tiny self, an unstoppable inevitability, as powerful as a tidal wave yet as gentle as a summer breeze. This love could mend every heartbreak and eradicate every stain of fear, regret, frustration, anger, despair, and grief. I could feel the flood in my heart saturating the parched and atrophied muscle.

With great clarity, I understood why someone would, could, and should devote his or her life to this. This was a taste of the exalted grail. Every other goal vanished in that instant. Tiny little me was absorbed into this cosmic sea. I felt seen and known, validated and accepted, and worthy and fulfilled, illuminating and dispelling the darkest recesses of fear, guilt, and shame. Afterwards I floated on a cloud of joy, my heart wide open to each of the other program participants.

My heart yearns wistfully to be filled with the incomprehensible, infinite, eternal, ever-present love that heals, guides, honors, inspires, exhilarates, delights, and transcends fear. I realize this was the desire behind each of my false idols, trying to quench this thirst with wine, Don, or material possessions. I know now that each VV that I purify opens my heart to this eternal, infinite flow. Removing these blockages is the most powerful thing I can do to draw this flow toward me.

This is what lays on the other side of our fear. This is what appears when our VVs are released. This process of recognizing and releasing VVs works in every problem I encounter; after I transcend Sir Ego's fears and delusions, the wise one reveals the truth and acts in the highest way to move through the situation. Understanding that each challenge comes to us so we will learn means that each problem is born of a lesson. Learning the lesson releases the problem. This works at all times for all situations. It is the only answer to every concern. I do not need to figure out what to do. Instead I need to purify the VV, align my will with the wise one, and wait patiently until his response and the lesson appear. I beseech the wise one, *Show me the truth that dispels this delusion.*

Sir Ego still is present in my awareness and often having a VV explosion, but he knows we will not act until that is purified. He has developed patience and impulse control. If it takes days before right action occurs, he will wait. He does not wish to make the monkeys extinct. His fix-it thinking is quickly silenced because he knows we will not act on his battle strategies. Instead of being wrapped up in monkey mind of fear thoughts, my mind is free to look more deeply into this higher reality. Sir Ego works with the wise one to dig deeply into the VV so it may be released at the root.

He asks, "Let's go to the bottom now, not halfway. I don't want to have to come back again and feel this pain again to release the remaining energy."

Once Sir Ego became aligned with the wise one in this way, even the biggest blocks and obstacles in my life melted away. Many times, Sir Ego found himself in the bleakest cave, in the darkness of ignorance, seemingly blocked in all directions with no way out. Yet, I had faith that the wise one knew the windy, crooked, narrow path that would lead me out to the sunlight of insight and victory. My circumstances were created to teach me a lesson, so the solution was born before the challenge and both are apparent to the wise one. And, as I leaned into him step by step, he would show me the only way out of this maze revealing the hidden path and removing the obstacles.

Each is a test of our faith or commitment to choose love over fear, the wise one over Sir Ego, and the truth over delusion. I knew that each had a purpose and would be resolved in its own time. My highest contribution was to release my VV and not resist the challenge. Each time, my resolve and confidence grew greater. Sir Ego knows that he needs the wise one to guide his thoughts, words, and actions for the highest good for all.

My journey out of darkness started after my mother's death when I sought to understand the higher realities. I became open to a different understanding of the cosmos and my role in it. Believing in the cycle of death and rebirth and the role of karma in our spiritual development paved the way for forgiveness, forgiving Don and myself. I came to see both of us as divine beings in a grand curriculum for our advancement and attunement to love's reality.

Accepting this as life's purpose caused me to align my ways to the path of goodness and forsake my vices. It no longer mattered whether I could get away with something. I knew karma would lovingly respond to each thought and action. If I don't want hard lessons, I must be vigilant to only create good karma in my thoughts, words, and deeds. I could forsake guilt because I knew each moment I failed, I could immediately reverse the karma with an opposite thought, such as blessing the person I had just cursed for his or her driving faux pas.

Trusting karma to teach myself and other, I am free of the need to judge and condemn. I can offer the unconditional love to each as I understand not what his or her lessons are or how they are performing on him or her. Two people might be in the same situation but be learning totally different lessons. And the opposite is also true. Two people might be in very different situations but learning the same lesson. I cannot know what their lesson is by considering my past. We are both peers on the quest and will all reach the grail in the end.

As I came to understand that our inner blockages and lessons magnetize lesson scenarios to us, I understood how to actively participate *now* in the creation of my future experiences. When a VV is triggered, it is time for it to be released. We are ready to learn the lesson. If we do not learn the lesson and suppress or express the energy, we make the VV bigger. This attracts the lesson in a louder format. It is our choice. If we refuse to get our lessons, we will continue to attract the circumstances that stimulate the VVs. We can either get the lesson quickly in the realm of thought, or we can attract the same addiction relapses and toxic relationships over and over until we do. This realization is very motivating to handle VVs in the highest way, knowing that we cannot hide from our karmic lessons. Nor should we want to. They are for our highest good.

When I learned how to dig into the VVs and the defenses that protected them, I came to understand Sir Ego and his motivations. This allowed the wise one to gently show him the higher path, the more effective path, and saved the monkeys, lions, and gazelles from extinction. My self-defeating and ineffective behaviors melted away to virtues of compassion, empathy, courage, generosity, patience, and humility.

Parenting my children taught me to have love without fear, unconditional love. And like forgiveness, it would be mine to the extent that I was able to open and purify my heart channeling this divine gift to them. I learned selfless service, giving our pure desire to bring light and love to another, absent any ego motivations or agendas. This is the prescription for profound healing miracles. It is our true purpose to channel this healing energy to ourselves, our family, our workplace, and our planet.

Sir Ego became convinced that his ways did not work. They failed or backfired. He learned the ways of love did work, elegantly and radically. He willingly chooses the wise one as his guide, the script of creation as his map and love as his grail. I have faith, devotion, and surrender in all things. I understand that I get what I give: forgiveness, love, and abundance.

I am grateful to each of my fellow knights whose quests have commingled with mine. Each has given me a valuable gift of this knowingness of love. Upon the commencement of the quest, Sir Ego gave each of these brave knights a supporting role in my quest and did not honor them in their true roles as divine brothers, holding the promise of mutual satisfaction of our quests. When I sought to condemn my brother guilty, I found evidence of his transgressions.

When I sought to see my brother as divine, I saw only his true nature and his mistaken behaviors as a call for love. As I offered each relationship to the service of the wise one, forsaking Sir Ego's special relationship, new aspects of love were revealed to me to replace the disillusionment. The wise one always accepts them where they are rather than where he wishes they were.

I have deep reverence and devotion for the teachers that have come to show us the way, especially Paramhansa Yogananda and Jesus Christ. They have gone beyond the need to reincarnate, yet they come back purely to help us. Yet we ignore, defy, deny, and curse them. None of this matters to them. They love us with a boundless love and an eternal patience. Being receptive and seeking attunement to them is all that is necessary to call them into our lives. Seeing how difficult it was to keep my heart open when my children struggled, I can't comprehend how great the divine love must be in this fully realized state.

Each day, the wise one becomes stronger in my consciousness. His thoughts, words, and deeds become mine, and my life is transformed. The exalted states will be revealed at the appointed hour. As I open my heart and remove the blockages, the Creator will do his part, reaching out to meet my outstretched hand that beseeches him to come to me. I recognize my personal transformation, the fruit of these practices as evidence of these truths.

A return to our exalted state of ever new, ever conscious love and bliss is the true grail. This is the destiny of the script of the Creator, for each and every one of us. It will be my honor to meet you there.

About the Author

With love, faith, and courage, Kindred Light finds powerful ways to work with dark emotions and disastrous life circumstances, transforming them into miracles of growth, healing, and loving relationships. Spiritual principles come alive as she applies them to her toxic marriage, alcohol addiction and recovery, workplace, and parenting challenges. She guides us step by step through her inner struggles, fears, and turmoil until they melt away into inner peace, love, compassion, and joy. As pearls of insight and wisdom are gleaned from each struggle, strongholds dissolve into a flow of grace, beauty, and abundance flowing through her life. Revolutionary new ways of facing life's trials and surmounting their obstacles are explored as she is transformed before your eyes.

CPSIA information can be obtained
at www.ICGtesting.com
Printed in the USA
LVHW080503180319
610997LV00033B/644/P